Sofia Perovskaya

Terrorist Princess

PROFILES IN TERRORISM ©

A SERIES

BOOK THREE: SOFIA PEROVSKAYA, TERRORIST PRINCESS

OTHER BOOKS IN THE SERIES (BY THE SAME AUTHOR):

BOOK ONE: JOHN BROWN, ABOLITIONIST TERRORIST*
BOOK TWO: JOHN WILKES BOOTH, THE TRAGEDIAN*

***

BOOKS FOUR THROUGH SIX: ANARCHIST ASSASSINS AND
TERRORISTS, 1890 - 1930 (TO BE CONTINUED)

BOOKS SEVEN THROUGH TWELVE: MODERN ASSASSINS AND
TERRORISTS, 1930 - PRESENT (TO BE CONTINUED)

* PENDING PUBLICATION

Sofia Perovskaya
Terrorist Princess

The Plot to Kill Tsar Alexander II
and the Woman Who Led It

Part of a Series
Profiles in Terrorism ©

by Robert R. Riggs

GLOBAL HARMONY PRESS

© Global Harmony Press 2017
Berkeley, California

Global Harmony Press, Inc.
2625 Alcatraz Ave., Suite 124
Berkeley, California 94705
Deluxe Color Hardbound Edition, 2017

Sofia Perovskaya, Terrorist Princess | The Plot to Kill Tsar
Alexander II and the Woman Who Led It | Part of a Series, Profiles
in Terrorism / Robert R. Riggs

Includes bibliographic references and index

ISBN 978-0-9991559-0-5 (Deluxe Color Paperback)
ISBN 978-0-9991559-1-2 (B&W Paperback)
ISBN 978-0-9991559-2-9 (Cloth Bound)
ISBN 978-0-9991559-4-3 (Deluxe Color Hardbound)
ISBN 978-0-9991559-3-6 (Electronic)

Library of Congress Control Number: 2017950822

Dedicated to Vittorio Varisco

Acknowledgements

This work would not have been possible without the constant support, guidance and encouragement of the author's wife, Dori Riggs.

A great deal of important help was provided by the author's Russian research assistants: Maria Hoffman, Varvara Kourova and Inna Volkova. More very appreciated work was done by his other assistants, Jackson Kaiser and Derek Turner. Invaluable comments and suggestions were given by Walter Moss, who reviewed a previous edition of the manuscript for this work. Amarjot Singh provided helpful suggestions.

Thanks are also due to the staff of the following institutions which opened their doors and collections to the author, making the research for this work a pleasure:

> The University of California at Berkeley
> The Hoover Institute at Stanford University
> The International Institute of Social History in Amsterdam
> The National Library of Russia in St. Petersburg
> The State Historical Archive in St. Petersburg

Additionally, the author wishes to acknowledge the innovative and well conceived facilities provided to the public as a whole by Google, Yandex and Wikipedia. They have created on demand resources which are enormously useful for a project of this kind.

Introduction

The Russian "revolutionist" group whose development culminated in the assassination of Russia's Tsar Alexander II by Sofia Perovskaya and Narodnaya Volya in 1881 inaugurated the modern practice of terrorism.[1] Narodnaya Volya's history, makeup and advocacy must be of extreme interest to any contemporary student of terrorism. The Narodnaya Volya explicitly called themselves "terrorists," though they would also, at other times, deny that they were terrorists when such a denial suited their purposes. Narodnaya Volya's theorists dwelt extensively on the philosophy of political terror as a method of struggle. They fabricated a rationale to justify its use. They devised a terrorist "constitution." They demonstrated how terrorism can be used to whip up recruits to the cause. Narodnaya Volya lends powerful insight into the phenomenon of terrorism because it represents a formative ontogeny, a sort of instinctual, toddling, unaided development into a terrorist organization. And the reaction of the imperial government against the Russian "Sixties" activists is also a prime source of insight. As we shall see, that reaction lacked in insight. Its harsh overreaction was short-sighted and largely counterproductive.

Sofia Perovskaya, in the end, emerged as Narodnaya Volya's most decisive leader. She resides on the thin razor's edge that divides a saintly heroine from a terrorist killer. Sonia, as she was called and as she called herself, has not yet been the subject of an English language biography. Prior authors have looked at Perovskaya in some depth as part of an examination of the feminist aspect of the Russian revolutionists of the "Generation of the Sixties," notably, Cathy Porter's *Fathers and Daughters* and Margaret Maxwell's *Narodniki Women*. Perovskaya has also been discussed in biographies of male members of Narodnaya Volya, particularly, in David Footman's *The Alexander Conspiracy: A Life of A. L. Zhelyabov*, and in Lee B. Croft's *Nikolai Ivanovich Kibalchich: Terrorist Rocket Pioneer*. Topical works on the Sixties era, such as Roland Seth's *The Russian Terrorists* and Walter Moss's *Russia in the Age of Alexander II, Tolstoy and Dostoevsky*, also feature her prominently. As well they should. It was Perovskaya's unyielding will which brought about Narodnaya Volya's most prominent terrorist exploit, the assassination of Tsar Alexander II. Inside Narodnaya Volya, as within the prior groups to which she had belonged, the others looked to Sonia for leadership due to her unstinting dedication to the cause, due to her energy, due to her zest for martyrdom, and due to her prominent asceticism. Her study is more difficult than is that of some others, because Perovskaya was mainly a doer, not a theorist; she was not a prolific writer, and she rarely spoke in public.

The ferment of a generation of Russians who matured in the 1860's and 1870's distilled out a small subset of people who had the requisite character traits to turn to the methods and mentality of terrorism. Perovskaya was a product of this distillation. Her passionate hatred, combined with her ability, drive, and determination, proved to be the key to fruition of the conspiracy to assassinate the closest 19th century Russian analog of Lincoln, the liberator of the serfs, Tsar Alexander II. Perovskaya's antecedents in the highest levels of Russian aristocracy* make her an archetype of one of the many striking paradoxes demonstrated by terrorists. By no means poor and oppressed beings, they are generally children of wealth and privilege who go overboard in adopting the cause of others.

Napoleon once wrote, "It is through many experiments made with precision, in order to arrive at the truth . . . that we advance gradually and arrive at simple theories, useful to all states of life."[2] It is in that spirit that we approach one of the thorniest and most perplexing unsolved problems of our era, the origins and motivation of the terrorist. Terrorism has become virtually a daily intrusion into Western consciousness. Yet at bottom it remains a poorly understood phenomenon. Governments, commentators and mass media tend to be distracted by the optics of contemporary groups who claim "credit" for the terrorist act of self-immolation. The distance of history yields perspective on these matters.

What we observe, in looking at historical terrorists such as Perovskaya and her associates, is a striking pattern of personal characteristics. Our "simple theory" is that the methods of terrorism appeal to a peculiar kind of personality, one not yet

---

* With reference to the title of this work, the objection has been raised, with justice, that Sofia Perovskaya did not have a formal title of "princess." We use "princess" as per the Oxford online dictionary definition 1.4 of that term: "A woman or thing regarded as pre-eminent in a particular sphere or group: 'the princess of American politics.'" This well describes Perovskaya, as we shall see. Moreover, her contemporaries – adversaries within the government, colleagues within Narodnaya Volya, and the public who turned out in hordes to watch her mount the scaffold – were fascinated above all with the fact that Sonia was a product of the highest level of the Russian nobility.

fully recognized in its details. All terrorist "causes" – be they Islamism, anarchism, right wing extremism, opposition to legalized abortion, racism, etcetera – serve merely as the "flavor of the day" for the terrorist persona. This is an expansion of a hypothesis offered by a thoroughgoing student of terrorism, Walter Laqueur.[3] There is an identifiable constellation of personality traits, what we call here a profile, that is strongly associated with persons who act out as terrorists, regardless of the particular cause or value structure that the terrorist happens to be supporting.

Like a particle, popping into existence at a fundamental quantum level, the terrorist persona appears to be an inherent fluctuation in the human personality. The terrorist materializes out of "nothingness" at any time, at any place, and in any social milieu. Terrorism has manifested itself in the United States, in Russia, in France, in Germany, in Japan, in India, and in the Middle East. There is no one political or religious structure that gives rise to terrorism, or that magically protects against it. Unfortunately, we see that under certain conditions terrorists can "grow" other terrorists by exploiting, cultivating and bringing out its inherent personality attributes, especially among young people. The terrorist emerges out of "nothingness" in the sense that terrorism is a sudden burst of passionate violent behavior which generally cannot be traced to compelling hardships, injustices or other social forces exerted on the terrorist personally. In the words of Laqueur,

> [T]errorism is not merely a technique. Those practicing it have certain basic beliefs in common. They may belong to the left or the right, they may be nationalists or, less frequently, internationalists, but in some essential respects their mental makeup is similar. They are often closer to each other than they know or would like to admit to themselves or others.

One of Laqueur's fundamental observations, which we

shall see verified in this work, is that terrorism is not carried on by "poor and desperate human beings."[4] Laqueur noted the following myths regarding terrorism: [5]

1.   Terrorism is a response to injustice; if there were political and social justice, there would be no terrorism.

2.   The only known means of reducing the likelihood of terrorism is a reduction of the grievances, stresses and frustration underlying it.

3.   Terrorists are fanatical believers driven to despair by intolerable conditions.

4.   They are poor and their inspiration is deeply ideological.

This biography will, in particular, add to the evidence which shows that the terrorist typically turns out to be a product of relatively affluent economic and social circumstances. Sofia Perovskaya started her life by being born into a wealthy, accomplished, family with royal status and with the highest social connections. Sonia ardently felt, and gave herself over to, the cause of others. We shall see that "adopting the cause" of others is generally a pivotal paradigm of the terrorist.

A strange paradox about terrorists is that despite their demonstrated capacity to engage in ruthless acts of murderous violence against unsuspecting, unarmed people, in their other life they generally are neither harsh nor cold blooded. Sofia Perovskaya, as we shall see, was lauded by her peers for being loyal to her friends, for being tender with the sick, for her sweet disposition, and for being devoted to her mother.

Chapter 1: The Power of a Literary Work

What Is to Be Done?, a novel published in 1863 by Nikolai Chernyshevsky, seems an unlikely candidate to inspire generations of terrorists. Chernyshevsky created it during a period of four months while confined in prison awaiting a trial and a harsh sentence that would require his permanent confinement in Siberia. Chernyshevsky had to request and receive special permission to write the novel from his jailors. The very paper he used was doled out specially to him for the purpose by the prison authorities. Each page had to be read and approved by the imperial censors. That they allowed a book to be written right under their noses which would soon serve as a blueprint for revolution has been considered one of the worst-ever examples of bureaucratic blundering.

The government censors did read *What Is to Be Done?* before its publication. Being mystified, like so many later readers, they even created their own plot summary.[6] What they failed to grasp was how the utopian anarchist outlook embedded in Chernyshevsky's work could water a soil that was fertile for growing terrorists. In Russia, the mix would prove especially fertile for growing women terrorists.

One hundred plot elements of *What Is to Be Done?*

1. A mysterious disappearance, apparently a suicide. The victim alerted police via a note. It seems he shot himself, falling off a bridge. No body was found – only a cap with a bullet hole was later pulled from the water.[7]

2. Vera Pavlovna, affectionately called Verotchka, receives a letter. Crying after reading it, she sends away her companion, a young man who is a mustache twirler. This companion is Alexander Mateivitch Kirsanov, although we don't actually meet him in the narrative until much later.[8]

3. The narrator provides a preface: "The motive of this story is love; the principal character a woman."[9]

4. The early life of Vera Pavlovna is narrated. She grew up in a multi storied house in St. Petersburg.[10]

5. Description is given of Vera's father, Pavel Konstantinovitch Rozalsky, and her mother, Maria Alexeyevna. Although she has a low opinion of her own looks, seeing herself as too skinny, Vera grows into an attractive, musically gifted young woman with thick black hair and black eyes. Vera's mother is very interested in getting her married, and married well. Her father Pavel is the building manager where the family resides. The family leads a middle class life.[11]

6. Vera develops a penchant for declining all of the proffered suitors.[12]

7. Verotchka's mother Maria Alexeyevna takes

her to the opera, elegantly dressed. Some gentlemen enter their box and converse among themselves in undertones, in French. Vera turns her head away from them. Later she insists on leaving early, telling her mother she feels ill.

8.   One of the gentlemen who came into the box at the opera was Mikhail Ivanovitch Storeshnikov. (Later, we learn that he is the son of the family that owns the building where Vera lives, and that her father manages.) Storeshnikov made a bet with his friends at the opera that he could get Vera to be his mistress. Afterwards, at a restaurant, Storeshnikov discusses the bet in the presence of a French woman named Julie. Julie is the live-in lover and companion of one of Storeshnikov's friends.[13]

9.   Verotchka in fact had overheard, and had understood perfectly well, the comment Storeshnikov made in the box about her becoming his mistress. She feels ashamed. The next day, when Storeshnikov comes by her flat to pay her a visit, she tells him to go away and to stop calling on her.[14]

10. Julie intervenes with a visit to Vera. The two of them discuss Storeshnikov's bet and the seduction he had propounded in connection with it. Julie decides to convince Storeshnikov to marry Verotchka, instead of trying to seduce her. Julie also tries to convince Vera to accept the proposal.[15]

11. Storeshnikov is won over by Julie's exposition of the reasons he should marry Vera. However, his mother is violently opposed. Storeshnikov defies her, and proposes to Vera anyway. Vera refuses. Reluctantly, in reply to Storeshnikov's now impassioned entreaties, she agrees to postpone her final decision. When Vera finally refuses Storeshnikov's marriage

proposal, his mother abruptly forms a better opinion of her.[16]

12. Storeshnikov continues his spurned courtship of Vera, with his mother's increasing support. Vera's mother Maria Alexeyevna is also enthusiastic.[17]

13. We meet Dmitri Sergeivitch Lopukhov. He is engaged by Vera's parents as a tutor for the "gymnasium," a type of college prep school, of Verotchka's younger brother Feodor. Lopukhov is a medical student from a middle class background who teaches in order to help pay his way through school. Like Vera, Lopukhov has some musical ability. He is philosophical and intellectually thoughtful. In a scene at the Rozalsky home, Lopukhov looks Storeshnikov in the eye and poses some rather direct questions to him. Vera's mother insists she sing an aria to entertain Storeshnikov and the other guests present. Verotchka chooses to sing *La donna è mobile* from Giuseppe Verdi's opera *Rigoletto*. Lopukhov is impressed.[18]

14. Lopukhov dances with Verotchka at her birthday party. While they dance, she confesses to Lopukhov her unhappy plight, in relation to Storeshnikov's unwanted courtship and the pressure she faces to marry him.[19]

15. Vera and Lopukhov develop feelings for each other.[20]

16. Verotchka and Lopukhov hide their budding relationship from Vera's mother. Lopukhov tells Maria Alexeyevna that he has a fiancée with a large dowry. Lopukhov also agrees to reduce the price of his lessons, so that he will be kept on as Feodor's tutor and will have more time to spend with Vera.[21]

17. To help Vera escape the pressure to marry Storeshnikov, Lopukhov busies himself trying to find

a position for her as a governess.[22]

18. Vera dreams her first dream of the novel. In this dream, she is released from a damp, gloomy cellar she had been locked in. She finds herself running and frolicking gaily in a field. There she encounters a beautiful girl who is constantly changing, and who changes before Vera's eyes from German to English, to French, to Polish, back to German, and then to Russian. The girl tells Vera that she is the bride of Vera's bridegroom. Vera sets about freeing many other young girls who are also locked in cellars throughout the city.[23]

19. Lopukhov's last effort to place Vera as a governess fails when the would-be employer, a Mrs. B, learns that Vera would be taking the job against the wishes of her parents. Mrs. B does not want to be sued![24]

20. To enable Vera to escape her plight, Lopukhov proposes to marry Vera. This is to happen after Lopukhov finishes medical school at the beginning of July. It was now the end of April.[25]

21. We hear more about Alexander Mateivitch Kirsanov, called Sasha, another medical student who is Lopukhov's close friend and roommate. Vera declares that she hates Kirsanov because he and Lopukhov are so close and intimate, always "sitting together, hugging and disputing."[26]

22. So that they will remain friends and she will not be enslaved, Vera proposes to Lopukhov that after they are married they will make their living arrangements with two separate bedrooms, each of them having their own room, and with a third neutral room in the middle for dining, having tea and receiving guests. Neither of them will enter the

other's room.[27]

23. Vera and Dmitri are secretly married ahead of schedule, before Lopukhov finishes his medical school exams. As a result, he does not become a doctor (he says he had no desire to become one, anyway).[28]

24. Lopukhov introduces Vera to his adored roommate Kirsanov. Vera promises to love Kirsanov just as much as she loves Lopukhov.[29]

25. Vera informs her mother that she has been secretly married to Lopukhov. Vera's mother is initially beside herself. When calmer, she has Vera's father pretend to the building owner's wife that they in fact arranged the marriage to Lopukhov so that Vera would not dishonor her son, Storeshnikov, by marrying him.[30]

26. The landlady accepts the explanation, but she reduces the pay increase she had previously granted to Pavel Konstantinovitch from 20 rubles per month to 5 rubles per month.[31]

27. The author, in an aside, gives the reader an apology and an enconmium for Maria Alexeyevna. In spite of her grasping, abusive behavior toward Vera, he says she was "not without reason" and "not stupid." Thus, he tells us, she is better than many.[32]

28. Vera and Lopukhov prosper in their new life together. Lopukhov takes on more pupils; Vera begins tutoring as well. They live in their separate rooms, and meet only in the common room.[33]

29. Vera gets the idea to start a sewing union.[34]

30. Vera engages with Julie to advise her and to help her promote the business of the sewing union. Julie and Vera drink champagne in honor of Vera's

marriage; they become very giddy celebrating the birth of the sewing union. They collapse together in a heap on a sofa, after wrestling together.[35]

31. Because of the repeated visits to Vera's sewing shop by Julie and her common law husband, who is an army general, public curiosity about the shop grows. Vera's father even comes to visit. He is coldly received.[36]

32. Verotchka dreams her second dream. It is very lengthy. All of the following people appear in it.

Lopukhov, her husband. He gives a discourse on the difference between "clean dirt" and "barren dirt."

Alexei Petrovitch, a regular caller in the neutral room at the Lopukhov household. Petrovitch engages in a philosophy discussion with Lopukhov.

Serge, Julie's live-in companion who is the army general.

Maria Alexeyevna, that is, Vera's mother, who is not, however, exactly herself, but rather a more philosophical version of herself.

An unnamed army officer, on whose knees Vera sits.

A lady, who declines to take on Vera as a servant because her father was a civil servant and, consequently, Vera is too close to nobility.

A drunken fellow, unnamed, who accosts Vera.

The real Maria Alexeyevna, who lectures Vera on how she should be grateful.

The "bride of her bridegrooms," also thought of as "the sister of one of Verotchka's sisters." The Bride takes Vera by the hand. Alluded to earlier in the work by Dmitri Sergeivitch Lopukhov as his betrothed, she appears to be a personification of a future Utopia characterized by libertarian anarchy. The Bride tells Vera, "kind people cannot get to their feet alone." They need the help of "ill-tempered" people in doing so. Afterwards, the "ill-tempered" will no longer be needed. The Bride likens Vera's mother to one of these necessary, ill-tempered people.[37]

33. The sewing union prospers. Although she is paying good wages, Vera insists on dividing the profits equally among all of the seamstresses.[38]

34. The seamstresses begin pooling their savings as capital, and living communally. In this way they save on all kinds of expenses. Vera avoids any appearance of rank or leadership on her part in connection with the operations of the shop.[39]

35. Vera begins organizing lectures, classes, and cultural events such as Italian opera outings for the seamstresses.[40]

36. Three years pass.[41]

37. Vera has a comfortable life, with lots of cream, and faithful servants who always get married and move on. Vera and Dmitri play host to many visitors.[42]

38. Vera and Dmitri attend a picnic where there are two other young philosophers, who spend much time debating with Dmitri. Dmitri ultimately exhausts himself racing and wrestling with these young men. As a result, he becomes very ill.[43]

39. Kirsanov, Lopukhov's good friend and former roommate, is by now a doctor. Kirsanov is called in by Lopukhov and Vera to minister to the sick Dmitri. Kirsanov concludes that Dmitri's case of pneumonia is not grave. Kirsanov tries to talk Vera out of staying up all night to watch over Dmitri. Kirsanov insists on taking over the vigil. Dmitri recovers after a few days.

Vera reproaches Kirsanov for not having been a regular caller at their home for two years until Dmitri had his crisis.[44]

40. In an aside to the reader, the narrator tells us, "a new romance is going to begin in Vera Pavlovna's life, and in this Kirsanov is going to play a part."[45]

41. Lopukhov and Kirsanov are each personified and compared. Both are self-taught, although they use somewhat different methods. Both are handsome, Kirsanov being lighter skinned, blonder and blue-eyed. Each of them, separately, experienced an important formative episode in which he had confronted and physically overpowered a member of the aristocracy who had disrespected him.[46]

42. Kirsanov resumes his visits to the Lopukhovs, but he has to struggle in order to hide the fact that he is falling in love with Vera.[47]

43. Vera takes Sasha Kirsanov on a visit to the sewing commune. There he is recognized and embraced by a girl named Anastasia, affectionately called Nastenka, who is ill and dying of consumption. Nastenka, later, tells Vera the story of how she and Kirsanov fell in love while he was curing her of the drinking problem which was the underlying cause of her illness, and how, as a result, she went to live with him in his house. She portrays to Vera the wondrous feeling of being in love, and assures her that Sasha is good.[48]

44. Nastenka recounts to Vera that Kirsanov decided it would be better for Nastenka's health if they did not see each other. He found her a place as the servant of an actress. Nastenka did very well with this mistress, but then, the actress retired from acting to live with her husband. The actress's father-in-law

made unwanted advances to Nastenka, causing her to leave the home to avoid causing family discord. After this, Nastenka joined the sewing commune. She did not see Sasha Kirsanov for two and one half years until the day Vera brought him to the sewing shop. During this time, her consumption has worsened.[49]

45. Though his former feelings of love have now faded to pity, Kirsanov remains at Nastenka's side constantly over the next month as she goes through the process of dying and then dies. Vera consoles Kirsanov about Nastenka's illness. Vera and Kirsanov walk together, and discuss topics such as the writings of Harriet Beecher Stowe. Kirsanov escorts Vera to the opera, sometimes without Lopukhov.[50]

46. Sasha begins again to struggle with himself over his feelings for Vera. He very subtly withdraws from seeing the Lopukhovs.[51]

47. Verotchka dreams her third dream. In this dream, Vera is visited by an apparition of a female singer from Verdi's *Rigoletto*. A new visitor then appears, who is just a hand. The hand directs Vera to read from her diary. The diary is magical and sprouts new contents every time the hand points to it. The magic diary recounts many of the events that have happened to Vera. At the end, the hand forces Vera to read more magical text. The text reveals Vera to be in love with Sasha Kirsanov. She wakes up cursing the hand for having shown her this text.[52]

48. Vera reacts against the dream by cuddling with Dmitri Sergeivitch Lopukhov and moving into his room. She also tells Dmitri some parts of the third dream, but not the part about the magical diary. However, after some days and weeks pass, Vera becomes discontented. Her thoughts keep drifting to

the more arts-appreciating Kirsanov.[53]

49. At Dmitri's insistence, Vera tells him more about her third dream, including the ending where the diary tells her she does not love him. Lopukhov cries over the revelation, but realizes he has no control in the matter. Vera does not mention Kirsanov, but Dmitri quickly realizes that there is an attraction between Vera and Sasha. He senses this is the real reason why Kirsanov has been shying away.[54]

50. Lopukhov goes to Kirsanov to tell him he understands the situation. He insists that Kirsanov resume his visits. Kirsanov protests violently. They engage in a lengthy ethical debate. Kirsanov finally agrees to resume his visits, but only if Lopukhov accompanies he and Vera everywhere.[55]

51. Lopukhov admires the way Kirsanov plays the role of not being head over heels in love with Vera.[56]

52. Vera weeps as she confesses to Lopukhov that she loves Kirsanov. Lopukhov, who had anticipated this, takes it coolly. He tells Vera that he is glad for her happiness and they will remain friends. Vera keeps insisting she wants to love only Dmitri. Lopukhov refuses to accept this.[57]

53. After a convulsive struggle, Vera writes Lopukhov a note in which she tells him, "I cannot live without him . . . forgive me!"[58]

54. Lopukhov leaves St. Petersburg for Riazan to see his family. He departs without Vera.[59]

55. A month and a half later, in the middle of June, Lopukhov returns to St. Petersburg. On July 21, he leaves again, going to Moscow. On July 23 occurs the mysterious disappearance that is the subject of the opening pages. The narrator sardonically comple-ments the reader on guessing that the person who was

the subject of the mysterious disappearance was probably Lopukhov.[60]

56. A character named Rakhmetov makes his appearance.[61]

57. Rakhmetov, we are told, is the descendent of a thirteenth century Tartar chieftain. Many of the descendants had prominent military careers. He is 22 years old. He enjoyed his nickname, "Nikitushka Lomov," because Nikitushka Lomov was a legendary larger than life figure who pulled boats up and down the Volga. A tall slender youth, Rakhmetov energetically practiced gymnastics, and then worked as a common laborer, until his strength became enormous. He lugged water, carried wood, chopped wood, sawed trees, cut stone, dug earth, and hammered iron. He ate only beefsteak, almost raw. To learn to tow boats, he booked himself as a passenger on a Volga expedition. He then voluntarily joined the crew of laborers towing the boat. He outtowed four of the strongest men in doing this labor, and that is how he earned the nickname, "Nikitushka Lomov."

Kirsanov prescribed for Rakhmetov a course of reading for self-study. He spent almost all of his time reading. Rakhmetov led a very severe and ascetic lifestyle. He did not touch wine or women. He spent his ample fortune, inherited wealth, on meat but very little else. He slept on a bed of straw and in all other respects lived the life of a Spartan. The only spot on his conscience was a weakness for good cigars.[62]

58. The narrator abruptly cuts in and recounts how he, the narrator, personally met Rakhmetov, and how everybody was satisfied with him, in spite of his strange manners, due to his straightforward manner.

Rakhmetov asked the narrator whether he felt he could give him his full trust. The narrator, who had been told good things about Rakhmetov, replied, "yes." Rakhmetov immediately pronounced him to be either a liar or a villain. But the narrator saw that this was justified because the narrator really was lying about trusting Rakhmetov.[63]

59. We are told that Rakhmetov disappeared from St. Petersburg, and nobody knows what eventually happened to him. The narrator recounts two stories Kirsanov told about him. In the first, Kirsanov was called to treat Rakhmetov for injuries he sustained while deliberately lying on a bed of nails. In the second, Kirsanov was called to treat Rakhmetov for leg injuries sustained when he dove to halt a runaway horse cart, in which a young and attractive widow was trapped. The lady afterwards fell in love with Rakhmetov while she was nursing him to health. With some melancholy, Rakhmetov declined her advances, stating "people like me must not unite their fate with anyone else." He tells her that his hands are tied in the matter of love because his life is already dedicated to a greater cause.[64]

60. The narrator teases the reader with the statement that nothing more will be said of Rakhmetov, other than his one conversation with Vera immediately following the mysterious disappearance. He then challenges the reader to guess why Rakhmetov had to be personified in such exquisite detail.[65]

61. Rakhmetov informs Vera that the reason of his coming is to bring her a message from Lopukhov. The note is 10 to 12 lines long. We never learn exactly what it says. However, after she reads it, Vera appears much happier. Rakhmetov says by delivering the note

he is "fulfilling a pleasant duty." He comments that Dmitri and the more mature Vera were not very well adapted to each other. Much more is discussed on the philosophy of love, to the effect that in an intelligent person jealousy has no right to exist.[66]

62. The narrator teases the reader some more about putting Rakhmetov in the story. The narrator imagines that the reader will bring a lawsuit against him for doing so.[67]

63. The narrator claims that his purpose with Rakhmetov was to illustrate, via a figure much larger than life, the ordinariness and normalcy of his main characters, Vera Pavlovna, Dmitri Lopukhov, and Sasha Kirsanov. He gives a parable:

"A man who never saw anything but little huts, would take an ordinary house drawn on a piece of paper to be a palace. How can you go to work with such a person to show him that it is a house and not a palace? It is necessary on the same paper to draw at least a corner of a palace."[68]

64. Vera receives a letter from an unnamed correspondent "who had a close relationship" with the late Dmitri Sergeivitch Lopukhov. The letter gets into the distinction between people who are "social" and "not social." There are more parables, and discussions about Dmitri's reaction to Vera's third dream. The author claims to be a complete stranger to Vera, and describes himself as "a former medical student."[69]

65. A letter to Kirsanov from the same correspondent is also included.[70]

66. The narrator stuffs a napkin into the mouth of the reader who is about to exclaim that he knows who it is that wrote these letters.[71]

67. Vera writes a lengthy response to the correspondent, explaining her gratitude to Dmitri and assuring him that she has gotten over the shock of his passing. In this letter, there are allusions to the fact that it was necessary for Vera to really believe, and genuinely grieve, that Lopukhov had committed suicide, in order that the "world" would accept his death as a fact, freeing her to marry Kirsanov, which she did one week later.[72]

68. Kirsanov also writes a brief and embarrassed reply to the correspondent.[73]

69. The reader pulls the napkin out of his mouth and, shaking his head, shouts – "Immorality!"[74]

70. The correspondence continues three to four months. It then peters out due to a lack of replies by the correspondent.[75]

71. Vera's new day-to-day life is detailed. She lives with Sasha near the hospital where her husband works. She establishes a new sewing union, on the other side of town from the old one, which is managed by a friend, Mertsalova. Although Vera feels some regrets about not having accompanied Dmitri to Riazan, she also feels joy at her ability to express her love for Sasha.[76]

72. Vera enters into a series of discourses on woman's capacity for equality or, indeed, superiority to men in terms of endeavors and accomplishments. At the conclusion, Vera informs Sasha that she intends to pioneer a new and long overdue class of women doctors. "It is much easier for a woman to talk with a woman than with a man . . . I must try it."[77]

73. Many years pass. Vera becomes a doctor. Her lifestyle with Kirsanov resembles that with Lopukhov, including the two separate bedrooms and

the neutral room. One difference though is that Kirsanov is expected to enter Vera's bedroom every morning, without asking. Three years after their marriage, a boy named Mitya is born to Vera and Sasha.[78]

74. The narrator goes on another digression to praise the new paradigm exemplified by the marriage of Vera and Sasha, wherein the husband and wife enjoy every minute together and feel their love for each other more warmly and poetically ten years later than on the day they were married.[79]

75. Vera dreams her fourth dream. This one takes place in a grand Utopia. Vera gets a narration from a tsaritsa, a queen who seems to be the sister of the Bride of her bridegrooms. There is allusion that the tsaritsa is a deified version of Vera. The tsaritsa says all of her power is founded in the equal rights and relations of men and women.[80]

76. The Utopia envisioned in the dream is populated by a young, contented people. It has futuristic aluminum furniture, which seems magically light, as well as aluminum and glass doors. The Bride also appears in the dream. The tsaritsa states that the Bride has done the work to produce all these wonders. The Utopia in the vision now extends well beyond the southern borders of Russia into the Arabian desert, which has now been turned into a fertile land. The inhabitants of Utopia, except for a very small contingent, migrate to this warm, fertile land every winter.

The tsaritsa explains that all this transformation was accomplished using the same means and methods that Vera used in her sewing shop. The Bride explains, "Every happiness here is suited to every one's special faculty. All live here in the way that is the best for each to live; there is a full volition, a free volition for every one here."[81]

77. The sewing unions are running well. Vera and Mertsalova open a sale shop for their clothing items on the Nevsky Prospect. Two more years pass.[82]

78. A woman named Ekaterina Vasilyevna Polozova, affectionately called Katia, writes a letter to a friend describing the wonderful sewing shops, extolling the free social system introduced by Vera Pavlovna, its virtues and economics.[83]

79. We are given a lengthy history of Katia's father, Polozov. Polozov was a retired cavalry captain who, after first losing everything, then amassed a sizeable fortune of three to four million rubles as a businessman. After thus "pushing up the hill" he declined to remarry (Katia's mother had died). However, he was a stubborn man in his business dealings. He quarreled with an important personage. He took on a huge contract to sell goods (the narrator claims he does not know what kind of goods) which went bad when his goods were rejected, perhaps due to intervention of the person he had offended, his business failed, and he was forced to eat crow. As a result of this deal gone bad, he lost his fortune of millions of rubles. All that remained was a few thousand rubles and some shares in a factory that made stearine (a derivative of plant or animal oils used in making soaps, candles and ointments).[84]

80. While Polozov was wealthy, Katia as his daughter had many suitors. However, she became sick and started wasting. The five biggest doctors in St. Petersburg – real Big Wigs of the medical profession – could not figure out her ailment. They called

in a noted consultant, Sasha Kirsanov. Through a private interview, Kirsanov determined that the real problem with Katia was that she was pining to marry Jean Solovtsov, a man of whom her father disapproved. Kirsanov actually agreed with her father that it was a bad idea for Katia to marry Solovtsov, a member of Storeshnikov's shallow venal circle. In fact, Solovtsov was one of the friends who had accompanied Storeshnikov to the opera mentioned in the opening pages, where Verotchka had overheard Storeshnikov making a lewd wager about her in French. However, Kirsanov obtained Polozov's consent to the marriage using a stratagem. He agreed with Katia that if he could not get Polozov's consent, he would help her commit suicide. Next, he got the five Big Wigs to agree that since Katia's case was hopeless, it would be humane to put her to sleep with a huge injection of morphine and let her die painlessly. Then he informed Polozov that with full medical consensus, Katia was to be put to sleep, to die that morning. Under this fright, her father finally relented about Solovtsov.[85]

81. Kirsanov continued to personally manage Katia's case. He made sure Katia saw the real aspect of Solovtsov. She, in response, promptly changed her mind about marrying him.[86]

82. We now return to Polozov. He convinces the other shareholders to sell the stearine factory. In the capacity of an agent for the purchaser, a British concern, we meet a new character named Charles Beaumont, pronounced Bee-mont, and affectionately called Charlie.[87]

83. Beaumont tells the story that his father James was a Canadian whose family emigrated to New York when he was a child. After James grew up, he was

engaged to supervise the planting of a cotton plantation in the Crimea. The project was absurd and destined to failure because the climate in the Crimea is
utterly unsuited to grow cotton. He was fired. He then
got a job in a Russian distillery, in which he saved up
some money. With this, he returned to America to re-
tire. Charlie, his son, thus grew up in Russia to the
age of 20. After father James died, Charlie determined to move back to Russia. He secured a position
with the New York office of a London firm that had
business in St. Petersburg. This is what brought him
to negotiate the purchase of the stearine factory which
Polozov was then selling. The narrator rather awk-
wardly tells us that "in conformity with this tale,"
Charlie spoke Russian like a native Russian, but spoke
English with an accent. [88]

84. Beaumont finds himself at dinner with
Polozov and his blond daughter Katia. Since Polozov
has lost his fortune, she no longer has suitors.

85. Beaumont gets into an extended conversation
with Katia, after saying he is an ardent abolitionist.
The subject turns to the emancipation of women. He
tells her women in America are free. Katia exclaims
to her father that she wants to go to America as soon
as the factory is sold. Charlie tells Katia, "One can
find something to do in St. Petersburg." "I should like
to see it," she replies. Charlie then mentions Vera
Pavlovna's "experiment" in political economy. We
are told this is how Katia learned of the sewing shops
and related social system, extolled in her letter.[89]

86. Charlie Beaumont expresses great interest in
the doings of "Madame Kirsanova." At the same
time, he asks Katia not to mention his degree of
interest to Vera. Katia thinks that this is strange.[90]

87. Charlie begins a courtship of Katia, one that is approved of by her father since she has no other viable suitors. Charlie stalls the closing of the factory purchase, so that there will be more time to spend on his courtship of Katia. Katia becomes rather attached to Beaumont and his daily visits, although their relationship remains intellectual and platonic. The narrator apologizes to the reader for his inability to make the characters who are involved in romances treat each other with anything but coolness.[91]

88. The sale of the factory finally closes, but when it does, it is decided by the buyer that Charlie Beaumont will remain on in St. Petersburg to manage the factory.[92]

89. Charlie finally proposes marriage to the eager and willing Katia. But, when he does, the proposal comes with an unusual twist. Katia must seek the advice and consent of Vera to the marriage. Katia dutifully pays a visit to the Kirsanovs. "Christ is risen!" Vera exclaims with joy when she learns about Beaumont. Of course she is all in favor of his marriage to Katia.[93]

90. At Vera's request, Charlie tells a story of what happened during his stay in the United States. To benefit the cause of abolition, he wrote articles for the Tribune on the pernicious effects of slavery in Russia.[94]

91. The two families agree to reside in adjoining apartments with interconnecting doors. In this way, they all dwell happily, in a variation of the separate rooms lifestyle originally designed by Vera Pavlovna. Three years pass. Katia and Charlie have a son. Katia takes over for Vera running the sewing shops, as Vera now concentrates on her medical practice.[95]

92. We now enter into the most mysterious and controversial portion of a tale that is already highly enigmatic, to say the least. The Conclusion is so weird, its meaning so veiled, that it was actually omitted from several English language translations of the novel. Chernyshevsky fooled the censors with an allegorical ending that would prove extremely meaningful to his radical following.[96]

93. As spring is coming, Vera yearns for a last day suitable for a frosty winter picnic. When hope is almost lost, an unexpected late snowstorm comes along. Afterwards the sky becomes bright.[97]

94. Two sleighs dash away. One, with the Beaumonts and the Kirsanovs, is decorous, filled with talk and jokes. The second dashes ahead riotously, beyond control. It is piloted in its headlong enthusiasm by a woman dressed entirely in black, whose name we never hear. Four young men ride with the woman in the second sleigh. They race and fight with snowballs. The race ends at the stearine factory. The Lady in Black sees Katia's father Polozov on the platform of the factory stairs. She says he is not old, and she caresses his gray whiskers. She teases her young men about her flirtation with him.[98]

95. Entering the salon inside the factory, everyone is exhausted from the sleigh racing. The Lady in Black asks all those present to tell her their story, beginning with Vera. Vera obliges. The Lady complements her on the story, but comments that it is very pathetic as it has a happy ending. It is intimated, obscurely, that the four young men traveling with the Lady in Black are the hope of the Fatherland. They are eager to give their lives for the cause by launching themselves headlong into death. Further intimated: the Lady in Black is their reaper.

96. The Lady dissuades the young men from committing suicide at that very moment. She announces that she is tired and would like to take a nap. As Katia escorts her to a bedroom, the others follow her condition with the utmost interest and concern. However, one of the Lady's young fanatics, Mosolov, urges everyone else in the party to continue to dance and shout and sing while the Lady sleeps.

97. Amidst the gaiety, Vera and Katia each ask their husbands in a whisper, "Could something like this happen to me?" Each husband tries to tell his wife that it could not. But their answers are doubtful and not reassuring.[99]

98. Nikitin, another of the Lady's young followers, asks Charlie if he saw an unnamed Russian in America. It is never stated that he is referring to Rakhmetov. Nikitin expresses the notion that this unnamed Russian would make a nice match for the Lady in Black.[100]

99. The Lady in Black awakens from her nap and rejoins the party in the salon. Now she tells something of herself. Much is presented indirectly, through verse. She was born of noble rank, in Scotland. After weighing it well, she made the choice to give up her rank and race for the glory of a cause. Her love was a poor man born for strife, an outlaw. He died a soldier. She must not be sorry. "I was told what to expect."[101]

100. Chernyshevsky adds a one-page Epilogue, entitled "Change of Scenes," that is still more cryptic.[102] The Lady in mourning is no longer dressed in black. Now she is sporting a bright pink dress and a pink hat. In her carriage ride three youths, including Nikitin and Mosolov, and another man, aged 30, who is never named. The Lady gazes admiringly on

Nikitin and comments that in him her hope had grown into assurance in the two years since the picnic with the Kirsanovs and the Beaumonts. The narrator breaks in and concludes with one last aside, challenging the reader to believe in the impossible. His final words: "I hope it will be very soon."[103]

What Is to Be Done? met with a thoroughly hostile reception from the Russian literary community. Fellow writers panned the work due to its clumsy narration, awkward characters and lack of overall coherence. One critic wrote, "It is quite burdensome to read. Chernyshevsky's novel from the point of view of art is lower than any criticism; it is simply laughable."[104] Leo Tolstoy had one of his characters label it "boring."[105] Ivan Turgenev, who popularized the term "nihilist"[106] in his famous work, Fathers and Sons, wrote of Chernyshevsky's work in *What Is to Be Done?*: "His manner arouses physical disgust in me, like wormseed.[107]

Cover of 1867 edition of *What Is to Be Done?*

Regardless of its literary flaws, Chernyshevsky's utopian novel found an adoring audience among a new and rebellious generation of Russians that emerged during the 1860's.[108] Strikingly reminiscent of America in the 1960's, in the 1860's energetic Russian youth renounced the values of the establishment. There was a pronounced generation gap.

Young men from good families defied their parents and grew their hair long. Young women defied theirs and cropped their hair short. Funky oversize blue spectacles became a symbol of the nihilist. There was a women's liberation movement, accompanied by a kind of sexual revolution. Love triangles, the *menage a trois*, open marriages and extramarital sexual partnerships all came into vogue.[109]

The rebellious Russian Generation of the Sixties found a profound message in *What Is to Be Done?* To them it conveyed faith in a vision of a future anarchist utopia. After the book was belatedly banned by the government censors, many of the faithful copied out the 400 plus page work by hand, word for word.[110] A schoolgirl was considered a dunce if she was not acquainted with the exploits of Vera Pavlovna. Young Russian women sought to emulate Vera's virtues. Abstemious marriages patterned on that of Vera and Dmitri Lopukhov abounded. Couples consciously modeled their lifestyles on Vera's, especially, adopting the odd practice of having separate rooms for each spouse. Bright young people turned their backs on inherited family property and existing business enterprises in order to establish communal ventures. Sewing cooperatives, in particular, were founded by the dozens.[111]

Chapter 2: The New Tsar Liberator

The rise of the Generation of the Sixties happened soon after the accession to the throne of Alexander Nikolaevitch Romanov, who upon the death of his father in 1855 was titled Tsar Alexander II. The new Tsar was only 38 years old. He had a tendency to lean to the liberal side of autocratic Russian politics. A sensitive sort, young Alexander had always displayed much more fondness for the pomp of military parades and the polish of military uniforms than the brutish imperial business of fighting battles against heathens and pacifying hostile territory.[112] His father, Tsar Nicholas I, felt it necessary to prepare Alexander for eventual rule. In 1837 Nicholas sent the 19-year old heir apparent on a tour of discovery throughout the vast regions ruled from St. Petersburg. While touring in a remote area of northeast Russia, on the way to Siberia, Alexander attended an exhibition where he was guided by a well educated young noble, Alexander Herzen. Herzen had been sentenced to live there for having attended a festival in which subversive poetry was read. After meeting Herzen in this way, the Tsarevich personally interceded for Herzen and obtained from his father a commutation of Herzen's banishment.[113]

Another place young Alexander Romanov sojourned on his voyage was Kurgan, Siberia. There, consigned to exile, resided a group of liberal nobles who had supported the so-called "Decembrist" revolt of 1825, opposing his father's accession to the throne, but who did not participate so overtly and directly in the rebellion to be hanged as ringleaders. Though the exiled Decembrists were not allowed to speak with the young Tsarevitch, Alexander had felt pity for these convicts. Immediately after his visit he had urged his father to show them clemency.[114]

Upon becoming Emperor, one of Alexander's first acts was to sign pardons and commutations for the remaining Decembrists exiled in Siberia.[115] The new Tsar was awed by the magnitude of the powers now reposed in him as supreme ruler of the enormous Russian empire. He humbly asked for divine assistance in assuming to undertake the role of supreme judge.[116] While vowing loyalty to his father's legacy, Alexander II promptly embarked on his own policies, which were in sympathy with the progressive elements of Russian thought, and thus stood in contrast to his father's conservatism. For instance, very soon after his accession, travel policies were loosened so that it became easy for Russians to obtain passports to travel abroad in Western Europe.[117]

More students were now allowed to pursue higher education. Entrance into the Russian university system, under Nicholas, had been basically restricted to privileged sons of the nobility. At the time of Alexander's accession, there were only 2,900 university students in a country of 70 million people.[118] Alexander cracked open the doors of the universities. Between 1853 and 1860 student enrollment in the five Russian universities (St. Petersburg, Moscow, Kiev, Kharkov and Kazan) climbed from 2,809 to 4,935.[119]

Though still very low in absolute numbers, the influx of new students and faculty would soon spray into Russian society a stream of young intellectuals and activists. Many of these men and women felt a strong urge to dedicate their lives to ameliorating the ills of Russian society. They were particularly concerned with the poverty, disease and often brutal discipline of the Russian peasantry, which young people from middle and upper class backgrounds found appalling. Eventually, most of the starry eyed students embarked on family life and productive careers. They favored the granting of academic and personal freedoms, as well as the abolition of serfdom, but they did not choose to sacrifice their own lives to attain these goals.[120]

However, a very small percentage of the students in the Generation of the Sixties would follow a different path. They would be drawn into a deepening fascination with the ideal of dramatic change through revolution, rather than gradual evolution. These "revolutionaries" would, themselves, evolve. They would organize. They would polarize, disdaining "liberals" and believers in constitutional reforms. They would theorize. They would rationalize. Ultimately, from the core of uncompromising "revolutionaries" would be distilled an even smaller circle, one composed exclusively of individuals who would refine and reinforce one another's delusions. This group would ultimately reject all other forms of direct action in favor of a vision of effecting dramatic change through spectacular murderous exploits. According to their own terminology, they were committed "terrorists." Their own deaths, and martyrdom in support of the cause, were integral to the vision. They created a virtual test tube laboratory for terrorism.

Early in his reign, Alexander delegated power to liberal ministers. He also gave much deference to the views of his younger brother Konstantin, always an outspoken reform advocate, and his aunt Hélène, a French-educated progressive. Konstantin and Hélène vehemently opposed the institution of serfdom. They bolstered Alexander in his resolve to make its abolition the key initiative of his reign.

The battle over Russian serfdom, a form of slavery, was fought out in parallel with the struggle to abolish slavery in the United States. In many respects, Russia's serfdom was even more challenging than America's problem with slavery. Out of an estimated 70 million total Russians, 50 million were in some form of bondage when Alexander became Emperor. Ending serfdom had been one of the principal "planks" of the Decembrists. Tsar Nicholas I, after crushing the Decembrists, sought to defuse the issue. He had, in fact, appointed his son Alexander to a secret committee to try to work out a solution.[121] The major issue and obstacle was: How to free the serfs, without at the same time granting them land? To give the serfs land, it was felt, the government must take away valuable land from land owners. And as in the antebellum southern United States, large plantation owners (in Russia, more commonly called "estate owners") formed a powerful and entrenched constituency. They depended upon and perpetuated the institutions of serfdom.[122]

Upon accession to the throne, Alexander rapidly appointed his own committee to find a path to emancipation.[123] However, in a pattern we will see repeated, a majority of the nobles and councilors whom Alexander placed on this committee were conservatives, basically hostile to the idea of a wholesale liberation. They were just as content to keep the system as it was or, at most, to enact slow and small changes. They expected to watch the new Emperor's anti-serfdom initiative die of its own weight, just like all the previous ones under Nicholas. In order to overcome this inertia, Alexander appointed his brother Konstantin to the emancipation committee. Alexander also took the bold

Alexander Nikolaevitch Romanov, Tsar Alexander II

step of publicly announcing his support f or ending serfdom.[124] Alexander thus earned his enduring nickname, "The Tsar Liberator."

Debate on how to end serfdom dragged on interminably during the first five years of Alexander's rule. Constant political battles raged over the issue. Alexander kept pushing for results. Finally, in January 1861, the Emperor personally intervened with the committee and insisted that a decree must be in place by mid February, well before the planting season could start. On February 19, 1861, the historic imperial decree abolishing serfdom was signed.[125]

Some highlights of the new emancipation law included:

- The serfs would receive the rights of citizens, and perpetual freedom.

- They also received the perpetual use of their homes.

- The serfs received an allotment of ground similar to what they had cultivated in the past; however, they were required to "purchase" this ground from the landowner.

- Only domestic serfs were emancipated without ground.

- A two year transitional period was decreed, in which the existing relationships would hold, prior to emancipation.

- During this two year transition period, the "purchase price" of the peasant plots was to be negotiated.

- Disputes over the land purchases would be resolved by "peace arbitrators" selected from the local nobility.

- To facilitate the transition, the government would make low interest loans, to enable the landowners to receive the money and to allow the peasants to pay off their land acquisition over a period of years.

- Much of the land, that was previously under collective cultivation, would remain under collective cultivation, in the form of the mir. The mir would also be responsible to pay the taxes.

- To figure out how much land each freed serf would receive, a complicated formula was used. In part, it was broken down geographically. Russia was divided into the "fertile" zone, the "non fertile" zones, and the "steppes," which were themselves subdivided into 16 categories. [126]

A rough parallel could be drawn between Alexander's emancipation decree and U.S. President Barack Obama's "Affordable Health Care" act. Both initiatives produced a legislative package that was, in the end, a patched up package of compromises, with many flaws, injustices, and loopholes. It was easy to underestimate the vast economic, administrative, and social difficulties and complexities involved in working out the emancipation law. As a result, advocates on both sides of the issue were left unhappy. Many were highly critical of the final decree. Among the more immediate problems, landowners naturally sold to the serfs those of their lands that were the least desirable due to issues such as sand or marshy conditions. The two year period of continued servitude prescribed prior to emancipation seemed like an eternity. Also, there was a provision in the law that allowed freed serfs to elect to receive only one quarter of their land allotment, and pay nothing, instead of "purchasing" their entire allotment. Many peasants of course opted to pay nothing, and as a result, they received an allotment of land that was too small to make a sustainable living. Due to protests over these problems and other perceived "tricks" embedded in the emancipation decree, the popular adulation Alexander received upon its issuance was short lived.[127]

In early 1861, just as the emancipation decree was in its final stages of preparation, major protests erupted in Poland against its rule by imperial Russia. Partly because of his German heritage (Alexander's mother was Prussian, and he had spent much of his youth visiting Germanic areas), Alexander had a tendency to look upon the partition of Poland between Prussia and Russia as justified and inevitable.[128] On the Poland question, he found himself strongly torn between the hawkish advice of his father's former aides, who urged a policy of repression, and the doves associated with his brother Konstantin and the liberal ministers, who urged conciliation. On March 25, 1861, Alexander announced a series of major concessions to Polish autonomy, including a Polish council of state, educational reforms, and increased freedom for the Catholic church to operate in Poland. He also installed a Polish nobleman, Alexander Wielopolski, as a sort of virtual vice-tsar of the Polish territory.[129]

Unfortunately, neither Alexander's autonomy concessions nor his appointment of Wielopolski were enough to pacify the nationalists dedicated to an independent Poland. Alexander's benevolent moves only led the militants to demand more. The Polish nobility, clergy, youth, and notable citizens all called for an end to Russian dominion over Polish territory. Polish partisans also agitated abroad, particularly in Paris.[130] Little by little, the "Polish cause" was widely accepted and championed throughout Europe. Wielopolski, despite being Polish, was viewed as an illegitimate imposition, resulting in hostility. Alexander was soon forced to recall him. Next, Alexander tried appointing his brother Konstantin to the post of vice-tsar for Poland. Despite Konstantin's strong credentials as an ardent liberal, his appointment again failed to quell the brewing nationalistic ferment within Poland.[131] Polish partisans declared that they preferred Siberia or the gibbet to the ignominious insult of an "amnesty" offered as one of the Tsar's conciliatory gestures.

The balance of power within the government was tipped back toward the reactionaries by a series of terrorist attacks that occurred in Poland, including an assassination attempt against Konstantin himself. The perpetrators were caught, and hung. Their martyrdom provoked more bitterness and recriminations among the Polish patriots. Alexander found himself emotionally affected by the attempt on his brother. In response, he approved the dispatch of Russian troops into Poland. Konstantin was recalled to Russia and, under the supervision of ruthless military governors who replaced him, a deadly purge commenced. Thousands of Poles were arrested, executed, and sent to forced labor in Siberia. Russian was made the obligatory official language in Poland. Even the church fell under strict scrutiny. Convents that were suspected of sheltering or helping Polish partisans were closed. Pope Pius IX protested in vain. Most of the surviving Polish partisan leaders fled to the West.[132]

Alexander's Polish policy obliterated his remaining goodwill among Russian progressives.[133] Alexander Herzen, who by now had left Russia and who had become one of the most influential Russian expatriates, cancelled his planned toast to Alexander's liberation of the serfs. Instead, in his London periodical *The Bell* [*Kolokol*], he chastised: "You, Alexander Nikolaevitch, why did you rob us of our joyful occasion?" Now Herzen drank "for the full unconditional independence of Poland."[134] Yet Alexander's hard line policy on Poland was thoroughly supported by mainstream Russian public opinion. Most Russians favored territorial aggrandizement, and did not want lands of the empire stripped off.[135]

By this time, some within the new generation of energized Russian youth had turned to writing as a means to push for social progress. At the center of the progressive Russian press was a radical periodical called *The Contemporary* [*Sovremennik*]. The writers who published in *The Contemporary*, including Chernyshevsky who was one of its principal contributors between 1858 and 1860, had nothing but contempt for liberals and their plans for peasant reform. Chernyshevsky was not an advocate of reform, but of revolution.[136] He privately criticized emigrés like Herzen and Mikhail Bakhunin as being hopelessly behind the times, in terms of the "liberation movement."[137]

Chernyshevsky was born in 1828 in Saratov, 840 kilometers southeast of Moscow. His father was a priest.

Young Nikolai himself grew up devout. He was groomed to follow in his father's profession. Thus he was sent to Russian Orthodox seminary, where he proved to be a precocious and gifted student. By the time he graduated, he had read most of the classics of contemporary world literature, including the works of George Sand, the alter ego and pen name used by the feminist French author Amantine-Lucile-Aurore Dupin, as well as Jean-Jacques Rousseau and Charles Dickens. He had acquired a working ability in eight modern and classic languages, including, French, Italian, German, and English, in addition to his native Russian. His parents, convinced that a brilliant future awaited their son, eagerly sent him to university at St. Petersburg, the capital of the Russian empire, in 1846. But upon his arrival in the capital, Nikolai was regarded as nothing special, just another boy from the provinces. He was awkward and very nearsighted, peering through thick glasses. He lacked social graces such as musical talent and dancing ability. His relative poverty was reflected in his wardrobe, which quickly made his origins obvious to his university peers, most of whom were children of the aristocracy.

Chernyshevsky's rather large and sensitive ego felt crushed. The experience altered him deeply. In his diary he spoke of a coldness that crept into his heart and produced a renunciation of emotion. He abandoned his former devout religious faith and, in its place, ardently embraced a philosophy of utilitarian materialism. This, essentially, is the utopian world view reflected in *What Is to Be Done?* As part of his transformation Chernyshevsky embraced with passion the political outlook of revolutionary socialism.[138] Thus, Nikolai finally succeeded in gaining acceptance by others who were following a similar path.

The year 1848 witnessed a wave of nationalistic and republican oriented uprisings against hereditary monarchies throughout Europe, including in France, Germany, Ireland, Denmark, Austria, Hungary and Italy. Russian students were acutely aware of current world events. Stimulated by the hope for radical change, Russian utopian socialists, including some prominent intellectuals and writers, formed a group called the Petrashevsky circle, named after its original organizer Mikhail Petrashevsky. The very idea of such a group was highly illegal under the repressive regime of Nicholas I. The Tsar's secret police soon learned of the Petrashevsky circle. They arrested all of its members whom they could catch. Many were sentenced to death, only to have the sentences commuted at the very last second by a special "dispensation" of mercy from Nicholas himself. Among these was Fyodor Dostoyevsky, who at the time was 28, seven years older than Chernyshevsky. Dostoyevsky spent four years in prison as a result of his involvement in the Petrashevsky circle. Chernyshevsky, as a university student, also was active with Petrashevsky, but apparently his involvement escaped the attention of the secret police.

After graduating in March 1851, Chernyshevsky returned to Saratov and became a teacher. Two years later, he was married.[139] However, his relationship with his wife Olga was never happy. Once married, she all but abandoned Nikolai, whom she found tedious and pedantic, and whose ideas she never found remotely interesting.[140] Unencumbered by any semblance of a family life, Chernyshevsky returned to St. Petersburg where he immersed himself in radical journalism. This he did predominantly in the form of *The Contemporary*, which he took over editing during the mid-1850's.

By 1861 Chernyshevsky was ready to launch into revolutionary agitation. To counter goodwill generated by the Tsar's proclamation freeing the serfs, Chernyshevsky wrote demagogic pamphlets. He did not, however, call for an immediate uprising. Instead, he urged the "people" to stay quiet and gather their strength until such time as their "friends" and "well-wishers" called for them to rise. He convinced himself that the revolution would occur in 1863. In order to build momentum in that direction, a group of St. Petersburg radicals inspired by Chernyshevsky formed a new secret organization, named Zemlya i Volya [Land and Freedom] to exploit the main frustration accompanying the Tsar's emancipation decree – the fact that land grants did not accompany the serfs' freedom. Zemlya i Volya would be the forebear of a series of underground groups organized by radicals who emerged from the Generation of the Sixties.[141]

Russian governments have long been very proficient in techniques of surveillance. In Alexander II's era, the Russian intelligence agency charged with spying on Russian subjects was called the Third Section of the Okhrana [meaning, Guard]. Chernyshevsky, rightly suspected of being an instigator of student protests, was a major object of its study. His janitor and cook provided the Third Section with the fascinating intelligence that he seemed to sleep only two or three hours per night, spending the rest writing behind the locked door to his study. He was observed being visited by army officers, by left wing dissidents, and by suspected Poles.[142] In late April 1862, Prince Vasily Dolgorukov, chief of police, presented a report to Alexander in which he concluded that liberal policies had led to an organization that was trying to take power. He recommended the arrest of 50 subversive persons including Chernyshevsky.[143] Alexander, however, did not immediately follow this recommendation. He took it under advisement.

In May of 1862, a series of major urban fires struck St. Petersburg. The largest of these, on May 28, 1862,[144] struck the Apraxin Dvor, a huge outdoor public market filled with shops and stores. Arson was suspected. Although no proof was ever produced, in the public mind the fires were associated with left wing agitators typified by Chernyshevsky and the writings of *The Contemporary*. A popular sentiment of fear and distrust, fueled by the fires, bolstered the conservatives in their push for repressive measures. On July 7, 1862, Chernyshevsky was arrested.[145] His prison based authorship of *What Is to Be Done?* would follow.

Alexander still moved forward with liberalizing. He continued with his opening of the universities, and he also supported initiatives to make the governance of the university system itself more enlightened. He took action to outlaw corporal punishment, in the form of control techniques such as beating and whipping, which were previously endorsed by codified law in Russia, and which were notoriously applied to the bodies of serfs. Alexander was aware that these punishments were was regarded as medieval and barbaric by "modern" societies. On April 7, 1863, Alexander signed a decree banning the *bastonnade* (judicial beatings), as well as branding with a hot iron and all corporal punishment. However, an exception permitted whipping to remain an approved method of discipline within the military and in prisons.[146] This exception would prove fateful for Alexander.

Alexander also instituted sweeping reforms of the Russian justice system. On November 20, 1864, he signed a decree that thoroughly modernized and overhauled the Russian court system. It introduced such concepts as confrontation of witnesses, the right to defense attorneys, public trials, independent judges protected from removal from office, speedier trials, and equality before the law. Criminal trials were now to be decided by juries. This change, too, would be intertwined in an unexpected way with Alexander's fate.

Chapter 3: The Prophet of Anarchism, Mikhail Bakhunin

    While Alexander was busy trying to reform the institutions of government in Russia, Mikhail Bakhunin was busy advocating the abolition of all government. Starting in the mid to late 1860's, he became the world's foremost advocate of revolutionary anarchy. Bakhunin is a fascinating character study. Although he did share some traits of the profile of the terrorist, and while his writings and ideas about anarchy served as a major inspiration to generations of terrorists, he was not himself a terrorist. He lacked above all the death wish and zest for martyrdom that is a recurring theme in terrorists. He certainly was not an ascetic. Further setting him apart, on rare occasion he compromised with authority figures. Terrorists usually disdain authority figures. As a direct result of such compromise, rather than ending his life rotting in a miserable Russian prison, Bakhunin survived and evolved into the venerated standard bearer of anarchism.

Mikhail Bakhunin was a product of the upper Russian nobility. His father, who had been educated in Italy, owned 500 serfs. Mikhail's early education consisted entirely of self-teaching through reading under the supervision of his parents. Bakhunin as a youth felt a great love for his father, whom he regarded as an authority on everything. He was not nearly as fond of his mother. "Vain and egotistical" were the criticisms.[147] These same terms could be applied with equal justice to the fully grown Mikhail Bakhunin.

Mikhail grew to be a large man, over six feet in height. When combined with his outgoing demeanor and his charming, fun loving personality, his stature was bound to get him attention from women. Over the period of his teens and twenties he was never lacking for female admirers, many of whom were devoted and passionate correspondents. It appears, however, that he was sexually impotent, an impediment which led him to avoid marriage proposals. Another likely factor was his strong affinity for "liberty," a value which might arguably find itself diluted by the constraints of conjugal life.

Bakhunin spent his childhood on the family estate in Pryamukhino, about two and one half hours by driving northwest of Moscow. It was as close as possible to idyllic. Certainly his later incitements to revolt were not born of an unhappy or impoverished childhood. At age 14, in 1828, Bakhunin was sent to live and study at the School of Cadets in St. Petersburg. The harsh military discipline he encountered there was a shock after his cozy boyhood. After enduring several years of the academy, he flunked out due to sustained lack of effort. After another year of desultory army service, he managed to resign his commission and go back to being a civilian.[148] For the rest of his life, Bakhunin would never hold what could be considered a regular job. Except during his time in prison, he would always basically be supported by wealthy family members, friends and patrons. Thus, it is one of Bakhunin's most profound ironies that such a man would attain renown for his zealous advocacy of the abolition of all social class, and especially, advocacy of the abolition of all inherited wealth. Virtually his entire life was spent living off people's inherited fortunes!

Before reaching the age of 20, Bakhunin took up the first of his many protest causes, railing against the arranged marriage of the oldest of his four sisters.[149] He was successful in preventing this union, although the sister herself would die soon after, of tuberculosis. When he returned home from his military service he continued to play the part of the family rebel, announcing that he wished to leave Russia to study in Berlin. Bakhunin was unable to get the money from his father to finance this greatly desired sojourn. His father gave the needed parental consent for the venture, but pleaded bad harvests, droughts, and other expenses as a reason for not providing Mikhail the money for it. Mikhail was, however, successful in getting a "loan" for the venture from Alexander Herzen (the same Herzen mentioned above), who lent him 1,000 rubles against a promise to repay him from funds Bakhunin's father would later send when times improved.[150] Herzen would turn out to be Bakhunin's lifelong friend, financial supporter, and an important figure in his own right in the history of the Generation of the Sixties.

While in Berlin, Bakhunin and Ivan Turgenev, the future author, met on July 24, 1840. They immediately became fast friends, so much so, that several months later, Bakhunin moved out of the apartment he shared with his sister and moved in as Turgenev's roommate. They were unified by their tall stature, their aristocratic elegance, and their Slavic charm. In October 1841, Turgenev traveled by himself to the Bakhunin family estate in Pryamukhino, where he stayed for six days and became very popular with the whole family.[151]

From Germany Mikhail informed his siblings he would

not return to Russia. He promised, "Turgenev will explain it to you." Then, after moving to Switzerland, Bakhunin lived largely by virtue of funds that he "borrowed" from Turgenev. He also did finally receive money from his father. The Russian secret police began taking an interest in Bakhunin. In November 1843, they visited Pryamukhino and asked his father to get Mikhail to return to Russia. They also asked the elder Bakhunin to stop sending Mikhail money. Russian diplomats in Switzerland served Mikhail with a formal order requiring him to return to Russia. Although he accepted the order politely, Mikhail had no intention of obeying. He shortly left Berne for Belgium. From this point on, Bakhunin was an outlaw in Russia.[152]

Upon his move to Belgium, Bakhunin became involved with the leading European leftists of the day. He met Karl Marx during a visit to Paris in 1845. The two of them would have a long and stormy history, characterized by bitter battles. From the very beginning, Bakhunin did not warm to Marx on a personal level, even though the two moved in the same political circles, and even though Bakhunin admired Marx for his intellect. Bakhunin wrote of Marx: "Being German and a Jew, he is from head to toe an authoritarian." This went against Bakhunin's libertarian grain. Bakhunin considered Marx to be conceited, treacherous and sneaky, all accusations more or less borne out by a variety of devious stratagems Marx eventually employed with success against Bakhunin.[153]

Marx was expelled from France in early 1845. He then relocated with his family to Belgium. Bakhunin remained in Paris, where he became a devotee of the progressive salon of George Sand. While living in Paris between 1845 and 1847, Bakhunin began earning his reputation for passionately championing other people's causes. Bakhunin's friend Vissarion Belinsky would write of him: "He was born and will die a mystic, an idealist, a romantic." A cause Bakhunin adopted was Polish nationalism. In late 1847, because of a public address which Bakhunin gave on the subject, Russian diplomats in Paris learned of Bakhunin's loudly expressed sentiments. They immediately protested his presence to the French government. On December 14, 1847, Bakhunin was officially expelled from France and ordered to leave the country within 24 hours. This added to Bakhunin's reputation and made him a hero to the French left, which strongly protested this government action.[154]

Bakhunin obeyed the expulsion order and, like Marx before him, went to Brussels. However, in Belgium Bakhunin was far less content than he had been in Paris. The very Poles whose cause Bakhunin was busy supporting did not trust him all that much. Marx through his allies spread rumors, which some of the Poles believed, that Bakhunin was really secretly a Russian spy. Bakhunin was becoming embittered in his relations with Germans. This was a fairly inevitable result of his persistent advocacy that Poles and other Slavic peoples should be "freed of the German yoke," by which he was referring to both the Prussian occupation of part of Poland, and the Germanic-dominated Austria-Hungarian empire which included numerous Slavic speaking territories.[155]

Dramatic events soon changed Bakhunin's mood. On February 22, 1848, barricades were erected by protesters in Paris. Stunningly, the French ruler Louis Philippe responded by abdicating and accepting exile. Bakhunin immediately obtained a false passport and went to Paris to take part in the ensuing power struggle. He preached the destruction of all authority, far more than any particular replacement of it. It was here that Marc Caussidiere, the "president of the barricades" and later prefect of Paris police, uttered the most famous epithet about Bakhunin. "The first day of the revolution he is an absolute treasure, but on the second day, you have to shoot him."[156]

In the spring of 1848, anti-monarchical fervor swept through all of Europe. At the beginning of March, new constitutions were adopted under pressure by rulers of numerous proto-Italian principalities. Metternich fled Vienna, the capital of Austria. The Emperor of Austria-Hungary, to save his throne, also promised a constitution. Even the King of Prussia, in Berlin on March 21, accepted the creation of a constitution. The French provisional government gave Bakhunin 2,000 francs to go to the Prussian-occupied portion of Poland, the grand duchy of Posen, to work for the cause of revolution there. Cynics viewed this largesse as mainly due to the government's desire to get Bakhunin out of France.[157]

Bakhunin's mission quickly got into difficulties. In Berlin, he was arrested at the instance of the Russian ambassador. However, the French ambassador intervened and demanded that Prussia not extradite him to Russia. The Prussian government complied, but after releasing him it forbade Bakhunin to travel to Posen. Instead, he was sent to Breslau in Silesia, ethnically Polish territory near the eastern German border. Here, Bakhunin was unable to start any serious trouble. Many Polish partisans were suspicious of Bakhunin because he was Russian, and because of the rumor spread by Marx that he was secretly an agent of the Russian government.

On May 15, 1848, full-scale revolution broke out in Austria. The Austria-Hungarian Emperor fled from Vienna to Innsbruck, where he was protected by his Slavic guard. Bakhunin and others asked, why would Slavs protect a Germanic Emperor? A peoples' congress dedicated to promoting pan-Slavic solidarity in confrontation to Germanic rule was called to occur in Prague. Bakhunin left Breslau to attend. As usual, however, Bakhunin was unable to accept participation in a political process. Instead he adopted what would become a terrorist's normal mechanism whenever confronted by the hurly burly inherent in politics: retreat into a secret society.[158] Then, just as the congress had ended, a revolt suddenly broke out in Prague on June 12, 1848. Even though he had originally discouraged it, Bakhunin could not resist going to the barricades. This pan-Slavic nationalist rebellion was put down fairly quickly by Austrian troops.

Bakhunin evaded capture and returned to Berlin, where he spent the summer of 1848. However, it was a frustrating time for him. While Marx was libeling him in print by accusing him of being the Tsar's spy, the Russian diplomatic corps was busy seeking his extradition on charges of conspiring to assassinate the Tsar. Bakhunin was arrested and his residence was searched. The police found ample evidence of his pro-Slavic, and hence anti-German, rhetoric. Now, Bakhunin was ordered to leave Prussia. He found a refuge in Dresden, capital of the independent German kingdom of Saxony. Dresden was, at the time, a haven for liberals. Here he wrote of how the world was awaiting an impending mass anarchist uprising by the peasantry. He looked to Russia for the start of this revolution.

One who spent time with Bakhunin while he was in Dresden was the opera composer Richard Wagner. Wagner remarked of Bakhunin:

> I was immediately astonished at the strange and imposing personality of this man who was then in his prime, being in this thirties. Everything about him was colossal and forceful. I don't think he gave me a second thought – he wasn't really looking for intellectuals. What he wanted was people with energy who were ready for action. It was impossible to oppose his pitiless arguments. He placed his hopes in the total destruction of our entire civilization. Putting this force of destruction in motion seemed to him to be the only object worthy of a sentient man. Otherwise, he was a likable fellow, with a delicate sensibility. At the same time he was preaching terrifying theories, Bakhunin, who had noticed that I had difficulty with my eyes, never stopped shading the

light for an entire hour with his oversized hand so that I would not be exposed to a light that was too bright.

Wagner also noted Bakhunin's voracious appetite. He did not go in for the German manner of eating dainty sandwiches. He would take everything intended for the sandwich and just gobble it down as rapidly as possible.[159]

Bakhunin kept conflating the idea of a pan-Slavic rebellion with the idea of an anarchist revolution. He was unaware, or at any rate refused to acknowledge, that the two concepts had almost nothing to do with one another. He kept urging an uprising in Bohemia. In a strange twist, while Bakhunin was busy trying without any success to foment unrest, a successful revolution by constitutionalists broke out "right before his very eyes" in Dresden. Otto Heubner, the leader of this uprising, did not even know Bakhunin. He called him "Boukanin." Heubner did not share any of Bakhunin's anarchist ideas. However, Bakhunin heartily jumped on the bandwagon and adopted the rebel cause. All of the eyewitnesses in Dresden testified that Bakhunin suddenly acted like he was in charge of the uprising. People saw him in City Hall giving out orders and making decisions.[160]

The rebellion was rapidly crushed after only four days, with the aid of Prussian troops who were sent to the aid of the deposed ruler of Saxony. Bakhunin fled, along with the provisional rebel government, 75 kilometers west to Chemnitz. There, in the middle of the night, Bakhunin was caught and arrested. As a result of his unplanned participation in a rebellion that was totally unrelated to his declared goals, he was sentenced to death for treason. But this sentence was commuted to life in prison. After a delay of around two years, a deal was finally worked out pursuant to which the Germans rid themselves of the diplomatic embarrassment of having Bakhunin on their hands. Bakhunin was sent to Austria, and from there, back to Russia. His Austrian chains were literally exchanged, at the frontier, for Russian chains.[161]

Tsar Nicholas I's government consigned the captive anarchist to Russian prisons which featured conditions so harsh and sickening that many convicts did not survive. In close confinement, Bakhunin became obese. He lost his teeth, as well as all vestiges of youthfulness.[162] In all likelihood, death in prison would have been the end of Bakhunin's story, but for two factors that intervened. One was Bakhunin's willingness to grovel, and to renounce his anarchist "principles," to try to win clemency from the authorities. The other was his willingness to allow, and even encourage, the intervention and aid of aristocratic family members.

While interned in the Peter and Paul Fortress in St. Petersburg, Bakhunin wrote a "Confession" to curry favor with Tsar Nicholas. The text of this "Confession" was buried in the secret police archives. It only came to light after the Russian revolution, in 1921. Its publication caused a bit of a sensation because in it, Bakhunin the "fearless revolutionary" was revealed to be a man capable of writing for the moment, as an almost smarmy admirer of the Tsar, and certainly not as an advocate of overthrow of the tsarist regime. In the "Confession," Bakhunin attempted to play up his pan-Slavist efforts and to portray himself as anti-German.[163]

In the spring of 1854 Tsar Nicholas, facing a threat from the British Navy to St. Petersburg due to the hostilities of the Crimean War, decided to transfer Bakhunin to Schlüsselberg Prison, another notorious Russian dungeon. In a letter from Schlüsselberg, Bakhunin expressed great patriotism, supporting the wartime cause. The premise of the Crimean war from Russia's point of view (i.e., freeing Slavic peoples in the Balkans from rule by Islamic Turkey) was consistent with his pan-Slavism. In December 1854, Bakhunin's father died after a long convalescence. This freed up his mother Varvara to devote herself full time to trying to get Mikhail released. She was very tenacious in her efforts.

The cause of getting Bakhunin released from prison was

helped when Nicholas died, bringing Alexander to the throne. Custom called for the proclamation of amnesty for political prisoners upon the accession of the new tsar. Also, of course, Alexander II had the reputation of being a liberal. Varvara immediately wrote to Alexander, arguing that grace should be shown to Mikhail due to his four brothers who had fought for Russia in the Crimean War.[164]

Alexander was not foolish enough to authorize Bakhunin's release. Bakhunin's name did not appear among the 1856 grants of amnesty (which went primarily, to the Decembrist survivors) that were announced at the new Tsar's coronation. Varvara however kept on, doggedly appealing to other government officials. Over and over, she continually pleaded that Mikhail was deathly ill and had not long to live. She asked that he be allowed to spend his few remaining days under house arrest. Although this was not granted, eventually she did win approval from Prince Dolgorukov, the chief of police, to allow Mikhail to write his own personal appeal to Alexander.

The groveling tone of this letter of Bakhunin to Alexander was judged even more harshly by post-Bolshevik posterity than was his earlier "Confession" to Nicholas. The theme of bad health that his mother had been pleading was mixed in with repentence, excuses, flattery for the new Tsar, and praise for the memory of his dead father. One week after it was written, Bakhunin was informed that he was being accorded the choice between remaining in prison and instead being exiled for life to Siberia. Bakhunin immediately accepted the "clemency" of Siberia.[165]

Bakhunin was sent to live in Tomsk, Western Siberia. Bakhunin's health, it seems, miraculously improved with his release from prison. He was soon able to resume the use of his winning social graces. As usual, he had financial issues. He needed money to buy a house and set up a household. He was not allowed to leave the Tomsk area, and he was denied permission to travel to the newly blossoming Siberian gold mines. In order to make ends meet, Bakhunin started giving lessons. Two of his pupils were Polish sisters. The older of these sisters, a slender, pretty 17-year old named Antonia Kwiatkowski, fell in love with him. People thought she and the aged, overweight and insolvent exile Mikhail Bakhunin made a very odd couple. However, with the help of his boyhood friend Nikolai Nikolaevitch Muraviev, who was now an important regional official, Bakhunin won over Antonia's parents to Bakhunin's proposal of marriage. The two of them were married March 3, 1859.

After more importuning, Prince Dolgorukov finally gave the newlywed Bakhunins permission to leave Tomsk and move to Irkutsk, where the Amur River was being exploited for minerals including gold. While in Irkutsk, Bakhunin remained good friends with Muraviev. Muraviev as governor found himself in continual conflict with Mikhail Petrashevsky, the same exiled Petrashevsky of whose utopian anarchist circle Chernyshevsky had been a member in 1848. Within the radical community, news from Siberia inevitably found its way to London. Alexander Herzen in *The Bell* strongly backed Petrashevsky's grievances against Muraviev. Bakhunin probably felt some jealousy for Petrashevsky because he was the acknowledged leader of the Irkutsk radicals. Bakhunin wrote long letters to his friend Herzen and fellow Russian expat Nikolai Ogarev, telling them they were misinformed, that the liberal minded Muraviev was like a reincarnation of Peter the Great, and that Petrashevsky was in the wrong. Despite thus giving an appearance of loyal docility during this period, however, Bakhunin refused the offer of a position as a minor government official.[166]

Muraviev was recalled to St. Petersburg in January 1861. But the new appointed governor, Mikhail Korsakov, had family ties to the Bakhunins. Thus, Mikhail Bakhunin was able to continue his comfortable lifestyle as a respected exiled aristocrat. Bakhunin took advantage of his trusted status to finally win special permission to go on a gold mining expedition on the Amur River. Even though Korsakov felt some reluctance to let Bakhunin leave Irkutsk, he relented partly because Bakhunin, besides giving Korsakov his word of honor that he would return, argued that he was leaving behind his pretty young wife and that he was certain to return to her.

In June 1861, Bakhunin was issued a travel passport together with an official government order authorizing him to be transported anywhere he wanted on the Amur, which constitutes the border between Russian Siberia and neighboring China. Out of a sense of delicacy, the civil governor agreed not to mention on the passport the fact that Bakhunin was under a sentence of exile. Instead the passport was more diplomatically written to call him a "retired lieutenant." This would be critical for the success of Bakhunin's plans.

By July, Bakhunin on the strength of the travel authorization made it all the way down river to Nicolaevsk, not far from the northern tip of Sakhalin Island, at the mouth of the Amur some 4,144 kilometers east of Irkutsk. Bakhunin had attached himself to an official government mission to eastern Siberia that was led by an official named Kazarinov. Kazarinov, who was supposed to be watching over Bakhunin, was the only person within a thousand kilometers who knew of Bakhunin's convict status.

The ebullient Bakhunin took an active part in Kazarinov's government mission, partying it up at a whole series of official dinners and receptions. In Nicolaevsk, he had a stroke of extraordinary luck, perhaps mixed in with some skill, in that within a few days after their arrival in the town, Kazarinov became enamored of a beautiful local girl. Bakhunin arranged to have a ball thrown, at which Kazarinov could court the young woman. By the late hour when Kazarinov made it back to their shared room, he found an empty bed. Kazarinov assumed Bakhunin was out on some romantic escapade of his own. In reality, while Kazarinov was out a large man dressed in a black cape had slipped away on a Russian clipper called the Strelok which had pulled up anchor heading south to a port called De-Kastri.

By another stroke of good fortune for Bakhunin, the Strelok, while still in the Strait of Sakhalin, encountered an American freighter, the Vickery, that was en route to Japan. The commander of Strelok, having no reason to think anything differently about his "retired lieutenant" passenger, immediately agreed when Bakhunin asked to transfer on board of the Vickery. Bakhunin took a huge chance by volunteering to spend the night with the Russian duty officer at the Vickery's last Russian port, just before it left for Japan. But once again, lady luck was with him. By the time news that Bakhunin was an escapee arrived at the port the next morning, he was already on his way to Yokohama with the Americans.[167]

Bakhunin got a ride to San Francisco on another American vessel, arriving October 3, 1861. He immediately wrote to friends, including George Sand, Herzen and Ogarev, to inform them of his escape. On October 21, Bakhunin set sail for New York, via the Panama isthmus. He arrived on November 15.

Little is known of what Bakhunin actually did while in America. In a letter to Herzen, he appended some comments on the American Civil War:

> Of course, the North has all of my sympathies, but the banality of material well-being where the heart is absent, and their cheap and excessive national pride, is infantile and appears to have depraved the people. Maybe this stubborn war will be healthy in that it will help them re-find their lost souls.

Like many others, Bakhunin was struck by the large number of similarities between Russia and America. However, he added an interesting comment in later correspondence:

> I have seen how this country [the United States] by following a path of demagogery has reached even worse results that we [Russians] have reached by the path of despotism.

Probably because he had to await the arrival of money from Herzen, Bakhunin stayed another month in the United States. He left New York on a steamship, December 14, 1861, and disembarked in London on December 27. He finally arrived at Herzen's London residence on New Year's Day,

Mikhail Bakhunin

1862. The sight of how Bakhunin had aged during his thirteen years of imprisonment and exile was a shock, but to Herzen, he still exuded energy.[168] In celebration of the prodigal son's return, an entire issue of *The Bell* was dedicated to a full biography of Bakhunin. Bakhunin himself also wrote for publication. In an article of February 11, 1862, Bakhunin reaffirmed his ultimate faith in "the People." He denied that the Tsar's liberation of the serfs had changed much. He wrote: "Let the reformers continue to play their little parliamentary games; the awakening is near and will be terrifying."

The honeymoon period between Herzen and Bakhunin would not last long. Disputes emerged within a matter of two months following Bakhunin's arrival in London. By March, Herzen was refusing to publish an article Bakhunin had written, because he disagreed with some of Bakhunin's statements. Then, in June, Herzen suggested that Bakhunin should relocate himself to Paris.[169]

A Russian peasant found his way to London, where he met up with Bakhunin and Herzen. Bakhunin was sufficiently impressed with this peasant's views to incorporate some of them into a piece he wrote. In this article, he expressed that he would be willing to follow "Romanov" [i.e., Tsar Alexander II] if Romanov would lead the way into a better society. This statement provoked a storm of criticism toward Bakhunin in the radical community, particularly from Herzen and Marx. Herzen criticized Bakhunin as advocating a sort of imposition of tyranny from above. Herzen could not see how an intellectual as distinguished as Bakhunin could allow himself to be influenced by the views of a mere peasant.

Herzen himself was now comfortably ensconced in his expatriate lifestyle, unwilling to immerse himself in radical activities that could mean hot water, as opposed to writing position papers. One example was his attitude about the series of Apraxin Dvor fires in St. Petersburg in early 1862 which led to Chernyshevsky's arrest. Herzen immediately distanced himself from them, and blamed the fires on "Young Russia." Bakhunin felt that this backbiting was not justified. The perception that Herzen's positions were tepid soon cost him support within the avant-garde of Russia's emerging Generation of the Sixties.[170]

Bakhunin now became obsessed with the idea of getting his wife Antonia from Irkutsk to London. Of course he had to convince Antonia to give up her relatively secure life in Irkutsk to join his uncertain existence as an exile. In June 1862 he promised that as soon as she arrived in London, the two of them would move to Italy. Tacitly accepting Bakhunin's transformation into a permanently escaped refugee, in September 1862 the Russian government granted Antonia Kwiatkowski permission to leave Russia to join to Bakhunin. She had to agree in writing not to carry any letters, and never to return to Russia. After spending Christmas 1862 and New Year's 1863 with Bakhunin's family at Pryamukhino, she left Russia. Upon her arrival in London, Herzen went into shock over her appearance as the "circus pony" to Bakhunin's "elephant." He viewed the marriage to Antonia as yet another of Bakhunin's follies.[171]

Moving together to Italy was a promise Bakhunin kept. He and Antonia finally arrived there in January of 1864, settling for the time being in Florence. Here he changed his focus for fomenting revolution from the "peasants" to the "workers" -- meaning those who worked in factories. Bakhunin became engaged in creating another secret society, the "Florence Brotherhood." This society was a precursor to the International Association of Workers, formed in London on September 4, 1864. Marx agreed to be the head of this "International." As a result of this movement to "internationalize" the cause of revolution, there was a fleeting rapprochement between Marx and Bakhunin. The two of them met for the second and last time in London in the fall of 1864. But the egocentric Bakhunin was temperamentally incapable of playing "second fiddle" to anybody for long, especially Marx.[172]

The swirling expatriate community in Western Europe, and Bakhunin's further development of the anarchist ideas expressed by Chernyshevsky, would play key roles in shaping a young girl who was destined to become a terrorist leader.

Chapter 4: Birth of a Princess

Sofia Lvovna Perovskaya was born September 1, 1853 in St. Petersburg. She was the fifth and youngest of the five children born to the union of Lev Nikolaevitch Perovsky and Varvara Stepanovna Veselovskaya.[173] At her christening the future terrorist wore a brightly colored sundress. She was decorated by her paternal grandmother, who doubled as her godmother, with a gold cross hanging from a bright crimson ribbon.[174]

The brilliant family into which baby Sonia was born was beyond noble. It was considered to be princely due to its royal connections. Hers was a family of immense wealth and prestige, situated at the highest level of the Russian aristocracy. And what is more, the family's members had reached the pinnacle of society not merely by virtue of high birth, but by dint of intelligence and hard work, combined with good looks and charm.

The newborn's great-great grandfather, on her father's side, was Kirill Grigorievitch Razumovsky.[175] Kirill Razum, his original name, was the younger brother of Alexei Razum, a courtier who due to his personal charm became the morganatic husband and royal consort of Empress Elizabeth, tsaritsa of Russia. Tsaritsa Elizabeth reigned from 1741 until 1762. The Tsaritsa fell deeply in love with Alexei, a handsome and musically gifted Ukrainian Cossack, and married him in secret. The happy relations between Alexei and Elizabeth were a boon to the entire Razum family. They were summoned to St. Petersburg, and on all of them was conferred a title complete with a new, ennobled name: "Razumovsky."

The Empress's new brother-in-law Kirill Grigorievitch Razumovsky was blessed with a handsome face and an even better intellect. He was known for his kindness, openness, generosity, and good-natured sense of humor. Catherine the Great, the empress who followed Elizabeth, described Kirill Grigorievitch in these terms. "He was good-looking, he was very pleasant to deal with and his mind was incomparably superior to the mind of his brother, who was also handsome." Kirill Grigorievitch, similar to Americans of the era such as Benjamin Franklin and Thomas Jefferson, was a Renaissance man. The formerly illiterate Cossack stunned Russian society by teaching himself mathematics and science to such a degree that he became not only a member, but ultimately a director, of the Russian Academy of Sciences.[176]

At the imperial court, all of the girls were crazy about the clever, handsome Kirill. To be his wife, Tsaritsa Elizabeth selected Kirill's second cousin, Katarina Naryshkin. Katarina came from an enormously wealthy noble family. As his reward for taking her, Kirill was given a huge dowry which included, among other things, several villages in the territory of modern Moscow. The favored brother of the Empress's consort suddenly became one of Russia's richest people. The lavishness of Kirill's lifestyle was legendary. In Razumovsky's kitchen every day were slaughtered a whole ox, ten sheep, chickens and a hundred other beasts and fowl in an appropriate amount. The cuisine was supervised by a famous imported French chef named Barid.

The Empress appointed Kirill to the post of Hetman, or supreme military commander, of the Ukraine. Although his performance in that position was tainted with accusations of corruption, ultimately leading to his dismissal, Kirill survived these political adventures to return to the estate in Moscow. He became even richer in 1771 when his older brother and imperial consort Alexei died childless, leaving him everything including an estimated "100,000 peasants."

Kirill Razumovsky had eleven children, of whom one of the most prominent was Alexei Kirillovitch Razumovsky.[177] This nephew of the original Alexei Razumovsky, born during his aunt Elizabeth's reign in 1748, grew to become a senator, minister of education and advisor to the throne. In 1774 his marriage was arranged to one of the wealthiest eligible brides in Russia. Alexei Kirillovitch was notably prolific. After having four children with his wife, he moved her into a home in town, and then produced a second family out of wedlock with a commoner on the suburban estate, Maria Sobelevskaia. Maria gave birth to eight illegitimate children by Alexei Kirillovitch between 1785 and 1798; eventually he had two more. Maria and her children were maintained in regal style on the Razumovsky family estate in Perovo, a suburb of Moscow. From this geographical point of reference, the out of wedlock children of Alexei Kirillovitch who were born on the

RAZUMOVSKY / PEROVSKY FAMILY TREE

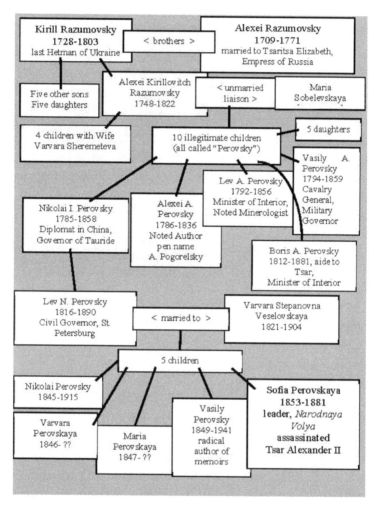

estate were all given a newly invented surname, "Perovsky."

Difficult as it is to imagine, the Perovsky children grew up to become even more accomplished than their "legitimate" Razumovsky forebears and cousins. Not only did they serve the sprawling Russian empire in a variety of military posts, and as cabinet ministers, they also distinguished themselves in scientific and artistic pursuits. Alexei Alexeivitch Perovsky, who fought with distinction during the victorious war of 1812 that repelled Napoleon's invading French army, was a botanist and a member of the Russian Academy of Sciences, besides being a noted writer as discussed below. Brother Lev Alexeivitch Perovsky was a noted geologist. He was the first to identify a mineral -- called "perovskite" -- that continues to be used today in making solar cells.

This portrait of Alexei Alexeivitch Perovsky, who went by the pen name Antony Pogorelsky, hangs in the Russian Museum in St. Petersburg

1835 painting by Karl Brullov.

Lev Alexeivitch was also important in Russia's political life, and became minister of the interior. We have small hints that Lev Alexeivitch was one of the more progressive members of the circle of advisors to the conservative Nicholas I. In 1846, after being appointed to head the Emperor's special committee to struggle with abolition, he took the lead in formulating a proposed measure to free the serfs.[178] He was trusted by the Emperor. In 1852, he was promoted to be the head of Nicholas's cabinet.

The Perovsky clan showed a talent for creative writing. Alexei A. Perovsky, the scientist and war veteran, also became a novelist. He wrote widely read children's stories under the pen name, Antony Pogorelsky. Alexei A. Perovsky / Antony

Pogorelsky was a good friend of Alexander Pushkin, still considered by many to be the greatest Russian poet. He was also the mentor and close companion of his nephew Alexei Konstantinovitch Tolstoy, another famed Russian poet. Alexei K. Tolstoy was in fact the son of Anna Alexeyevna Tolstoy (b. 1796), one of the "Perovsky pupils" (i.e., illegitimate offspring) of Alexei Kirillovitch Razumovsky. Anna's sister and fellow "Perovsky pupil," Elisaveta Alexeyevna (b. 1795), was the mother of three "Zhemchuzhnikov" brothers (Alexander, Alexei and Vladimir Mikhailovich). Collectively these brothers, together with their cousin Alexei K. Tolstoy, gained notoriety for publishing a series of satirical verses and aphorisms under another fictitious pen name – "Kozma Prutkov." Kozma Prutkov published much of "his" material in *The Contemporary* – the same publication that would sow the intellectual seeds for the Generation of the Sixties -- during the last part of Nicholas's reign, and continuing into the early years of Alexander's.

As young people both Lev A. Perovsky and Vasily A. Perovsky distinguished themselves in the war of 1812. On Vasily Alexeivitch the war left its lasting mark. He was wounded, tearing off the index finger of his left hand.[179] For the rest of his life he wore instead of a finger, a silver tip. He also was captured by the French, escaped from captivity and, as a result, he became the dashing prototype of Pierre Kirillovitch Bezukhov in Tolstoy's novel *War and Peace*. Tolstoy in 1877-1878, after writing *War and Peace* and *Anna Karenina*, conceived (but did not get around to writing) a new novel, the central figure of which would have been Vasily A. Perovsky.[180] In real life, Vasily Alexeivitch was promoted to be a prominent general, and the governor of Orenberg province at the southern end of the Urals. After some reverses, in the 1850's he ultimately conquered for Russia several of the wild regions in Central Asia, and he constructed a fort to hold them, known as "Fort Perovsky."

The oldest "Perovsky pupil" was Nikolai Ivanovitch, born in 1785. He too went on to a state career of importance. After serving for a time as a diplomat in China, he was appointed mayor of Feodosia, on the Black Sea in the Crimea. He then became governor of the Tauride, an administrative region in the southern part of the Russian empire that included most of the Crimea. Nikolai had three surviving children, the second of whom, born in 1816, was named Lev Nikolaevitch Perovsky.

This younger Lev attended the Tsarskoe Selo High School, which had been founded by Alexei Kirillovitch Razumovsky while he was minister of education and which gained repute as the leading Russian prep school. In 1831, he continued his "studies" by taking courses in railway engineering at university. He then gave every indication that he would follow in the footsteps of family glory by pursuing a career in military service. There being no suitable war in progress, as a junior military officer holding ranks such as ensign and lieutenant, Lev Nikolaevitch was engaged during the 1830's in "practical activities" working on government railway and canal construction projects in the St. Petersburg area. Later he worked on highways.[181]

By 1839, Lev Nikolaevitch became an aide to Major General A. K. Ushakov. While on duty in Mogilev province in the town of Chechersk (in what is now Belarus) in 1844, he met a 22-year old girl from a local family that was landed, but modest in terms of its wealth. This girl was Varvara Stepanovna Veselovskaya. The two of them fell deeply in love. Very soon they were married. It was a whirlwind romance, and for Varvara, Lev was passionate. He took extended leave for most of 1844, and then resigned his military commission entirely, without returning to duty, in early 1845.[182] Without doubt a baby was soon on the way, and indeed, Nikolai Lvovitch was born to Varvara on June 8, 1845. A marriage of this kind, based on an impulsive "love match," was a break from family precedent and was also contrary to Russian custom, particularly in the high aristocracy. The story of his marriage tells us that Lev Nikolaevitch Perovsky, despite the major conflicts he had later on with a rebellious son and daughter who were avid participants in the Sixties Generation, started out as a young man with something of a progressive, idealistic and "liberated" point of view on social issues.

Any doubt about the young Lev's liberal leanings are put to rest by the identity of the woman with whom he fell in love, and whom he so eagerly married. Varvara Stepanovna was, according to her son, a person with a "loving soul and an affection for all things progressive."[183] Varvara was highly intelligent, and she was raised in an intellectual family. Her father, Stepan Semenovich Veselovsky (born 1781) when 18 years old began to serve in the Guards of the Semyenovsky regiment, whose chief was Tsar Alexander I himself. Stepan Semenovich distinguished himself in the Napoleonic Wars, taking part in several historic battles. According to Varvara Stepanovna's brother, Konstantin Stepanovich Veselovsky, "for the Veselovskys it was a matter of honor to devote their noble youth to military service, and only then, after reaching a certain rank, to leave the village and live a country life."[184] Stepan Semenovich followed in this family tradition. After the war ended, in July 1817 he married the 18-year old daughter of a Mogilev landowner and officer, and in 1820 he retired as a colonel. Varvara Stepanovna was born soon thereafter, in late 1821 or the beginning of 1822.[185]

Stepan Semenovich, Varvara's father, was openly liberal in his attitudes and his politics. He was "much loved" for his kindness and for improving the lives of the local peasants. The revenues derived from his Mogilev estate were marginal. Still, the Veselovsky children including Varvara were sent away to schools in St. Petersburg. Konstantin Veselovsky wrote later: "Our parents made the greatest possible effort to ensure to deliver the best education to their children, and for this they made material sacrifices, ones that were disproportionate to their modest incomes."[186] Varvara's brother Konstantin graduated from Tsarskoe Selo High School and thereafter became an outstanding scientist, active member and secretary of the Russian Academy of Sciences. He was an economist whose statistical studies on the Russian economy were recognized internationally and were relied upon in the writings of Karl Marx.[187]

It has been speculated that Lev Nikolaevitch Perovsky after falling in love with Varvara at first thought to follow in the Veselovsky tradition by retiring, with his new bride, to the life of a country gentleman.[188] However, Lev Nikolaevitch had no land of his own, he had not yet reached the age of 30, and most importantly, his "love match" did not come with a dowry. So in 1846, almost exactly one year after his discharge from the army, he took on a civil service job with the post office. From there he moved to a series of other civil service jobs in St. Petersburg.

Here we encounter an aspect critical to the understanding of Lev Nikolaevitch Perovsky. Within the perspective of the glorious Perovsky family, he was something of a disappointment, a bit of a "loser," as it were. In early 1850, when Lev was seeking advancement within the customs service, he prepared a sort of curriculum vitae which covers the history of his professional life to date. The very existence of this resumé is a hint of trouble. A glorious Perovsky should not need to submit a humble resumé; he should move up the ladder with ease based on energy, charm and talent. And the contents of that resumé are of interest. In it, Lev Nikolaevitch Perovsky attempted to smooth over some of the problems with his military service record. His lengthy "leaves" – three months in 1837, four months in 1840-41, and then the entire time, except for one month, between March of 1844 and March of 1845, as well as his discharge itself – were explained as being due to an unidentified "illness." Blame was also placed on the discharge of General Ushakov in early 1844, which was said to have "affected his job" adversely.[189]

Lev Nikolaeivitch Perovsky would eventually succeed in using his family connections to climb the ladder to a high position within the Russian civil service. However, he would continue to be plagued with job related difficulties, conflicts and heartbreak. Ultimately, his career would turn out to be a disappointment to him. Lev developed a persistent complex around his insecurity and anxiety about inability to live up to the family name. This complex grew over time and profoundly influenced his family, especially his daughter Sonia.

Chapter 5: He Called Her Gloomy Girl

Lev Nikolaevitch received his big career break in late 1856. While working in a mundane job as an associate director of expeditions with the State Bank in St. Petersburg, he was appointed by the newly crowned, liberal and reforming Tsar Alexander II to fill the office of vice-governor of Pskov, an ancient town located to the southwest of St. Petersburg, on the western edge of Russia next to Estonia. Undoubtedly, Lev Nikolaevitch owed this executive appointment to lobbying from relatives and friends in high places, including his uncle Lev Alexeivitch whom Alexander had inherited as a key member of Nicholas's cabinet. But Lex Alexeivitch died unexpectedly on November 10, 1856, shortly after the family had arrived in Pskov.[190] This triggered nervousness in Lev Nikolaevitch that he would now wind up being stuck in a long term provincial assignment.

In Pskov, the Lev Nikolaevitch Perovsky family moved into a large two-story home that was more comfortable than their St. Petersburg apartment. The Perovsky children were

The Perovsky Family, in 1856. L to R: Nikolai, Varvara Stepanovna, Sofia, Maria, Lev Nikolaevitch, Vasily.

Source: V. Perovsky Memoir, National Library of Russia

happy there. The vice-governor's home was situated next door to the home of the Pskov governor, at that time Valerian Nikolaevitch Muraviev, brother of the Nikolai Nikolaevitch Muraviev who was governing at the time in eastern Siberia and who helped Bakhunin, as we have reviewed. Valerian Muraviev was a widower, his wife having died in childbirth. The Perovsky kids regularly played with his son Nikolai. Together they enjoyed a variety of children's games. In the Perovsky garden in the summer they swung on swings, and in winter an ice mountain was constructed. In the governor's garden, where there were thick high plants, Vasya Perovsky and Kolya Muraviev made themselves wooden swords and then used them to "fight" in games such as "cops and robbers."

Sonia from the age of four to five years took an indispensable part in these "battles." Decades later Vasily Perovsky would vividly remember a private ferry boat that the children could take to and from the Pskov governor's house. While riding the ferry, the young children liked to imagine that they were sailing on an ocean ship and fighting with pirates. [191]

During the Pskov years, the Perovsky family was relatively harmonious. They all regularly gathered in the same formation at the dinner table, with Lev Nikolaevitch sitting to the left of Varvara Stepanovna, and with Sonia seated across from him, to the right of her mother. Lev Nikolaevitch frequently entertained everybody when he returned from his office in good spirits. He would recite to the family silly nonsense poems. He liked to amuse everyone by approaching the youngest, Sonia, with thought provoking questions. These elicited characteristically short dry responses from little Sonia that left the entire family rolling with laughter. They thought it was funny how Sonia maintained such a serious facial expression when answering her father's questions.[192]

On April 22, 1858, Lev's father Nikolai Ivanovitch Perovsky died, leaving substantial estates in the Crimea to 42-year old Lev Nikolaevitch and his younger brother Peter Nikolaevitch. Lev visited St. Petersburg where, after prolonged efforts, he ultimately secured a transfer to the post of vice-governor of the Tauride. The family, after selling all of its furniture in Pskov, moved to the family country estate at Kilburun in the Crimea in the summer of 1859. They traveled by a newly rebuilt rail line to St. Petersburg, and continued from there to Moscow. From Moscow, they went on to the Crimea in their own private horse drawn carriage. Vasily Perovsky recalled that as they traveled along in the carriage the family looked with amazement upon the natural beauty of southern Russia with its dramatic mountain peaks and its verdant river valleys lined with orchards.[193]

In the Crimea as in Pskov, the Perovsky family led a close-to-idyllic existence. Nikolai entered the fourth grade, and Vasily the second grade, in Simferopol gymnasium. The family stayed on the estate in summer and occupied a town house in Simferopol during the winter. Maria Lvovna, the second oldest, went to a finishing school in Kerch. For six-year-old Sonia a home teacher was hired. There were dance lessons, there were music lessons, and there were dress-up parties for the children. But with every passing year Sonia engaged more and more in energetic, active type games. At the seaside in Yalta she was already competing successfully with her brothers in the arts of swimming and diving. She soon became a phenomenal swimmer, surprising and even frightening those in her age group (and adults!) with the distance of her swims.

In Kilburun at the tender age of eight years, Sonia also became a serviceable gunner. This is depicted in the memoirs of Vasily Perovsky. "At my grandfather's estate there were up to a dozen different sizes of copper cannons, with French inscriptions on some of them. With Sonia we amused ourselves considerably by firing them in wide directions, being considerably benefitted by the cheap cost of gunpowder. I, as usual as I was the older, tried to play the role of commander, and Sonia regularly, on command, applied a match to the wick of the fuse. She was not frightened, and did not hesitate to fire off the gun, despite how the gun recoiled and bounced back when fired." [194]

Vasily could not recall an instance when he had ever seen Sonia act frightened of anything. To the contrary, she appeared fearless, even at a young age. He gave an example from life at Kilburun. "One time when Sonia left the house and went towards the stable, I saw one of the workers waving at me and telling me to be careful, saying there was a rabid dog on the loose. I then saw the dog with his tail tucked under its legs and foaming at the mouth. I dashed to my room, grabbed my gun, and ran out looking for the dog. I saw that it ran around a long building, and went on a path that was made in the grass. At that time I saw Sonia walking towards the dog. Very scared, I yelled at her to get off the path and to stand still so as not to attract the rabid dog's attention. Sonia slowly walked four to five feet off the path and just calmly looked at the dog while it ran by. After that I was able to shoot the dog."[195] On another occasion several years later, when Sonia was ten years old and Vasily fourteen, the two stayed out until Russian summer midnight stalking a bear, whose lair they had detected in an oat field. Vasily was equipped on this expedition with a shotgun, Sonia with just a large hunting knife. Probably they were lucky that the bear did not make an appearance.[196]

Varvara Stepanovna played the role of full time homemaker during her time in Pskov, followed by the Crimea and Simferopol. Her passionate devotion to her children throughout these formative years was a huge influence on them. The children were deeply impressed by her heartfelt pious sentiments, which were often expressed by crying along with them while reading and rereading the account of Christ's crucifixion in the Bible.[197] One of the family's friends in the Crimea described Varvara Stepanovna as "holy in the full sense of the word." Vasily said of the time when he was five years old, "Mother, who was then very religious, taught me every day before going to bed to say a prayer, kneeling before an icon, in the corner of the room. She did the same with Sonia in the first years of her childhood." However, father Lev Nikolaevitch was not a openly religious man. While careful to state on his resumé that he was "Orthodox," he avoided immersing his children in what is commonly called religious education.[198] What he did share with his wife, and even projected to their children during these early years, were progressive values. To the entire family, he read aloud from Hugo's *Les Miserables*, then as now a humanist classic.[199]

Meanwhile, Lev Nikolaevitch began having trouble in his

government service. He came into conflict with his immediate superior, Lieutenant General Grigory Vasileivitch Zhukovsky, who was then the governor. Zhukovsky was just as ambitious as Lev Nikolaevitch, and he held a higher rank, which enabled him to undermine not only the quality of the work, but also the personal reputation of anyone on a lower level, including the vice-governor. Zhukovsky often absented himself from work, and Lev Nikolaevitch in such cases substituted for him. But upon his return from absence, Zhukovsky got his vice-governor in trouble by blaming him for problems and scandals that had happened while he was gone. In the end, after a series of accusations to the minister of internal affairs P. A. Valuev, Zhukovsky brought about the resignation of Lev Nikolaevitch as vice-governor and the removal of his protégés from the provincial government.

In the wake of this debacle, Lev Nikolaevitch was reassigned to St. Petersburg, and there, "thanks to an influential family," was appointed to the same level position, vice-governor, but now in the capital. St. Petersburg was really where Lev Nikolaevitch wanted to be, anyway. At the time, of the immediate family of Lev Nikolaevitch there remained alive only his uncle, Alexei Kirillovitch Razumovsky's youngest son Count Boris Alexeivitch, who was then serving as a teacher for the Tsar's sons. Probably Boris advocated his nephew for the appointment. But, it appears Lev Nikolaevitch's candidacy also was supported by the circle of liberal advisors to Alexander who were then in vogue, including the St. Petersburg Governor-General Alexander A. Suvorov and the head of the secret police, Vasily Dolgorukov.[200] So, on July 7, 1861, State Councilor Lev Nikolaevitch Perovsky was appointed vice-governor of St. Petersburg. The family soon relocated from the Crimea to St. Petersburg.[201]

The St. Petersburg civil governor, Lev Nikolaevitch's new superior, was Alexander A. Bobrinsky. He extended a warm welcome to the Perovsky family. He invited them to live in the governor's mansion, as Bobrinsky, the wealthy scion of an industrialist family, had his own private residence in the city. Thus the lives of the children, including Sonia, continued on a fairly even keel. The boys were enrolled in gymnasium, while the girls had

Sofia Perovskaya, posed portrait, circa 1865.

source: V. Perovsky Memoir, National Library of Russia

private home tutors. But Lev Nikolaevitch's fortunes took a bad turn when Bobrinsky left the governorship in late 1864. He was replaced by Vladimir Yakovlevitch Skuryatin, a man known for his love of hunting and gala parties. Skuryatin required the Perovskys to vacate the governor's house. What was worse, Skuryatin and Lev Nikolaevitch got into an immediate personality conflict. This once again placed Lev's career footing in jeopardy.

The added stress of Lev Nikolaevitch's responsibilities in St. Petersburg took a huge toll on the family. Now enmeshed in the turmoil and politics of the capital, Lev devoted an inordinate amount of attention to cultivating relationships. He chafed at his wife's poorly concealed disdain for high society life. She made her lack of enthusiasm obvious whenever she was forced to accompany him to balls, functions, and visits.[202] Lev Nikolaevitch became impatient with her attitude. Apparently he felt himself to be under financial stress related to the need to keep up appearances with a celebrity lifestyle. The fact that his wife's family was relatively impoverished and could not contribute to lavish St. Petersburg entertaining now caused him to chafe. Oddly, though, it was the cooking of the household chef which turned into the special object of Lev's ire. He flew into ugly rages directed at Varvara, ranting that the fare she had the cook prepare was too "simple," meaning country style. On these occasions he suffered repeated meltdowns in which he lost his temper completely, angrily swearing at his wife, in front of others, in a most humiliating manner. He badmouthed her family members for being provincial rubes. As Lev's political troubles increased, these unpleasant scenes became more frequent. They disturbed and affected the children. Sonia strongly sided with her mother. Her relationship with her father was damaged, and it would never recover.[203]

Lev and Varvara, after leaving the governor's house, moved the family to live with a former colleague of Lev Nikolaevitch in the military service, Feodor Ivanovich Truzsona. Vasily later remembered Truzsona fondly. "He was with us often and we all liked him very much." Truzsona was struck by Sonia's dour personality. He called her "gloomy girl." He did so "because when she was with him (or when she was at a party) she was rarely found to be cheerful or talkative."[204] Sonia absorbed and reflected her mother's attitude about balls. When the children were required to take part in these rotating events, called *jour fixe* because they were hosted by each of the aristocratic families on a particular day, Sonia with her brother Vasya would avoid talking to the other guests. Instead, they would just stroll around by themselves, or would just sit on the side, sarcastically criticizing dressy ladies and their low necked gowns.[205]

Luckily for Lev Nikolaevitch, Skuryatin's tenure as civil governor of St. Petersburg was short lived. After only a few months he was promoted to be a Marshal on the personal staff of the heir to the throne, His Majesty Nikolai Alexandrovitch (eldest son of Alexander II). Skuryatin moved to Anichkov Palace, at that time the main bastion of conservatism in Russian politics. To replace him, Lev Nikolaevitch was appointed civil governor effective January 1, 1865. His key support for the position came from his uncle, Boris Alexeivitch, and the liberal governor general, Alexander A. Suvorov. The family now moved back to the governor's house, which Skuryatin had in the meantime decorated luxuriously.[206]

In the spring of 1865 Lev Nikolaevitch received an alarming telegram from Geneva. It concerned his brother Peter, who was serving at the time as the Russian consul general in Geneva. The telegram stated that Peter was dangerously ill. The telegram was signed by a friend and neighbor of the patient in Geneva, Alexander V. Poggio.

Alexander Poggio, born in 1798, was a former Decembrist exile. Although he was from an Italian family, Poggio was born and raised in Russia. As of 1825 he had been a lieutenant colonel of the Russian army. He became an active participant in the Decembrist conspiracy, a close associate of the executed Decembrist leader, Pavel N. Pestel. Poggio was Convicted of first degree treason with a sentence of death by beheading. However, the sentence was commuted to etermal servitude and Poggio, together with other Decembrists including Nikita Muraviev, Prince Sergei Trubetskoi and Prince Sergei Volkonsky, was confined in the Schlüsselburg fortress and then sent into exile in Siberia, where he stayed for the next 31 years. After the amnesty by Alexander II in 1856, he lived in Irkutsk, in other cities of Russia, and then, from the end of 1864, in Geneva. There Poggio became close to Peter

Nikolaevitch Perovsky, who already knew him from Irkutsk, which Peter had visited while traveling to Beijing on diplomatic missions as the head of the First Section of the Asian department. In Geneva, Poggio was by no means politically neutral. He associated with Alexander Herzen, the left wing writer, who, with Ogarev, had recently relocated to Geneva from London. Poggio and Herzen engaged in long conversations on political issues.

The circumstance that a Decembrist expatriate like Alexander Poggio was in communication with Lev Nikolaevitch while Lev was the governor of St. Petersburg, the fact that Poggio was one of Peter Nikolaevitch's close Russian associates in Geneva, and the fact that Lev Nikolaevitch sent Varvara, Sonia and Vasily to see Poggio in Geneva, all provide strong evidence that Lev Nikolaevitch was, as of 1865, an occupant of the reform minded side of the Russian political spectrum. St. Petersburg conservatives would not deal with any ex-Decembrists, who were still considered by them to be traitors and intellectual precursors to the Sixties Generation troublemakers.

Lev Nikolaevitch was too busy with his responsibilities as civil governor to leave St. Petersburg right away, but Varvara Stepanovna quickly packed up, taking Sonia with her, and left for Geneva. When Varvara and Sonia arrived in Geneva,

Sofia "Sonia" Perovskaya and Varvara "Varya" Poggio, photographed together in Geneva, 1865

Source: V. Perovsky Memoir, National Library of Russia

Poggio met them and introduced them to his daughter Varvara "Varya" Poggio, who was a year younger than Sonia. Varya showed Sonia her geography book, Louis Figuier. La terre et les mers. Paris, 1864, which Herzen had given to her with the inscription: "From a deep, deep admirer of your father in memory of Geneva" - and with the very recent date of December 24, 1864. Eleven year old Varya was well versed in the history of the Decembrists and the subsequent European revolutions of 1830 and 1848-1849. Sonia immediately took a liking to

Varya, and the two remained close companions throughout Sonia's six months in Switzerland. From Varya, Sofia Perovskaya thoroughly absorbed the cause of rebellion in Russia.[207] From now on, Sonia would be an avid member of the Generation of the Sixties.

Chapter 6: A Shot that Changed Russia Forever

At 4 p.m. on April 4, 1866 Tsar Alexander II, after taking his daily walk in the St. Petersburg summer garden near the Imperial Palace, was saying goodbye to two of his friends. He prepared to climb into a waiting carriage. As was usual in those days, he had no special security detail. A small crowd of persons had gathered nearby, eager for the opportunity to see their ruler. One of these onlookers suddenly drew a flintlock pistol from his pocket and pointed it at the Tsar. A man standing next to him saw the outstretched pistol. Crying out, "What are you doing?" he made a grab at the assailant's arm. This jostled the assailant's elbow enough to cause his shot to barely miss its target. For an instant, everyone was frozen in shocked silence as the shooter tried to flee the scene. He did not get far before police pounced on him.

The Tsar's savior, a peasant named Osip Komissarov, became an overnight celebrity. He was elevated to the nobility and was given a new, more noble name, Komissarov-Kostromskoi. He became a marketing sensation. Within two weeks, Russian consumers could eat Komissarov pies, candies, and chocolates, drink specially issued Kostromskoi beer, and smoke "Komissarov-Kostromskoi cigarettes."[208]

Immediately after his arrest, the would-be assassin posed as a peasant, Alexei Petrov. That he was not really a peasant was soon obvious to the police from his manner of speaking and vocabulary, as well as his ability to read and write in a correct manner. It took days of feverish investigation to uncover his real identity: Dmitri Karakozov, a landowner's son from Saratov province. Karakozov was a graduate of Penzenskaia gymnasium, and an ex-student of the Kazan and Moscow university law faculties. Once his real identity was finally uncovered, the authorities quickly also learned that in the summer of 1865, after dropping out of law school, Karakozov had become preoccupied with his health. He had eventually entered the Moscow University clinic, where he was diagnosed with several ailments, including gonorrhea. During his two month stay in the hospital, Karakozov appeared to be severely depressed and tried to commit suicide. After his discharge from the hospital in January 1866, less than three months prior to his attempt on Alexander, those around him continued to perceive him as quiet, solitary and a hypochondriac who was convinced that he was soon to die.[209]

The fact that an assassination attempt was made blatantly in public without any effort to hide it caused unease. The fact that Karakozov was an unknown loner was a source of extreme nervousness. It was also troubling that the accused was educated. Although the authorities initially maintained silence, and although their theories on Karakozov kept shifting, they never could accept that he was just a stray, senseless lunatic. Conspiracy was the only theory given any credence. No one found the attempted assassin quite believable in the role he professed, that of a melancholic suicide. Evidently, it was far more natural to suspect that Karakozov was part of a conspiracy.[210]

Alexander's conservative counselors at first made an effort to tie Karakozov to the Polish nationalist cause. Deeper investigation revealed another connection. Karakozov was linked to a small circle of nihilists inspired by *What Is to Be Done?*, whose members called themselves mortusy (which means "dead men"). The mortusy were a splinter group from a larger organization of radicals called, whimsically enough, "The Organization." The name of the splinter group has been most frequently translated as "Hell." Hell's goal: tsaricide and the annihilation of authority with murder and poison.

Whether Karakozov's assassination attempt really was sponsored, or even sanctioned, by Hell remains a deserving subject of controversy. Although Karakozov knew of Hell, he also, on his own, independently advocated tsaricide. A consistent theme in Karakozov's ideation was that he was ill and destined to die soon, so he wanted to be "useful" in his death. "A death for a death," as he put it.[211] One of Karakozov's close connections was Ivan Khudiakov. Khudiakov was one of the founders of Hell. Khudiakov, however, did not personally favor immediate tsaricide. Instead, Khudiakov's efforts at the time were devoted to a plot to rescue Chernyshevsky from his captivity in Siberia.[212]

The most tangible clues to his mind frame were items found on Karakozov upon his arrest. Turning out the pockets of his peasant style overcoat, the arresting officers discovered extra bullets and gunpowder, two powdery substances, a small, pear-shaped vial containing a sticky liquid, a scrap of paper bearing the word "Kobylin," a letter, and two copies of a printed pamphlet entitled "To My Worker Friends." The powders were identified as morphine and strychnine, the liquid, hydrocyanic acid. These were all strong organic poisons intended to enable a quick suicide, without antidotes, and difficult to trace post mortem. "Kobylin" turned out to be Alexander Kobylin, a St. Petersburg doctor who was a political liberal with probable connections to a faction of palace schemers that favored the elevation of Konstantin to the throne. Although he was acquitted of involvement in Karakozov's crime, there is evidence to indicate that Dr. Kobylin had helped Karakozov financially, that he had provided him with the poisons found on his upon his arrest, and that he had allowed the penniless Karakozov to stay in his home for several days immediately prior to the assassination attempt.[213]

The letter, phrased in terms that were deliberately veiled and ambiguous, was written by Karakozov to Nikolai Ishutin, a Moscow member of Hell. To the government, this cemented a link between Karakozov and Hell, although it remained unclear to what extent Hell had approved of Karakozov's timing and method.

The pamphlet "To My Worker Friends" contained a proclamation that was in essence Karakozov's terrorist manifesto:[214]

> It saddened and burdened me that my beloved people is perishing like this and thus I decided to annihilate the tsar-villain and die for my beloved people. If my intention succeeds, I will die with the idea that my death will be useful to my dear friend the Russian muzhik. If not, then I nonetheless believe that there will be people who will take my path. If I do not succeed, they will. My death will be an example for them and inspire them. Let the Russian people recognize their main, mightiest enemy be he Alexander II, Alexander III, and so forth, that's all the same. Once the people makes short work of their most important enemy, the petty remainder of his landowners, grandees, officials, and all the rest of the rich folk will become afraid, for their numbers are not at all noteworthy. And then there will be real freedom.

On September 3, 1866, Karakozov's suicidal wish was fulfilled as he was publicly hanged on a scaffold before a huge crowd in St. Petersburg.[215] Karakozov's failed assassination attempt accomplished one very tangible result -- a sudden, sharp and lasting lurch to the right in the power structure of imperial Russia. His attempt on the Emperor brought to a grinding halt what progressive tendencies lingered from Alexander's era of great reforms. Karakozov's attempt inaugurated an era of political reaction so severe that it has gone down in history as the "White Terror." Many arrests took place. No one with a liberal bent of mind felt safe. Thousands in the empire's major cities were censored, searched, questioned, arrested, and harassed.[216]

A major shakeup ensued in St. Petersburg. Any of the Tsar's ministers who was tainted with even a hint of liberalism were immediately fired and replaced with conservatives. Alexander A. Suvorov, the progressive governor- general of St. Petersburg, was among the officials dismissed. The governor-general position was abolished; in its place General Fyodor Trepov, director of the brutal Warsaw reprisals, was made prefect of police in St. Petersburg.[217] Another official who lost his job at the same time was Suvorov's protégé and associate, Lev Nikolaevitch Perovsky.[218] Lev Nikolaevitch was removed from his position as civil governor and reassigned to a desk job in the ministry of the interior. The family was required to vacate the governor's house. The demotion was a major humiliation which sent Lev Nikolaevitch into a tailspin of depression. It would soon lead to the breakup of the Perovsky family.

Lev Nikolaevitch and Varvara Stepanovna decided to live apart. Varvara sought, and Lev granted, the Russian equivalent of a legal separation. Varvara returned with the two girl children to Kilburun in the Crimea. There Sonia spent the next three years reading books from her grandfather's library, as well as more contemporary works brought to her on visits by her older brother Vasily, who was busy attending university in St. Petersburg and developing into a fairly typical Sixties Generation radical. When arrested and asked, years later, about her upbringing, she would respond, "Educated at home, by my parents." Sonia was basically self-educated.

From her reading, Sonia eagerly absorbed the utopian world view of Chernyshevsky's *What Is to Be Done?*[219] She also read works of other progressive Russian writers, including Nekrasov and Turgenev, as well as the English utilitarian John Stuart Mill. The pastoral setting of the family estate gave her the opportunity to engage in physical pursuits at which she excelled, such as swimming and horseback riding.[220]

Meanwhile, living in St. Petersburg Lev had serious financial problems, the details of which are not fully revealed to history. He acquired a mistress and a penchant for card games, both of which were likely contributing factors to his mounting insolvency. After three years, his financial situation was so bad that he had to put Kilburun and other family properties up for sale to pay his creditors. As a result of the sale, the family in 1869 was required to rejoin Lev Nikolaevitch in an apartment in St. Petersburg. To travel there, Sonia, her brother Vasily and her mother Varvara first took a boat from the Crimea to Odessa. Along the way, they met a young radical named Anna Vilberg, eight years older than Sonia, who was also traveling to St. Petersburg. Anna was the first in a series of "nihilist" women who became Sonia's friends and companions during her late teen years. Sonia's stormy family atmosphere, her pensive nature and the difficult complex relationship between her father and mother caused her to reflect at length on the position of women in Russian society.[221] She returned to a St. Petersburg environment that was swirling with protest and the continuing repression of the White Terror.

Chapter 7: A Select Harvest of Rebellious Seedlings

Shortly after the public hanging of Karakozov, Vera Zasulitch, a young woman of 17, arrived in St. Petersburg. Vera, of middling height, was strong and robust. She was not what would be considered a beauty, but she had very fine, well shaped gray eyes with long lashes that shone when she became enthusiastic. She was negligent about her appearance and disdained all makeup, jewelry or other feminine adornment.[222] Vera had been born to a noble family in the region of Smolensk. At age three, her father died. She was sent to the country to be raised with her cousins. She was very bright and taught herself readily. As a girl, she read and re-read the New Testament gospels. She felt a passionate love for Jesus. She was particularly obsessed with Jesus's execution on the cross, which she found very engrossing and stimulating. She felt a kind of excited dread about his fate.[223] Inspired by the example of Jesus to a path of renunciation, the maturing Vera felt her upbringing as a member of the upper classes was more a misfortune than it was a privilege.[224] She bridled against the "future" available to her as a woman. A boy would have had far broader prospects. The idea of revolution appealed to her because it made her the equal of a boy. She could dream of action, of exploits, of waging the supreme battle and of making the supreme sacrifice. She seized avidly upon the idea of dying for a cause.[225]

In the 1860's in Russia, there were no formal university programs for women. Women who came to universities, like Vera, did so purely out of their own energy and a sense of solidarity with the male students. Once in St. Petersburg, Vera soon gravitated toward circles composed of those of the Sixties Generation who were searching for an answer to the Chernyshevsky question, "What Is to Be Done?" Many students were frustrated, impatient and felt that the revolutionary movement was at a standstill.

After publication of *What Is to Be Done?*, many sewing cooperatives had been started, "like mushrooms" as Zasulitch says in her autobiography. Her account reveals the degree to which these utopians lacked contact with reality.

> The associations were generally created by women who had the means to buy a sewing machine, to rent an apartment and to pay the wages of one or two other experimenters. Among the members, most of the time one found nihilists who knew nothing about sewing but who ardently desired to 'work for the cause,' while the rest were seamstresses who were hoping to earn a good salary. The first month, everybody wielded the needle with great conviction. But sewing eight to ten hours per day just to show the principle of the utopian association, especially when most of them were not used to manual labor, was something in which very few found the patience to persevere.
>
> The workers started complaining and in fact, the

best ones left because they could make more money working for a regular boss. This was true even though the founding proprietor abandoned her own earnings to the collective. Eventually some of the workers took the sewing machines. At the trial that ensued, the workers said that the proprietor was not good for 'anything except talking' and that they had the right to take the machine in order to earn a livelihood. The court, however, required its return to the proprietor.[226]

The children of the Sixties who were yearning for action were now largely silenced due to the White Terror. Young men and women who had come to St. Petersburg with high hopes for radical change found themselves demoralized and anguished. People in universities started saying, "there needs to be a student movement," and that "something," at least, needed to happen. This was the situation as school opened in the fall of 1868. Rebellious, progressive youthful energy coalesced around a campaign to protect scholarships for deserving students, which became, superficially, the focus of student protest.[227]

Organizers emerged, who started forming smaller circles out of the more committed students. By Christmas the first wave of student gatherings started. Some of these were held in homes of the wealthy that were made available for the purpose. Several hundreds would crowd into a room to hear speeches by student orators who, one after the other, stood on chairs to give their declamations. One of the organizers was 21-year old Sergei Nechaev (pronounced "Netch-A-yev"). Nechaev himself rarely spoke in the chair climbing rallies. Instead, he concentrated on observing and tracking who, among the militants, made the most willing and effective speakers.

Sergei Nechaev grew up the son of a sign painter in Ivanovo, a dreary textile mill town aptly dubbed "the Manchester of Russia." He was almost entirely self-educated. Without ever being enrolled as a student in a formal school, he progressed directly to being a teacher. He attached himself to a small group of intellectuals in blue collar Ivanovo. While only 13, he served as the librarian for a school which his older friends were running in Ivanovo. From librarian, he progressed into teaching. With the financial help of his father, at age 17 he escaped Ivanovo and traveled, first to Moscow, and then on to St. Petersburg where he first obtained a teaching certification and then secured a paid position as a bible school teacher.

Physically, there was nothing attractive about Sergei Nechaev. He was smallish, sickly looking, with thin lips, straight black hair half covering his ears, and he wore wrinkled clothes. He was constantly biting his nails.[228] But his demeanor quickly betrayed a ferocious energy churning within him. He was in perpetual motion, always needing to be busy. He had a mania for surrounding himself with books, nervously jumping from one to the other. After his arrival in St. Petersburg, Nechaev became obsessed with the Karakozov assassination attempt.

Sergei Nechaev

He avidly read all of the back issues of *The Bell* which dealt with the subject. He also studied, with fascination, the methods of The Organization and of Hell.[229]

From a young age Nechaev demonstrated an uncanny ability to manipulate people. Some of his extraordinary power in this regard can be attributed to an unusual personal capacity he possessed for simultaneously terrifying and fascinating. Another vital element was his ability to convince others that he was fully resolved and prepared for the supreme sacrifice of martyrdom.[230] Nechaev was obsessed with control techniques, which he used to dominate. One of his roommates described him as follows:

> The first impression Nechaev makes is unpleasant yet actually seductive. He is psychologically touchy – and one feels this at first contact, although Nechaev tries to restrain himself. He reads a great deal . . . especially books of historical and sociological content, and thus knows a great deal, although when he cites various authors he is sometimes quite careless. In debate he will try to trick and humiliate his opponent – he is a talented dialectician and knows how to touch the most sensitive areas of a young conscience: truth, honesty, courage, etc. He won't tolerate people who are his equals, and with those stronger than he, maintains a strict silence and tries to cast a shadow of suspicion over them. He is extremely firm in his convictions, but out of self-esteem, to which he is prepared to sacrifice everybody. Thus, the main traits of his character are despotism and self-esteem. All of his declamations are full of passion, but very bilious. He stimulates interest in himself, and the more impressionable and naive simply worship him, the latter a necessary condition of any friendship with him.

Another who knew him in the early "student protest" period commented,

> On the one hand, he was a good comrade, honest, truthful, willing to share all of his material possessions with his friends, but on the other, he was unbearable,

always asking questions and saying nothing about himself, taking everything the wrong way, extremely callous in his treatment of others . . . But his most repellent trait was his extreme despotism with respect to one's ideas. He couldn't reconcile himself to the fact that his acquaintances had ideas, convictions unlike his own, and looked at things and acted in a different way than he did. But he didn't scorn these people. No, on the contrary, he tried with incredible persistence to convert them.

The St. Petersburg student gatherings in the fall of 1868 were not clandestine. In fact, their times and locations were sometimes announced in the papers. Even the police did not hesitate to attend. From the first, there was a split between the "radicals" – whom Nechaev winnowed and cultivated – and the "mainstream," of whom a student named Stepan Ezersky was the spokesperson. The primary issue driving the split was the means to be used to achieve the goals of student grants-in-aid and securing the right to assembly. The radicals advocated submitting signed petitions, and publicly demonstrating. The mainstream, on the other hand, pointed out that this method would be foolhardy as well as counterproductive, because it would put the all the names of the dissident students directly into the hands of the government and the police. Nechaev and his faction did not directly dispute these arguments. They just kept criticizing and reproaching anyone who argued the moderate line, accusing them of being insincere cowards.

In more intimate discussions, Nechaev privately admitted that demonstrations and petitions had no chance of achieving the protest goals. In fact, he admitted the goals being advocated by his chair orators in the student gatherings were not even his real goals. Nechaev's real expectation was that the petitions and demonstrations would, indeed, get a large number of students expelled from university. These expulsions, he calculated, would then set off a wave of discontent throughout the Generation of the Sixties. More students would be expelled. Then their brethren in seminaries would also take up the cause, with many of them also being expelled. The expelled students would return, discontented, to their home villages. Thus, according to Nechaev's vision, large numbers of the disgruntled, unemployed students would make their way en masse to the country, where they would rapidly foment rebellion among the peasants. The peasants were always assumed to be, if properly led, ready, willing and able to rise in revolt. It was an article of faith within the Sixties movement that the peasants were exploited, miserable and on the verge of rebellion. The smallest doubt on this subject was criticized and reproached as a politically incorrect insult to the character of "the People."

Nechaev called another activist gathering. This time, he personally spoke. He challenged all of those present who were not scared for their skins to prove it, simply by signing a paper that he had prepared for this purpose. Students in attendance agreed and started to sign. But after many had signed, others present started to ask, why? Some independent thinkers protested that it was stupid, in fact suicidal. They demanded that the paper be torn up. But it was too late. The signed paper was already in Nechaev's pocket. Next day, the rumor swirled and circulated that Nechaev and two other students had been summoned by the university chief of security, who threatened that if the meetings did not stop, all three of them would be arrested and put in prison.

Yet another activist gathering was hastily organized. This time there were only 40 to 50 persons in attendance. The mainstream student movement, fed up with Nechaev's signature ploy, basically did not show up. But then, to everyone's surprise, Nechaev did not show up either. Instead, his protégé and de facto aide de camp, a youngster named Evamply Ametisov, stepped up and announced the startling news that Nechaev had been arrested.

He informed the gathering that Vera Zasulitch had received in the mail a strange letter which read:

> Today crossing Vassilevsky Island, I came across a jail carriage. From the carriage a hand was sticking out a window. The hand dropped a note. I heard a voice call out from the carriage, 'if you are a student, take this to the address written on it.' I am in fact a student, so I considered it my duty to obey his request. Make this letter disappear!

There was no signature. With this letter there enclosed was another, scratched in pencil in the handwriting of Nechaev. It read:

> I am taken to prison, I don't know which one. Send this message to the friends in the movement, that they will continue with the path of action. I hope to see you again.

The news of Nechaev's arrest caused an immediate sensation among the students. The event became even more dramatic and attention grabbing because the authorities persisted in denying it.[231] Everyone assumed the authorities were lying. They speculated feverishly about the reasons for Nechaev's arrest and why it was kept a secret.

It would be a matter of years before the students would finally learn that Nechaev's sudden disappearance was not, in fact due to his arrest. Rather, it was a cover for a carefully planned departure from St. Petersburg, coupled with a completely false and concocted story of his arrest that was intended to, and did, generate a mystique with respect to Nechaev himself, while at the same time whipping up an angry reaction among the activists. After a preliminary stop in Moscow, where he borrowed someone else's passport, Sergei's ultimate destination was Geneva.[232] He arrived there in March of 1869. Very soon after his arrival, he sought out Mikhail Bakhunin.[233]

Chapter 8: Terrorism Gets a Catechism

The Bakhunins, Mikhail and Antonia, after moving to Italy, had spent most of 1865 living in relative tranquillity in Tuscany. Perhaps to escape the contentment, they decided to move to Naples late in the year. Here, they soon made friends with Princess Olga Sergeyevna Obolenskaya. She was the semi-estranged wife of the governor of Moscow. Olga had left him to move to Naples with her whole household, which included her children, her lover, a Polish exile, and a suite of domestic assistants including her doctor. Being wealthy, she was surrounded by a coterie of would-be revolutionaries and other sycophants. Mikhail Bakhunin and Princess Olga were made for each other. He promptly became a regular in her entourage. Mikhail and Antonia turned themselves into the animators of the Obolenskaya household, continually organizing picnics, concert and theater outings and other social events.

Antonia now became involved in a love affair with a Neapolitan revolutionary, an attorney named Carlo Gambuzzi.

Bakhunin was pleased to tolerate this relationship, partly because of his own inability to satisfy her sexually, and partly because Gambuzzi was a dedicated revolutionary and a member of the Florence Brotherhood. Ultimately, Gambuzzi became an accepted part of the Bakhunin family. While Antonia was living with Bakhunin, Gambuzzi would father two children with her.

Only now, at the age of 50, did Bakhunin begin to express hostility to the church. In part this was triggered by living in Italy, where the wealth and power of the Roman Catholic church was very visible. As a counterpoint to church dogma, Bakhunin penned his own anarchist maxims and doctrines. The proper devotee, he wrote, must be:

> Atheist
>
> Socialist
>
> Federalist
>
> An enemy of authoritarian principles
>
> Love more than anything liberty and justice
>
> Convinced that there is no liberty without equality
>
> And also, to:
>
> Wish for the destruction of all religious and political institutions
>
> Seek to reduce nationalist principles
>
> Bring about the suppression of inheritance
>
> Bring about the overdue recognition of the equality of women
>
> and
>
> Adhere to the necessity of violence for suppressing the privileged classes

Additionally, he wrote, it was not enough that the candidate be convinced – he or she must also possess a "revolutionary passion."[234] This set of prescriptions is a precursor to the "catechism" Bakhunin would later co-author.

After spending the winter of 1866-67 in Naples, the Bakhunins moved to the nearby island of Ischia. During this period Bakhunin wrote a large number of articles, many of which were published in a journal called Liberty and Justice that was published by a group of Bakhunin's Italian circle of friends including Gambuzzi. In these writings, Bakhunin for the first time referred to himself as an "anarchist," as opposed to a "revolutionary" or a "socialist."

In June 1867, Bakhunin began to express concern that he might need to leave Italy. The Russian ambassador, Kissalev, was the same official who had obtained Bakhunin's expulsion from France 20 years earlier. By now, the White Terror had gone into full swing in Russia following the Karakozov assassination attempt. The former government attitude of tolerance toward his expatriate status had evaporated. Kissalev was lobbying the Italian authorities to deport Bakhunin and was arguing to them that Bakhunin was linked to political unrest that had occurred in southern Italy and Sicily in September 1866. But although Kissalev was given as an excuse by Bakhunin, political pressure was probably not his most pressing problem causing him to leave Italy. The more important reason was the departure of his financial patron, Princess Olga. Being a noted liberal, as part of the White Terror she was cut off financially by her husband, and thus had to economize on expenses. She wound up moving to France with a greatly reduced entourage that did not include Bakhunin.

The opportunistic Bakhunin now found a way to regain the financial support of Herzen and Ogarev. Bakhunin took on a role as one of the headline speakers in the inaugural conference of the newly formed "League of Peace and Liberty" that gathered in Geneva from September 9 to 12, 1867. Before a euphoric audience, Bakhunin strode dramatically on stage to embrace the renowned Italian freedom fighter, clad in his emblematic red jacket and dubbed the "Hero of Two Worlds,"

Giuseppe Garibaldi.[235]

In Switzerland as opposed to Italy, Bakhunin was able to advocate revolution more openly. Moreover, in Switzerland there was a substantial community of Russian expats, such as Herzen, Ogarev, and Poggio, who like Bakhunin supported radical change in Russia. Bakhunin quickly assumed leadership in that community, although the wildcat nature of the people in the community meant it was anything but cohesive. Bakhunin once again headlined at the second congress of the League for Peace in Berne, Switzerland, starting September 25, 1868. This event, however, turned into a struggle that did not end well for Bakhunin. He made enemies of Marx and other "left wing" delegates with the following declaration which pretty well summed up his lasting philosophical differences with the Marxists:

> I detest communism because it is a negation of liberty and because I cannot conceive of anything human without liberty. I will never be communist because communism concentrates and absorbs all powers of society within the State, and because it necessarily leads to the centralization of property in the hands of the State, and I myself want to abolish the State. Wanting to abolish the State, I want to abolish the inheritance of property, that is nothing but an institution of the State, in fact a consequence of the concept of the State. It is in this sense that I am a collectivist and not at all a communist.

Despite Bakhunin's superior personal charisma and rhetorical skills, Marx was by far the more adept politician. Bakhunin lacked the qualities of an effective organizer, especially, the ability to enforce party discipline. He also lacked the stern judgment about people that usually is required to build an organization. He tended to be surrounded by a collection of misfits and refugees. As a result of Marx's maneuvering behind the scenes, Bakhunin's position was handily rejected by the Lausanne congress of what would be called the "First International." The prideful Bakhunin resigned and, with a rump composed of his sympathizers, started his own separate organization called the International Alliance of Socialist Democracy (commonly called the "Alliance," in contradistinction to the "International" dominated by Marx), on November 21, 1868. This was also to be based in Geneva. Bakhunin claimed that he had signed up 500 members within a month. Marx's sidekick, Friedrich Engels, countered this move by publishing articles deriding Bakhunin as senile, deluded by a combination of his paunch and a young woman.[236]

Bakhunin did, however, find some natural allies among the Swiss. Switzerland, especially its Jura Mountain cantons, had a strong tradition and inclination toward autonomy and lack of government interference with private citizens. Thus Swiss socialists were largely immune to the appeal of Marxism. A young Swiss socialist named James Guillaume, who was from the Jura region, was eventually to become Bakhunin's primary biographer. Guillaume moved to Geneva and soon entered into an intimate friendship with Bakhunin, who was not deterred by differences in age and social class. One reason the relationship lasted was that Guillaume had enough sense not to be seduced by Bakhunin's many fantasies and projects. For example, he refused to join Bakhunin's Alliance, saying he was already a member of the Jura branch of the International.

Guillaume invited Bakhunin to Le Locle, two hours by train northeast of Geneva along the French border, to address his local branch. He did this on February 20, 1869. As usual, the charisma of Bakhunin was impressive. But despite his personal popularity, he could not convince the branch members that they needed to leave the International and join the rival Alliance. By the end of March 1869, Marx temporarily patched over his differences with Bakhunin by allowing

Bakhunin's "Alliance" itself to be admitted as a member of the International.[237]

At precisely this moment, Sergei Nechaev suddenly made his appearance in Geneva. The intenseness of his personality drew Bakhunin to him like a powerful magnet. He instantly appealed to Bakhunin's weakness for younger male protégés. Bakhunin affectionately referred to Nechaev as "Boy." Bakhunin at the time felt lonely, in terms of Russian comrades. He was becoming politically distanced from the more moderate Herzen, who had left Switzerland to live in Paris and Nice. Using his instinctive gift for reading and controlling others, "Boy," with Bakhunin, played up his alleged persona as being from the *narod* – a "man of the Russian people."

Their enduring work, *Catechism of a Revolutionary*, was produced jointly by Bakhunin and Nechaev during a six month period of intense collaboration that ensued. It is simultaneously a chilling credo for a terrorist, and a chilling constitution for a terrorist organization. It is a terrorist Bible whose precepts continue to be applied and followed today. In *Catechism of a Revolutionary*, Nechaev's diabolical ideas on organization building were elaborated with the benefit of Bakhunin's more polished writing. "Catechism," borrowing core ideas previously developed by "Hell," went far beyond Bakhunin's prior collection of anarchist maxims.[238]

1.   The revolutionary – is a doomed man. He has neither his own interests, nor affairs, nor feelings, nor attachments, nor property, nor even name. Everything in him is absorbed by a single, exclusive interest, by a total concept, a total passion – revolution.

2.   In the depths of his being not only in words but in action he has sundered any connection with the civil order and with the entire educated world and with all the laws, proprieties, conventions, and morality of this world. He is its merciless enemy, and if he continues to live in it, then it is only in order the more certainly

to destroy it.

3. The revolutionary despises any kind of doctrinarism and has rejected peaceful science, leaving it to future generations. He knows only one science – the science of destruction. For this and only for this he now studies mechanics, physics, chemistry, perhaps medicine. For this he studies night and day the living science of people, of their personalities and positions, and all the conditions of the present social structure in every possible stratum. The goal is the same – the quickest and surest destruction of this foul structure.

4. He despises public opinion. He despises and hates the existing public morality in all its motives and manifestations. Everything that facilitates the victory of the revolution is moral to him. Everything that hinders it is immoral and criminal.

5. Merciless toward the state and generally toward the entire society divided into estates and by education, he does not expect from them the least mercy toward himself. Between them and him there exists a concealed or manifest, but constant and implacable life-and-death struggle. Every day he must be ready to die. He has to train himself to withstand torture.

6. Stern with himself, he must be stern with others as well. All tender, effeminizing feelings of kinship, friendship, love, gratitude, and even of honor itself must be suppressed in him by a total cold passion for the revolutionary cause. For him there exists only one comfort, one consolation, and one reward, and satisfaction – the success of the revolution. Day and night he must have one thought, one goal – merciless destruction. Striving coldbloodedly and tirelessly

toward this goal, he must always be willing to perish himself and to destroy with his own hands everything that hinders its realization.

7. The nature of a true revolutionary precludes any kind of romanticism, any kind of sensitivity, enthusiasm, and excitement. It precludes even personal hate and vindictiveness. Revolutionary passion, having become in him normal and constant, must be united with cold calculation. Always and everywhere he must be, not a person guided by personal inclinations, but the kind of person prescribed by the general interest of the revolution.

The Catechism provides maxims to govern "the Attitude of the Revolutionary Toward His Revolutionary Comrades." The following is a typical example:

10. Every comrade must have at his disposition several revolutionaries of the second and third rank; that is, not fully initiated ones. He has to look upon them as part of the general revolutionary capital placed at his disposal. He must expend his portion of the capital economically, striving always to extract from it the maximum utility. He looks upon himself as capital foredoomed to be expended for the victory of the revolutionary cause, but as a type of capital which he himself cannot dispose of without the agreement of the entire association of completely initiated persons.

The "Attitude of the Revolutionary Toward Society" is also prescribed.

13. The revolutionary enters into the official world, the world of social rank, and the so-called educated world, and lives in it only with the aim of destroying it more completely and sooner. He is not a revolutionary if he pities anything in this world, if

he can hold back before the annihilation of a position, a relationship, or some person belonging to this world, in which everyone and everything must be equally despicable to him. All the worse for him if he has in it family, friendly, or love relationships; he is not a revolutionary if they can stay his hand.

14. With the goal of merciless destruction the revolutionary can and frequently even must live in society, pretending to be something other than what he is. The revolutionary must penetrate everywhere, into all strata . . .

The Catechism also speaks to the relationship between the terrorist "revolutionary" and the sustaining "people" (*narod*):

22. The association has no other goal besides the complete liberation and happiness of the narod, that is the laboring people. But being convinced that this liberation and the achievement of this happiness are possible only by way of an all-shattering revolution of the narod, the association with all of its power and means will facilitate the development and dissemination of those troubles and evils, which must at last drive the narod beyond the limits of its patience and incite it to a massive rebellion.

. . . .

24. The association does not intend to thrust upon the narod any organization from above, no matter what kind. A future organization, without doubt, will be produced from the narod's movement and its way of life, but this – is the concern of future generations. Our concern – is passionate, complete, general, and merciless destruction.

Nechaev rapidly transformed this blueprint for a terrorist organization into a semblance of reality. Herzen and Ogarev had joint control of a substantial fund of money, some 20,000 francs, that had been left in their hands by a mysterious young Russian who went by the name of Pavel Bakhmetev (itself a false name, one suspiciously similar to "Rakhmetov") when he departed to found a utopian colony in New Zealand.[239] Nechaev, with Bakhunin's help, induced Ogarev to give him "his half" of the Bakhmetev fund to support "revolution in Russia." From Ogarev, Nechaev also acquired a tribute in the form of a poem telling the story of Nechaev's martyrdom in a snowy labor camp in Siberia. This was a myth that the brazen Nechaev intended to perpetuate upon his repatriation. From Bakhunin, Nechaev acquired a signed document attesting to the status of Nechaev as the secret representative of the "Russian section" of the "World Revolutionary Alliance." To add more weight and credibility to this fictitious organization, Bakhunin affixed "No. 2771" to the document. Armed with money, his phony "certificate," Ogarev's phony martyr's tribute, and the Catechism, Nechaev returned to Russia at the end of August 1869 in time to be on hand for the beginning of the university school year. The university was the fertile field for organizing in which Nechaev had his prior experience. He re-entered Russia with a fake Serbian name and a passport that Bakhunin had helped him fabricate.[240] After a short time spent plotting in Odessa, he made his way by train to Moscow.

There, Nechaev already had a willing follower in Peter Uspensky. Uspensky was a university dropout who now maintained a "legal" job in a bookstore. He had remained in contact with Nechaev after his faked disappearance, and he had helped supply Nechaev with money for his travels. Only Uspensky and the owner of the bookshop, a radical veteran of "the Organization" named Prince Varlam Cherkezov, were allowed to know Nechaev's true identity. In order not to immediately shatter the myth of his Siberian martyrdom, Nechaev now presented himself to all others under the false name of Ivan Petrovich Pavlov. Of course, "Pavlov" would not be his only fake identity. He went by a whole variety of aliases: Panin, Petrov, Kiniavsky, Nachalov, Dmitri Fedorovich, and Ivan Korol. He also kept an array of disguises to accompany them – a priest's cassock, a soldier's uniform, a peasant costume, the accoutrements of a bureaucrat.

Sympathizers such as Cherkezov were brought under Nechaev's spell almost involuntarily. Later, Cherkezov would tell the authorities that Nechaev had a personality which "was not particularly attractive." He described him as:

> a person neither particularly clear minded, broadly developed, nor equipped to direct the movement, nor even to be a serious and consistent political agitator. But he possesses one quality – decisiveness to the point of fanaticism, a passion for work in the popular cause and an equally fanatic devotion to it. In this last quality one must seek whatever influence he has over any particular group of people. He didn't give them anything. Didn't help their development – they're more developed than he is – didn't clarify the program or the state of the popular cause – they knew it anyway and better than he did. Without having given them anything he got them involved in the movement because he is an energetic and active person; though he was tainted he appeared as a person standing for the cause.

Instinctively using the techniques of a cult leader, Nechaev impressed recruits with his own passion and made them feel as if they were parasites if they did not attach themselves to the cause with equal fervor. At first, he might demand just a small act of commitment – a seemingly trivial errand or a copying task. He would then interpret its acceptance as an indication of total subordination to him. He did not convince people with words or arguments. Rather, he would push them into motion with his energy, by setting them to a task, and then by initiating them into the secret organization, showing them its rules, its proclamations, and its documents stamped with an official-looking oval seal of "the Committee of the People's Revenge of February 19, 1870."[241]

Nechaev grasped that a terrorist act would be all the more terrifying if it could be presented as carried out in the name of a larger, more mysterious and more sinister organization, rather than by just a single individual or even by a few fanatics. Nechaev's simple principle of exaggeration, which would be adopted as a matter of philosophy by the Russian terrorists who would follow in Nechaev's footsteps, has subsequently grown to dominate the thought and behavior of modern terrorists.

Nechaev devoted much energy to revamping the organizational framework of the young student activists who were already overflowing with disruptive energy. He turned it into a pyramid scheme involving terrorist cells. Each member was given one very simple priority: to recruit a secondary group of revolutionaries from among the dissidents in the student community. The organization's members, with the exception of the group leader, would know of each other not by name, but by number. And, even the very numbers they were given would be chosen with the intent to exaggerate the overall size and importance of the organization. Thus, revolutionary "number 2" would form a group whose members were given the names "21" to "24." Member "21" would in term form groups whose members would be known as "211 to 214," and so forth. All members in the lower strata were pledged to give full reports on their activities every week to their "group leaders."[242] Nechaev had a trusted crony whom he sometimes sent to "drop in" on meetings of the lower strata cells. The crony was instructed to always present himself as an observer from the mysterious overarching "Committee of the People's Revenge." Cell meetings themselves, as well as the free time of all of the group members, were diverted away from rhetoric, instead being filled with busy work such as writing out long lists of potential recruits, making profiles of the personal characteristics of "liberal" students, and cataloging potential sources of money.[243]

All of the busy work naturally irritated some of the members. One whose nerves became particularly frayed was Ivan Ivanov, a robust young man who was already a dedicated activist well before Nechaev's arrival in Moscow. Ivanov, as usual, was assigned a long list of duties by the "Committee," including fundraising, arranging literary gatherings, arranging lodgings for organization members, influencing public opinion, and establishing ties with sympathetic local bureaucrats.

Ivanov began to question Nechaev, known to him as "Pavlov," over the tasks that were ordered to be performed. Each of their disagreements was settled by a stamped decision from the "Committee." The "Committee" decisions invariably backed up the views of "Pavlov." On November 4, 1869, "Pavlov" and Ivanov had a violent argument over the former's insistence that Ivanov paste a provocative propaganda poster, entitled "From Those Who Have United to Those Who Are in Disarray," in public places throughout the university. Ivanov feared clashes with the authorities over the posters, which would lead to expulsions and arrests of the most activist among the students. Nechaev, just as he had done in his previous year's incarnation in St. Peterburg, insisted that these provocations must go forward. Again he reasoned that the students, once expelled, would become even more dedicated followers of the "Committee." And as always, the "Committee" settled the dispute between "Pavlov" and Ivanov in favor of Nechaev's position. In response, Ivanov disclosed his decision to leave the group.[244]

After a brief visit to St. Petersburg to re-establish ties there, Nechaev turned his entire attention to dealing with Ivanov immediately upon his return to Moscow. He informed core group members that the "Committee" had imposed a sentence of death on Ivanov for insubordination. He ordered all of them to help carry out the verdict. Pursuant to a plan he dictated, Nechaev with other conspirators laid in wait in a dark grotto within a park on the campus of the ironically named Pavlov Academy, while two of his followers summoned Ivanov to assist in digging up some hidden printing equipment which supposedly had been buried in the cave by other revolutionaries. At least one follower had to steel his nerve with vodka, but all of them complied with the instructions. In the confusion after their penetration into the cave, Ivanov realized the treachery and almost escaped, but just as he reached the entrance, group members were able to tackle him. With three other men helping to hold down Ivanov, Nechaev sat on the victim and finally succeeded in strangling him. During the death struggle, Ivanov was able to bite into one of Nechaev's hands, inflicting a deep wound that would leave a permanent scar. After the victim was finally throttled, Nechaev took his revolver and shot Ivanov through the head for good measure. The conspirators then tied bricks to the body and dumped it through a hole in the ice covering a nearby pond. But they did a hurried job of it. Ivanov's body floated up to the surface and was discovered only four days later.[245]

By that time, Nechaev had already left Moscow to return to St. Petersburg. There, he met with a chilly reception. A number of other students who had opposed Nechaev's deceitful tactics during the previous winter had by now organized themselves into a stronger group which although radical was, in some measure, a reaction against "Nechaevism." One of this group's key organizers was a medical student named Mark Natanson. In the short time he spent in St. Peterburg during the fall and early winter of 1869, Nechaev made no new headway with his terrorist organizing tactics.

By pure coincidence, Moscow agents of the Third Section, in following up on a prior investigation, searched Uspensky's apartment on the very same day that police found Ivanov's body in the pond at Pavlov Academy. In Uspensky's apartment they found an encoded version of *Catechism of a Revolutionary*, copies of the propaganda poster titled "From Those Who Have United to Those Who Are in Disarray," other radical posters and literature, and enough identifying information on members of Nechaev's group to enable them to begin a systematic roundup. Under police questioning, two of the arrested followers quickly cracked and confessed their roles in the Ivanov killing. They also implicated and identified other group members. Nechaev heard the news. He hastily returned to Moscow to try to stem the damage to his organization. Then, Nechaev traveled south 190 kilometers to Tula, the site of a major gun factory and arsenal, to plot a takeover in the style of John Brown. Nothing came of this, other than Nechaev acquiring from sympathizers some 300 rubles and a woman companion named Varvara Alexandrovskaya. Traveling with Alexandrovskaya and a false passport, Nechaev left to head to Prussia. He ultimately sent Alexandrovskaya back to Russia, loaded with propaganda publications, and went on in January of 1870 to Switzerland, where "Boy" was heartily welcomed back by Bakhunin.[246]

The murder of Ivanov had made big press worldwide. Bakhunin initially was inclined to dismiss the official version and blame Ivanov's death on the Russian secret police. He helped Nechaev publish yet another detailed fictitious account of his own martyrdom, this one involving his transportation to Siberia, and his death while en route by a brutal beating at the hands of three escorting police guards. Later, of course, Nechaev found it necessary to further embroider this tale to explain his continued existence. He published a further tale that Nechaev had survived miraculously because in fact the gendarmes, while thinking they were killing Nechaev, had accidentally beaten to death one of their own number while the real Nechaev made his escape.[247] Bakhunin eagerly aided Nechaev in promoting this story, publishing accounts of his own which backed up Nechaev's fictionalized version of events.

The pair collaborated some more on further expanding the philosophical justifications for terrorism. Bakhunin put this theory into the following terms:

> It is . . . impossible to be either a revolutionary or a true reactionary without committing acts which, from the point of view of criminal and civil codes are incontestably delinquencies or even crimes, but which, from the point of view of actual and serious practice, appear as inevitable misfortunes. . . . .
>
> But that which is permitted to the state is denied to the individual. Such is the governmental maxim. Machiavelli said it, and history, and the practice of all actual governments alike prove him right: Crime is a necessary condition of the very existence of the State, which therefore creates an exclusive monopoly of it, from which it follows that the individual who dares to commit a crime is twice guilty: first of all, against human conscience, but then and above all against the State, in arrogating to himself one of its most precious privileges.[248]

Nechaev, in a journal several months later, presented his own twisted version of the theory:[249]

> Aristotle called man a political animal; he might have called him a criminal brute. Law, so to speak, organizes murder and . . . brings about plundering; law is that talisman, which permits a small band of cheats and parasites to exploit and savagely beat masses of people – with impunity! You can be the worst son of a bitch, the vilest scum, and you are an inviolable and sacred person, if you are outside the law (to be outside the law means to make the laws) and if you are the most virtuous subject, the law all the same can christen you a scoundrel! . . . Force gave

birth to law; the instinct for exploitation of those nearby, the instinct of parasitism, the instinct for plunder gave birth to law. . . . Mankind must recognize that to the present moment law, having given birth to crime, itself was the greatest crime, and the criminals were not the ones who were punished, but those who punished.

Nechaev's manipulating personality rapidly enveloped Bakhunin. Months earlier, to generate some needed cash Bakhunin had undertaken to produce a Russian translation of Marx's Das Capital. He had received an advance on the project. However, as he disliked Marx, Bakhunin found a task which basically involved filtering the abstract details of Marx's political theories very slow going. He was still laboring over it when Nechaev arrived. Nechaev rapidly concluded Bakhunin needed to give up the translating project and dedicate himself full time to producing propaganda. Without informing Bakhunin, Nechaev took it upon himself to write to Bakhunin's Russian publisher who had previously paid the advance. He curtly told him that the translating project was over. If the publisher made any trouble, the "revolutionary committee" would be coming to pay him a visit. The publisher could be sure that it would use "uncivilized" methods.[250] Marx was later able to use this letter written by Nechaev as grounds for expelling Bakhunin from the International.

With Bakhunin's help, Nechaev promptly got his hands on the other half of the money from the mysterious Bakhmetev. Then Alexander Herzen died suddenly on January 21, 1870, shortly after Nechaev's return to Switzerland. Using Ogarev and Bakhunin, Nechaev now tried to gain access to the ample financial resources of Herzen's family. Nechaev sucked Bakhunin into a scheme to milk Herzen's daughter Natalie of her inheritance. Natalie Herzen, an attractive but troubled young woman, was 25 years old when her father died. She traveled from Paris to Geneva to console Ogarev, whom she looked upon almost as another parent. She had grown up in a complex emotional melange of governesses, teachers, family retainers, revolutionary writers and politicians of several nationalities. She had suffered a psychotic episode after a brief relationship with a blind Italian nobleman. Bakhunin and Ogarev had to repel a coalition of Natalie's family and friends who tried to protect her from any involvement in revolutionary schemes.

During her visit to Geneva, Natalie was introduced to a "Mr. Volkov" (another of Nechaev's aliases), who immediately poured his energy into seducing her. "Volkov" used one of his stock techniques, asking Natalie if she was truly interested in "the Russian cause" and asking her to, if so, perform small tasks to support it, such as addressing envelopes. Nechaev convinced Natalie that her cooperation was a matter of life and death for imperiled revolutionaries. He declared himself to be in love with her and asked her to marry him. Natalie, who was feeling physically ill at "Volkov's" overtures, declined. At one point, she refused to meet him again unless he first gave his word that he would not try to kiss her. But despite this, like numerous others who found Nechaev's personal behavior uncomfortable and embarrassing she tolerated it for the sake of the cause. She also apparently felt an involuntary fascination with the persona of the righteous fanatic.[251]

Nechaev got Natalie to grant him permission to continue publishing her father's newspaper *The Bell*, which was revived for a total of six new issues in April and May of 1870. Then Nechaev, under growing police pressure, was forced to flee Geneva. He went to London. When he went, he took with him a series of compromising letters he had stolen from Bakhunin. He calculated he could use these later on to blackmail Bakhunin, Ogarev, and the Herzen family.

Bakhunin and Ogarev kept up their support for Nechaev, even in the face of such crude behavior. They did so although they were also confronted with direct testimony, brought to Geneva by a Russian radical named German Lopatin, attesting to Nechaev's treacherous murder of Ivanov. The attitude and conduct of Bakhunin and Ogarev toward Nechaev, including such highly questionable matters as delivering the psychologically vulnerable Natalie Herzen into his clutches, typify the support often provided to terrorist outlaws by sympathizers who are more securely positioned within society. By June 1870, however, Bakhunin finally grudgingly admitted to himself that Nechaev had lied about many matters. He resolved to make a total break with him. However, at the same time Bakhunin felt a great deal of ambivalence about forsaking "Boy." Over the next two years, Bakhunin would continue to allow his contacts and resources to be used to shelter Nechaev, who was living under a variety of new aliases, and to protect him against extradition to Russia for as long as possible.[252]

Not until the summer of 1872 did Russian diplomats finally succeed in securing Swiss government cooperation for Nechaev's arrest and extradition. They were able to argue successfully that Nechaev was a common criminal, as opposed to a political refugee, in the matter of the murder of his own ally Ivanov. Nechaev was returned to St. Petersburg in chains for a show trial that took place in January of 1873. He impressed the onlookers with his defiant projection of utter disdain for his captors and their judicial proceedings. Rejecting any suggestion of putting on a defense, he thoroughly acted the part of the hissing feline. He shouted slogans such as "Down with despotism," that he was a political prisoner, and that the court had no authority to judge him.[253]

Nechaev was, naturally, convicted. He was sentenced to civil execution followed by deportation to Siberia. However, yet again his "Siberian exile" proved to be nothing but a deception. Only this time, the deception was instigated not by Nechaev, but by an evidently somewhat intimidated Russian government. Rather than ship Nechaev to Siberia, the government secretly incarcerated him in the Alexei Ravelin, the ultra-secret, ultra-secure solitary confinement wing of the Peter and Paul Fortress. There through force of will he would overcome the dungeon-like conditions to linger on in obscurity, his presence in St. Petersburg remaining a closely guarded secret that was totally unknown to a new crop of Russian terrorists who were born of the Sixties Generation. Yet even though these fierce young men, and even fiercer young women, were never his personal protegés, and even though some of them had earlier rejected "Nechaevism," they would eventually come full circle to execute Nechaev's blueprint for terrorist organization. It would have stunning effects.[254]

Chapter 9: Going to the People

The liberalization of university admissions under Alexander II was limited to men. The extent of higher education for young women in Russia consisted of finishing schools for the daughters of the nobility, the most prominent of which was called the Smolny Institute.[255] Women were on occasion permitted to attend university lectures, but only as outside auditors not allowed to take any of the qualifying examinations. There was little incentive for women to engage in a rigorous course of studies.[256] At the beginning of the Sixties, however, a "Sunday School movement" arose, in which regular school teachers volunteered their time on the sabbath to try to provide access to learning for young women otherwise excluded from the educational establishment. The Sunday School embodied something of the spirit of the women's self-help collective idealized in *What Is to Be Done?* The movement rapidly gained momentum. There were soon 2,500 volunteers teaching in the Sunday Schools throughout Russia.[257] But this was short lived. The very wildfire nature of the Sunday Schools, as well as the ministry of education's inability to supervise their curriculum, caused the government to entertain grave doubts about the wisdom of allowing them to exist. Those in power feared that the unregulated schools were spreading "liberal ideas," or worse. In 1862, most of the Sunday Schools were abruptly disbanded by government decree. The more radical teachers were arrested and the schools were closed down "pending their reorganization on a new basis."[258]

When Sofia Perovskaya returned to St. Petersburg at age 16 in 1869, the situation in women's university education was basically unchanged. That spring, another unofficial school for women, consisting of a series of evening classes, had been launched by university professors teaching on a volunteer basis. Because the classes were given in a school building near the Alarchina Bridge, they were called the "Alarchinsky" classes.[259] Anna Vilberg, on the boat with Sonia, was headed to St. Petersburg to study in the Alarchinsky classes. Sonia rapidly made up her mind to enroll in Alarchinsky as well.

Sofia Perovskaya as a student in Alarchinsky was quiet and taciturn. Only a few of the other students learned much about her.[260] A fellow woman student recalled the impression which Sonia made at this time:

> [A] girl very young, almost a little girl, who stood out over the other women by the modesty of her attire: a very simple gray dress, that almost resembled a high school uniform, with a small white collar that did not fit her that well. One sensed a complete indifference to her exterior aspect. The first thing that stood out about her was her exceptionally high and large forehead which swallowed up the rest of her small round face.
>
> Watching her closely, I noted, under the forehead, blue-gray eyes that looked around from beneath lowered lashes at everything around her with an air of

distrust. In that look, there was something inflexible. When she was not speaking, her childlike mouth was pressed shut, as if she was afraid of allowing any superfluous words to escape. Her face was profoundly serious and thoughtful. From her whole persona emanated something ascetic and monastic.[261]

Perovskaya embodied an incongruous combination of feminine gentleness and masculine hardness. Although her appearance was juvenile and unprepossessing, something about Perovskaya made her attractive to men. One would later preface his biography of her with the comment, "[i]t was not the beauty which dazzles at first sight, but that which fascinates the more, the more it is regarded."[262] Over the course of the next ten years, several men in the radical community developed real crushes on her.[263] But Perovskaya cultivated a studied indifference to the opposite sex.

In terms of the Alarchinsky course program, Perovskaya's main academic pursuit was mathematics. But her real interest was quickly drawn to the flaming women who attended the class sessions. With their lack of feminine adornment, short cropped hair, wide brimmed hats, and plain white blouses, their whole manner of dress exuded the distinctive nihilist attitude.[264] The effect was topped off with the nihilist trademark, enormous blue spectacles. Sonia liked the aura and audacity of these women. She soon become close friends with several of them. The stocky, masculine looking Alexandra "Sasha" Kornilova became one of the closest. Like Sonia, Sasha had a passion for remaining independent of all forms of male control.[265]

Sonia as well as other girl students soon went outside the formal curriculum of Alarchinsky to become involved in organizing independent group meetings. Feminism and the oppression of women were always the issues at the center of the debate, even if political and social themes also were discussed. Perovskaya, although the youngest, already was the de facto leader of a study circle. She was cautious about which girls she agreed to admit into the group. It was decided to delve in depth into review of an edition of John Stuart Mill that Chernyshevsky had annotated. She walked everybody through this text slowly, analyzing each new idea and argument presented. Sonia took these studies very seriously. With biting sarcasm she criticized the girls who did not show up for the study sessions, or who chronically arrived late.[266]

Sonia's father, with Varvara, left St. Petersburg for an extended period to visit Germany to seek relief in a sanitarium for his physical and mental ailments. By the time her parents returned, Sonia had become accustomed to hanging out in her new circle of nihilist women. One time Sonia's mother made some of Sonia's friends stay for dinner. Lev immediately detested these women due to their irreverent attitude, boisterous conversations and nihilist form of dress. He forbade Sonia from ever bringing them into his home again. He even threatened to forbid Sonia from continuing with the Alarchinsky courses if she continued to see them.[267] This edict greatly upset Sonia. She rejected any thought of obeying Lev's orders. Sonia decided to move out and rent her own room. In order to do so, she had to possess an internal passport stating that she was allowed to reside in the town. Because Sonia was underage, the passport could only be provided by her father. This, he refused to do.

But Sasha Kornilova's father, a wealthy merchant and the father of four radical daughters, was far more tolerant. Before long, Sonia became a regular at the Kornilova household. There she engaged in long discussions with Sasha and her sisters, as well as a steady stream of other women who constantly dropped in to visit. One of the Kornilova sisters, Vera, worked out a fictitious marriage with a willing young man in order set up her own separate flat. One night Sonia failed to return home and instead stayed with Vera Kornilova. She intended to remain there, in hiding, until Lev relented and granted her the papers necessary to live on her own. She stubbornly stuck to her resolve, even though her father instigated a major police investigation aimed at finding her and returning her home.[268]

Lev was appalled at his daughter's impertinence. He accused her brother Vasily of putting her up to it. Vasily at one point met with his father's doctor to discuss the situation with Sonia. This doctor scoffed at Sonia's demand for independence. Vasily pointed out to the doctor that Sonia, if denied the independence she sought, could very well commit suicide. This was taken as a serious threat. Vasily was summoned to the police station and

Sofia Perovskaya (on floor wearing man's trousers), with companions (L to R) A. Vilberg, S. Lechern and A. Kornilova, 1870.

Source: V. Perovsky memoir, National Library of Russia

threatened with arrest if he did not disclose where Sonia was hiding. Fortunately for him, he really did not know where his sister was. Varvara intervened, trembling with emotion. She tearfully insisted to Lev that she would go along to the police station with Vasily, and that she would insist on being arrested herself if Vasily were to be arrested. In response to his wife's impassioned reproach, Lev softened his attitude.

The following day, Lev himself joined Vasily in the trip to the police department. He seemed bent on avoiding trouble.

After speaking alone in the office with the chief of police, he left in the carriage. When Vasily's turn came to be interviewed the chief did not arrest him, but merely gave a lecture about the foolishness of Sonia's behavior. He warned that hanging out with the wrong crowd could ruin her life. He added that he hoped the uproar caused by Sonia's evasion could be resolved peacefully and without police involvement. In the course of the interview, Vasily repeated to the police chief what he had told the doctor, that he knew his sister, and that if police become involved, she may take a "tragic step" (implying suicide). Faced with this threat, continued pressure from Varvara, and his doctor's medical advice against any further stress of confrontation, Lev finally relented and signed to allow Sonia an internal passport. When doing so, he lashed out to Vasily that he never wanted to see Sonia in his house again.[269] The wish, made in anger, would be granted.

After getting her passport, Sofia Perovskaya moved into a communal dacha along with Sasha Kornilova, Anna Vilberg and Sofia Leshern, a woman a decade older than Perovskaya who had been involved with the Sunday School movement. The housemates spent much of their time focusing on a self-directed reading program. To avoid unwanted sexual attention, the four of them wore men's clothes when they went walking. Sonia's ascetic personality included a prominent rejection of any sexual experiments. Vasily recalled a conversation he had with Sonia during this period in which the topic turned to sexual relations. Sonia expressed a strong opinion that early marriages were against the normal development of the human body, and that a person was not ready for sex until around age 30. Earlier sexual urges, in her opinion, were caused by "living in the city" and "ballet." Perovskaya and her friend Vilberg shared the view that early marriages serve to halt a person's development in the activities of public life.[270]

With Sasha Kornilova, Sonia began to attend meetings of the Chaikovsky circle, so named after one of its early organizers, Nikolai Chaikovsky. Their participation in this group, because it was organized by men, caused a bit of a stir at first among Sonia's women friends who were accustomed to her "keep males out" attitude that had prevailed to that point.[271] The Chaikovsky participants were basically the same St. Petersburg radicals who, just a year earlier in 1869, had declined to become involved with Nechaev and his phantom "Committee." They tried to build an organization on a higher level of moral development than the crude Nechaev model, one dedicated to mutual respect, trust, and equality of all members. Mark Natanson was an influential participant. The circle united around the point of view that the "people" – workers in the urban areas, peasants in the country -- needed to be "prepared" before the revolution would come. The Chaikovsky members themselves needed to be "prepared" as well. For this purpose they organized classes and study programs for themselves. Natanson frequently served as the "professor." The young men and women lived communally in dachas rented by Natanson and other wealthy adherents. In the mornings they worked out with gymnastics and also rowing, another physical activity at which Perovksaya excelled.[272]

At the time of Sonia's arrival, the Chaikovsky circle functioned much like a utopian collective from the pages of *What Is to Be Done?* Nikolai Chaikovsky himself was an idealist of the highest order, a true believer in the vision of Chernyshevsky. One of the participants later wrote:

> There were no rules, for there was no need of any. All the decisions were always taken by unanimity. . . . Sincerity and frankness were the general rule. All were acquainted with each other, even more so, perhaps, than the members of the same family, and no one wished to conceal from the others even the least important act of his life. Thus every little weakness, every lack of devotion to the cause, every trace of egotism, was pointed out, underlined, sometimes

reciprocally reproved, not as would be the case by a pedantic mentor, but with affection and regret, as between brother and brother.[273]

Perovskaya rapidly immersed herself in Chaikovsky. She passed a year in its almost cloistered surroundings. During this time she became one of the group's more respected and influential members. Despite her small stature and youthful appearance, her air of stoic severity, her indefatigable energy, and her mental capacity brought her a moral authority over others. Her disciplined lifestyle was admired. She slept on bare boards. She insisted on personally carrying large buckets of water and performing other physically strenuous household chores.[274] The anarchist theoretician Peter Kropotkin, who spent much time with Perovskaya during the Chaikovsky days, described his memory of her:[275]

> Seeing this worker dressed in a wool dress, wearing ugly shoes, with her head very simply covered with a cotton scarf, nobody ever could have recognized in her the same girl who, just a few years earlier, had glittered in the most aristocratic halls of the capital. She was our favorite out of everyone.... Hard as steel, she displayed no fear at the thought of death, the vision of the scaffold. One day she said to me, 'We are undertaking something big. Two generations perhaps will die at the task, but it will be accomplished.'

Those in the Chaikovsky circle strongly embraced "Going to the People." This was a movement that swept over and through the "Sixties" activists during the early 1870's. The "spirit of *Narodnichestvo*" arose. This means, roughly, "a love and reverence for the working classes of one's country, coupled with an altruistic desire to serve them." It was inspired in large measure by the published advocacy of Herzen and Bakhunin. Bakhunin's writings, in particular, urged activist students to leave the university in order to raise consciousness of the need for revolt.[276] Hundreds if not several thousands of young people left the cities, left their families, left the universities and colleges and, hastily acquiring some semblance of a practical trade and peasant dress, headed for the villages. They felt an urge to mingle with the mujiks, to breathe their smell, to share in their suffering. The idea was to prepare and bring about the revolution by working directly among the vast Russian peasantry to enlighten them and to improve their lot. There was an almost religious feeling among these "populists," as they called themselves, a sense that by serving the humble and blessed "people," a child of wealth and privilege could somehow expiate the moral debt of original sin.[277]

In the spring of 1872 Sonia left the communal Chaikovsky dacha in St. Petersburg for Stavropol, a medium sized town nestled inside a meander of the Volga in the province of Samara.[278] There she stayed for a time with a local doctor named Evgraf Alexeivitch Osipov. Osipov sympathized with the progressive point of view on Russian society. From what we can gather, Osipov and his family acted as generous benefactors to Perovskaya. Sonia, however, rapidly grew to feel disdain for the doctor and also for his wife, whom Sonia disparaged as being "infected with liberalism." In contrast to her monastic singular commitment to the cause of radical change, Osipov was in her view bogged down with "family, aristocratic, petty life; all the attention he gives to community medical activities."[279]

With help from Osipov, Perovskaya volunteered to start a program of smallpox vaccinations, an activity she could combine with proselytizing for revolution as she made her way from village to village, boarding each night with a different peasant family. She lived with spartan "Rakhmetov-ness," according to a colleague's anonymous memoir, meaning, she lived without comforts, slept on straw pillows, ate milk porridge, etcetera. The peasants, in general, were friendly. They enjoyed 18-year old Sonia's energy, her robust health and rosy cheeks,[280] but they proved very resistant when it came to selling them on social upheaval. The "people" were, in fact, far more firmly anchored in reality than were the idealists who came to them in droves from the Sixties Generation. Few "Going to the People" ventures ended well. The populists possessed little in the way of skills relevant to rural life. They failed to appreciate that the romanticized view of the peasantry reflected in Russian literature was not widely embraced by the peasants themselves. The prevailing mentality of peasants throughout Russia was to be stubborn, protective of old ways, and suspicious of strange people and doctrines. Peasants especially did not trust privileged, educated youth who were preaching revolution. They immediately suspected them of being spies, spirits, or worse. Most of the populist missions devolved into a series of disappointments.[281]

We have a window into the inner gloom Perovskaya felt upon sensing the vast disconnect between her visions and the reality. She wrote a letter to a friend and Chaikovsky companion, Alexandra Yakovlevna Obodovskaya, shortly after her arrival in Samara in late April 1872.

> 6 May (1872).
>
> Alexandra Yakovlev(na), Why you don't write to us. How do you live and how long do you intend to stay there. I'm here, in the Samara province for the second week already. I just moved to the village, before I lived in Stavropol with Dr. Osipov. This gentleman gave me a nasty impression. He married an empty lady who is infected with liberalism, and now he gradually begins to get bogged down completely with family, aristocratic, petty life; all the attention he gives to community medical activities. He has a brother, who also serves in zemstvo, he seems better. I have met two rural teachers, they seem

good, but don't seem developed. When I look around, I feel the smell of dead deep sleep, I don't see the thought of active work and life; and in the villages and cities, everywhere is the same. And the peasants are similarly working every day, like machines, no longer thinking, just dead machines that started once and now always move in a routine. This situation deeply affects the young teachers, they are just silent, sad, and it seems that they could start the activity, but there is only emptiness and death everywhere. I now understand why the persons traveling alone to the province start to feel down with time. First of all, the people's consciousness is not thoroughly enough developed. Then, when they find themselves in this state of torpor, they inevitably begin to converge with other personalities that have anything good, and therefore that way, they gradually start to get used to the vulgarity, and then later they become vulgar themselves. After all it's necessary for a human to have a rest, and if you don't have noble people around, you can stick with vulgar and immoral ones, with the exception of only the strong, energetic personalities.

I had such a strong yearning these days, it was impossible to study, and yet everything around me brings such a wistful melancholy, including even these teachers, because they are so sad, add to this also the fact that I feel that the only way out from this situation is to stir it up and to help these individuals to break out of their situation, and yet for this I have no knowledge, no skill. It is true that skill and knowledge can be gained, but now the situation is still despicable. I want to stir up this dead world, but all I can do now is to look at it.[282]

A month later, Sonia wrote Obodovskaya again. She claimed that her prior "apathetic despair" had passed, yet the written evidence in the form of Perovskaya's own words persuades us otherwise. Sonia was already looking at moving on from Stavropol; much of the message was spent urging her friend to find her some kind of accounting job working at the Tver cheese factory where Obodovskaya was employed. "Please take care of it," she implored. "I don't want to live with my mother." By this time, Perovskaya had largely ceased her "work" in the villages. She was concentrating on indoctrinating student teachers. On June 13 she wrote:

> Then I will say that I live now in the heart of Stavropol, helping one lady to work with teachers and four peasant boys. Mainly, I read now; now more than ever, I feel the need to study, because of the awful situation around. All around I see only torpor, and the other people fight, fight, but their efforts are wasted and accomplish almost nothing, and due to that fact, it seems to me that there is little knowledge as to existing conditions as well as theoretical, they cannot correctly and finally decide what to do next.

> Recently, I received a letter from Mikhail Fedotich.[283] He is in distress, — all the bread he planted, dried up, so he has only the debt left now and doesn't have money to pay it back, to move further, and to finish a course in University, otherwise he will be forced to become a Cossack. Maybe he will visit me while passing by my place. I really want to see him, to know what impression was made on him by the year of peasant life.

> You ask me to write you more, but to write about my inner state disgusts me, also it is now very volatile; one thing I can say is that my apathetic despair state that I had due to the surrounding conditions in which I was when I wrote you the last letter has passed, and I hope, will never return. A general characteristic of

my condition both external and internal, both at present and in the future, is the uncertainty. It seems that only two girls out of those with whom I study and the lady who arranged these sessions are good people. The first two are beginners in becoming part of the new direction, and their moral qualities, in my opinion, are hopeful. But their outer situation is horrible -- first, because of the family, and secondly, because of poverty, so whether they can break out of this wilderness, is still unknown.[284]

Sonia's letter reveals much about an aspect of her mentality she shared in common with terrorists of more recent vintage. She drew a sharp distinction between "good people" – meaning persons she perceived as candidates for total dedication to the "cause" -- and everybody else.

Perovskaya sent a third letter to Obodovskaya about a month later. Again, the basic theme was a plea for help in finding work elsewhere. The authorities had by now identified Sonia as a subversive threat. They had banned both the "vaccinations" and the "studying sessions with the teachers." She talked as if the inertia of her situation was making her feel listless and almost physically ill.

Alexandra Y., you, probably, have not received my answer to your letter, where I begged you to learn from Vereshchagin[285] whether there is any accountant clerk position or something like that. I wrote you this letter a long time ago, and still didn't get the answer. I am in a very nasty situation; here, in Stavropol, I do nothing, because of the terrible awfulness, I need to find a job somewhere to survive; due to lack of money and any prospects in this place I can't move anywhere. Anyway, please Alex. Yacob., even if you didn't find out about an accounting position, yet answer me as soon as possible, and it is better finally to know that the answer is no, than rely on a maybe. I absolutely don't know what I am going to do in the future. I know one thing, that I need any activity, even in the most ordinary sense of the word. I can't be happy with only theory and books; it is my strong desire to do some work, even though it is purely physical, only that it is reasonable. And in inaction, a whole day alone in four walls with books mixed with talks to one or another, leads me, finally, into such a state of apathy and mental dullness that I cannot stand any book, and everything, starting with myself and ending with all people and everything around me, is getting me sick. Sometimes I so desperately want to do something, except reading books and making conversations, that I end up in an abnormal state -- running from one corner to another or prowling through the woods, then fall into another strongest apathy. I need five or six hours a day to work, even to some extent physically, and then my theory will go smoothly. At first, when I came here, it was a totally unfamiliar environment, the vaccination, acquaintance with the teachers gave me quite a bit of living material, and my theory went well, I read Buckle and some other books and I started to identify a number of issues for which I was trying to come to a practical final conclusion. But now the vaccination is stopped, and the studying sessions with teachers ended, due to the fact that the authorities banned it, and because I now have nothing to do and am waiting for a job and my lack of money doesn't allow me to move. I don't have anything to write about now and don't want to.[286]

Sonia's statement that she read Buckle near the start of her sojourn in Stavropol is of interest. The Englishman Henry Thomas Buckle (1821-1862), much like Perovskaya, was an "auto-didact" – meaning, he was self-educated. Being the son of a wealthy merchant who inherited a fortune while relatively young, Buckle had time for leisure, and, by dint of his high intelligence, he developed into a brilliant chess player. He was a prolific writer as well. *The Miscellaneous and Posthumous Works of Henry Thomas Buckle* were published in 1872, at just about the same time when Perovskaya arrived in Stavropol. This volume included an essay with the tantalizing – for Perovskaya – title, "The Influence of Women on the Progress of Knowledge."[287] Sonia apparently felt enraptured by passages such as this:

> On every side, in all social phenomena, in the education of children, in the tone and spirit of literature, in the forms and usages of life; nay, even in the proceedings of legislatures, in the history of statute-books; and in the decisions of magistrates, we find manifold proofs that women are gradually making their way, and slowly but surely winning for themselves a position superior to any they have hitherto attained. This is one of many peculiarities which distinguish modern civilization, and which show how essentially the most advanced countries are different from those that formerly flourished.[288]

Shortly after sending her third letter, Sonia abandoned Stavropol to join Obodovskaya in Tver, northwest of Moscow.[289] There she earned a teaching credential and taught for a time in a rural school. But by the end of the school year, she felt isolated and out of touch with the main populist movement. So she returned to St. Petersburg, where in the summer of 1873 she once more became a prime mover in the Chaikovsky circle. By now Natanson and many other Chaikovsky adherents had been arrested for subversive activities. Along with one of the Kornilova sisters, Sonia began to specialize in visiting jailed comrades. Taking full advantage of her innocent girlish appearance, she brought them books, groceries, clothing, and letters from the outside.

The police had now learned much about the group.

Subterfuge was beginning to be required to avoid easy arrest, and Sonia played her part. She moved into a flat, posing as the wife of a member named Dmitri Rogachev.[290] Fictitious marriage, so prominently featured in *What Is to Be Done?*, was considered by the anarchists to be a particularly virtuous form of subterfuge. With other Chaikovsky adherents, Perovskaya became involved in "educating" factory workers. This eventually brought her to the attention of the authorities. In January 1874, the police arrested Perovskaya.[291] She spent the next six months in jail, reading a series of books brought to her by her brother. Already thoroughly accustomed to a spartan lifestyle, Sonia found this incarceration relatively easy. By means of bribery, she received adequate supplies of both books and interesting visitors.[292]

Eventually, Sonia allowed her father to intercede. By now, Lev Nikolaevitch was permanently separated from Varvara Stepanovna. Chronically ill, he lived with a mistress in St. Petersburg.[293] When Lev Nikolaevitch intervened, Sonia was released on bail. She was directed to remain in the Crimea with her mother, under strict police surveillance. While in the Crimea, Sonia worked on improving her healing skills, taking a formal medical training course at Simferopol. Ultimately she was certified as a *fel'dsher*, a Russian medical professional similar to a paramedic.[294] While studying, she worked in a hospital in Simferopol. Due to her zeal and diligence, she managed to acquire such regard from the doctors that they often trusted her with patients, despite the fact that she had not yet finished the *fel'dsher* course. She was the darling of the sick. In addition to her coursework and her hospital rotations, Sonia volunteered to care for a helplessly ill cancer patient, going to her home every day to change her dressings. This dying woman was very impressed with Sonia.[295]

Perovskaya took a break from her medical internship to join her brother Vasily and others on a horse camping trip in the mountains. At some point, Sonia's mount tripped and fell.

All her companions were very worried. However, Sonia got the horse back on its feet all by herself. One man in the party, named Peter Telalov, was very funny and charming. However, this did not attract Sonia to him in the slightest way. She kept deliberately sending her horse off into a gallop, so that Telalov's horse would take off after it. Telalov was terrified, although later he was able to laugh over the episode.

When the vacation was over, Sonia left the horse with her brother and returned to Simferopol where there was an urgent need to treat the many soldiers wounded in the Russo-Turkish war, a sort of pro-Christian, anti-Islamic crusade which Alexander had recently decided to undertake. This sad work made an impression on Sonia. However, after only a month, in the summer of 1877 she was finally summoned by the police to go to St. Petersburg to stand trial on nebulous charges related to her role in "Going to the People."[296]

The prosecution of Perovskaya and her fellow "Going to the People" populists was part of a get-tough policy by the Russian government focused on radicals from the Generation of the Sixties. From a political standpoint, the policy reflected a continuation of the White Terror of the late 1860's. It in many ways backfired. For example, the "Going to the People" wildfire was fueled by an imperial edict issued in 1873 which required all female Russian students then studying in Switzerland to return to Russia by the end of the year.[297] This decree was intended to prevent young women from becoming contaminated with Western liberal notions, but in reality it had an opposite effect. Young students, and especially girls, were already attracted to progressive ideas. When required by the edict to return to Russia, large numbers of them returned as populists. The government decided to arrest anybody caught "Going to the People." Some four thousand were arrested by the end of 1874. Of these 770, including 158 women, were charged and held over for trial.[298] A large number of the arrestees were held in custody pending trial at the newly built

St. Petersburg House of Detention. Another manifestation of imperial policy in the 1870s, this was a new facility built to lock up radicals.[299]

Chapter 10: The Tsar's Second Family

Alexander had, by now, pretty well abandoned the broad liberal vision he had brought to the throne. He was very preoccupied with his personal life. His wife Marie was sickly and had long ago stopped having sex with him. She had already suffered through eight pregnancies and doctors had advised her she could not survive any more. Alexander sought solace with other women, while Marie, weak with tuberculosis, turned a blind eye to his flirtations. Starting in 1865, Alexander focused his attentions on a young girl of illustrious ancestry whose parents had recently gone bankrupt. She was an indigent ward of the state, benefitting from the Tsar's financial aid to attend the Smolny Institute. Her name was Catherine "Katia" Dolgorukov. Katia was only 18, and Alexander 47, when she became the main object of his romantic intrigues. It was an attention she coyly encouraged with the full complicity of her mother. Alexander was already courting Katia, meeting her regularly on the Palace grounds for walks and the like, in April 1866 when the Karakozov assassination attempt occurred. The

Catherine Dolgorukov, c. 1866

two began a physical sexual relationship three months later.

Young Katia was not the most beautiful, nor the most intelligent, nor the most cultured of women. She was moody, intensely jealous, and possessive, as reflected in her extensive letters to and from Alexander which were written in French with only a few words of Russian thrown in here and there.[300] Katia rapidly did what was necessary to solidify her grip on the monarch. In Alexander's own words, they "clenched each other like cats."[301] But Katia's Italian sister-in-law Louise, working to keep the affair a secret while it was still possible to salvage the young woman's reputation, arranged to take Katia away to live with her in the home she shared with Katia's brother in Naples, Italy.[302]

Alexander had much German blood in his ancestry, and he had spent time in Germany with his relatives during his youth. He tended to chart a pro-German course in the balance of power politics that prevailed in nineteenth century Europe. He maintained "neutrality" when Prussia waged war on Denmark, ending with the annexation of Schleswig and

Holstein in 1864. Alexander was well aware of Bismarck's grand plan for unifying Germany. In 1866, Prussia took a giant step toward unification by defeating the Austrian army at the battle of Sadowa. Only then did some of Alexander's advisors urge a rapprochement between Russia and France to balance the expansion of the north German confederation. In an effort to improve Russia's image in France, Alexander declared a general amnesty for the Polish insurgents of 1863. This paved the way for a personal visit to Paris by Alexander in May 1867. His ulterior motive in making this trip was to arrange a rendezvous with Katia, whom he had not seen for six months. He put her up in a Parisian luxury hotel a short distance away from his guest quarters.[303]

Alexander received a cold reception from the French public, which kept chanting *"Vive la Pologne"* when he appeared in public. On May 25, Alexander joined fellow emperors Napoleon III of France and Wilhelm I of Prussia for his favorite military activity, a full dress parade at the Longchamp horse track. As the troops were streaming by, a man stepped forward brandishing a pistol and fired twice at Alexander. One of Napoleon III's guards spotted the assailant first and grabbed him, disturbing his aim just enough so that the shots missed, grazing a nearby horse and a bystander. The brazen attempt greatly perturbed the Tsar, although he maintained a facade of indifference. The assassin was a Polish refugee, Anton Berezowski.

After the shock of another assassination attempt, Alexander found comfort in the loving arms of young Katia. But he would long hold the Berezowski attack, as well as the hostile hecklings he had received, against the French people. He was even more insulted when France failed to put the assassin to death, finding "extenuating circumstances" which warranted sentencing him to life in prison instead. He would have been happier if the culprit would have been first sentenced to death, and then granted a Russian style reprieve on the scaffold.

When Alexander returned from France to St. Petersburg, he brought Katia back with him. There she took up residence as the Tsar's concubine, thinly disguised as one of the Empress's maids of honor. Katia had the discretion to stay away from imperial functions, being content, for the time being, to remain largely in the Palace shadows. But Alexander began taking Katia with him on junkets, even when he traveled on important affairs of state. In June 1870, Alexander held meetings in Germany with Wilhelm I, his chancellor Bismarck, and Alexander's own foreign minister Gortchakov. Alexander favored Prussia in her disputes with France, giving vital encouragement that led to the Franco-Prussian War of 1870. Napoleon III would lose this war, after a disastrous defeat at Sedan, and he would also lose his throne. Alexander viewed this as a righteous punishment for France's attitude during his visit in 1867.

On April 30, 1872, Katia gave birth to her first child with Alexander. This occurred in secrecy at the Winter Palace. But of course the news leaked out to the imperial court. Some of Alexander's relatives, especially his brother Konstantin and his aunt Hélène, expressed consternation over Alexander's extramarital conduct with Catherine Dolgorukov. However, the Tsar's wife Marie seemed resigned to her fate. She projected a feeling of being used up, that she had almost lost her will to live. The next year, Katia bore Alexander another child, this time a daughter.

By this time, Alexander's extramarital relationship with Katia was common knowledge at court.[304] Thus, it was almost certainly known to Perovskaya, who remained in touch with sympathetic nobles, including some in the highest echelons of government. Alexander's lifestyle was one of which Sofia Perovskaya strongly disapproved. Probably her hostility to it was heightened due to her own father's promiscuous behavior. Sonia reacted in an opposite direction. Not only was Sonia herself sexually abstinent, she expected similar restraint from others within the communal society of the Chaikovsky circle. Traditional Russian vices, such as heavy alcohol consumption, she criticized sharply when engaged in by any of the Chaikovskists. And if there was one area where Sofia Perovskaya was particularly judgmental, it was the tendency of Russian men, especially those in the upper classes, to womanize. Within the Chaikovsky circle, Sonia was known for ostracizing young men bent on sex. She criticized them as philanderers even when the objects of their attention were unattached and available. When a Chaikovsky member found himself torn between a love affair and political commitment, she insisted that the member be ostracized and excluded from the group.[305]

The idealistic Chaikovsky circle died out, largely due to attrition from the mass arrests of 1874. Nikolai Chaikovsky emigrated to the United States, where he started a utopian commune near Wichita, Kansas. However, the Chaikovsky circle veterans formed a ready-made nucleus for further revolutionary organization. In the fall of 1876 Mark Natanson, having finished his period of administrative exile, returned to St. Petersburg. Along with Georgi Plekhanov, he became one of the leading spirits in the formation of a new organization of St. Petersburg radicals, many of whom were former Chaikovsky participants. The group's name, Zemlya i Volya, bespoke an intent to revive the Sixties group of the same name that Chernyshevsky had helped form. One of the revived organization's first major actions was a demonstration under a red banner proclaiming "Zemlya i Volya" in front of the Kazan cathedral in St. Petersburg. Although sparsely attended with only 250 participants, the public rally was regarded by the government as a serious affront. The police responded in force, greeting the activists with clubs and arrests.[306]

One of those arrested in front of the Kazan cathedral was a 24-year old student named Alexei Emelyanov. He gave authorities the false name of Bogolyubov. Bogolyubov was swiftly sentenced to 15 years of hard labor. Awaiting deportation, he was placed temporarily in the St. Petersburg House of Detention, which was already full of young radical men and women being held pending trial in connection with "Going to the People." An ambiguous attitude existed toward these prisoners on the part of the jailers. Although official government policy toward them was harsh, the prison guards recognized the reality that these were not ordinary criminals. The overwhelming majority were children of the nobility and upper and middle classes. The detention center accorded the "politicals" a certain amount of liberty within the prison walls. However, Fyodor Trepov, the former director of the 1863 Polish reprisals, had been promoted to the post of Governor of St. Petersburg. One day he came to the House of Detention for an inspection. He did not appreciate the relaxed attitude of the political prisoners. His anger seethed as he saw them walking about the yard in groups and chatting. Among them was Bogolyubov. Upon approaching Bogolyubov, Trepov became infuriated because Bogolyubov did not remove his cap. Trepov reached out and knocked off Bogolyubov's cap. Trepov's aggressive motion caused Bogolyubov to flinch and lose his balance. The enraged Trepov regarded this sudden movement as an assault and a further unacceptable affront.[307]

One cardinal feature of Alexander's judicial reforms in 1864 had been the abolition of corporal punishment. But this reform left one exception – beatings remained legal inside prison walls. Trepov summarily ordered Bogolyubov to be lashed with one hundred strokes. The sound of the slow, steady strokes of the whip cracking against the naked body of Bogolyubov while he was held on the whipping block caused a near riot. The prisoners went into an immediate frenzy, making all kinds of noise and throwing just about anything that they could fit through the bars.[308] Word of the vicious lashing, which resulted in lasting injury to Bogolyybov, soon spread and, indeed, caused indignation in many levels of society, not just among the nihilists. Avenging Bogolyubov became a special rallying cry for the radicals.

Hundreds of versts away from St. Petersburg, news of the ugly Bogolyubov incident reached a new collection of radicals who had split with the "populist" philosophy of Zemlya i Volya. Variously called "insurrectionists" or "the disorganizing group," these anarchists were loosely based in what Russians called "the South" – primarily, the Ukrainian cities of Kharkov and Kiev, and the Crimean city of Odessa. No longer were these "Southerners" enthralled with the notion that it was good to work gradually to educate the peasantry in order to build support for revolution. They now theorized that the "people" were already miserable and in inchoate revolt against the existing system. So, the revolutionaries simply needed to engage in strokes bold enough to set off a spark to catalyze a lightning-quick chain reaction. They felt strongly that the government was an organized injustice, and that there was no form of resistance too dirty to use against it.[309] They embraced dramatic, violent "disorganizing" tactics, which featured publicly proclaimed acts of assassination and banditry that were designed to intimidate ordinary citizens.

One of the key Southern leaders, Valerian Osinski, repeated a classic Nechaev strategem by inventing a fictitious "Executive Committee of the Russian Social Revolutionary Party," complete with its own seal, to take credit for acts of terrorism. Osinski, the son of a wealthy landowner, was personally debonair and charming. But he was chilling in his approach to perceived "spies," as well as government leaders viewed as leading instruments of repression. These persons would be cut down on the street, killed without warning. As another legacy of Nechaev, spreading falsehoods was used as an instrument of fomenting fear and panic. Osinski had his

Seal of the "Russian Revolutionary Executive Committee," used on communications in 1877 by Osinski's group to evoke terror.

"Executive Committee" publicly take "credit" for terrorist assassinations of spies and local police officials.[310] In the spring of 1877, Osinski and some of his associates went out at night and plastered Kiev with false communiqués of Russian disasters in the Russo-Turkish war. They developed skillful methods for forging passports, evading surveillance, and communicating through sophisticated signals and ciphers. They acquired revolvers, and they practiced shooting them.

The budding group of "Southern" insurrectionists now included Vera Zasulitch. The years since her association with Nechaev in St. Petersburg had been a long odyssey for Vera. Due to the government's discovery of letters addressed to her from Nechaev, she had been arrested and held in a detention center for a year. Then she was confined for a second year in solitary confinement within Russia's maximum security facility, the Peter and Paul Fortress. After that, she was released to a series of administrative exile postings in western Russia and the Ukraine. Eventually the authorities relaxed their supervision. Vera was able to slip into a clandestine life first in Kharkov, and then in Kiev. She tried "Going to the People" by posing as the married proprietress of a tea shop in the village of Tsibulevka, near Kiev. She utterly failed in convincing the "people" of the role, as all she did was read books. She refused to do any cooking or cleaning in the shop, and was unable even to make a decent pot of tea. Her fictitious "husband" Mikhail Frolenko took up drinking with the peasants to try to allay their suspicions about Vera.

Shortly after the Bogolyubov episode, Zasulitch with an attractive red-haired female companion, Maria "Masha" Kolenkina, made their way from Kiev to St. Petersburg. They arrived just as the mass trial got under way of the activists arrested while "Going to the People." Drawing attention to the sheer numbers on trial, this event was dubbed the "Trial of the 193." The collective nature of the trial, with its huge number of defendants, was another serious miscalculation by the imperial authorities. The proceedings brought together and united the most radical and intransigent activists left over from the Generation of the Sixties. Those of the accused who were not already friends with each other, now became friends in the courtroom. No longer were these defendants starry eyed students. They were now veteran revolutionaries. They would react with harshness of their own to the government's harsh policies.

Perovskaya herself became much more involved with underground radical activity after she was removed from Simferopol in the summer of 1877 and ordered to stand trial in St. Petersburg. She was not under true arrest, and spent most of her time being in charge of the "Prisoner Red Cross." She pretended to be engaged to a Chaikovsky member, Lev Tikhomirov, in order to visit him in the House of Detention. In addition to Tikhomirov, she also visited other political prisoners. Typically she brought them supplies that they could use. Even more important, she could tell them much of what was happening outside the walls. In the trial, Perovskaya was brought up first, apparently in hopes that she would make statements implicating other defendants. However, acting in accordance with a prearranged plan, Sonia pointedly refused to say anything at all.

The Trial of the 193 accomplished little, except to provide

a pulpit for a few of the accused to voice very public criticisms of the government's repressive policies. The most vocal was Ippolit Myshkin, a printer by trade, who had been arrested in Siberia while plotting to rescue Chernyshevsky from exile. In his speech to the court, Myshkin branded the trial a farce. He accused the judges of being worse than girls in a brothel. Such impudence caused him to be dragged away by the bailiffs, and ultimately, to be sentenced to ten years at hard labor. But in general the defendants who declined to speak, including Perovskaya, were acquitted, or were released based on credit for time already served, when the trial ended on January 23, 1878. Much rejoicing ensued, and a great deal of energy was released among the revolutionaries. One who was not on trial would recall: [311]

> It was an uninterrupted session of a revolutionary club, where 90 to 100 visitors attended in a day. Friends brought with them strangers who wished to shake hands with those whom they had looked upon as buried alive.

In the wake of the acquittals, Perovskaya hosted in her apartment a celebratory gathering welcoming the newly freed defendants from the Trial of the 193. The discussions digested and recapitulated much that had happened during the trial. The participants were stimulated by this event and, far from learning a lesson, felt themselves spurred on to further revolutionary commitment.[312] Perovskaya, however, was not happy about the trial or its outcome. Her thoughts continued to dwell on Myshkin and the others who had been sentenced to hard labor in prison. She retained channels of communications with those close to the halls of power and, from them, she was informed that there had been sentiments to commute those sentences to mere exile, but the sentiments had been vetoed. It kindled a bitterness Sonia would never relinquish.[313]

Despite the notoriety that was given to her disdain for men, Perovskaya was remembered by many for her tender qualities toward male activists who were sick or imprisoned. One of her fellow feminists, Kovalskaya, left this portrait of her.

Among the defendants [in the Trial of the 193], there was a very young male student, A.L., who was put in prison in the flower of his adolescence. He left, under surveillance, four years later dying of tuberculosis. He had an attitude beyond reproach during the entire trial, rigorously honest, but he did not join the outspoken protestors because he felt that the presence of those who were unjustly accused and remained silent would have an even greater effect on public opinion. He was a very good friend and before leaving St. Petersburg I wanted to stop by to see him. Fearing to wake him, I very softly opened the door to his room and entered without making a sound. The long straight room was bathed in the afternoon sun. L. was lying on a metal bed. His fine handsome face displayed the flushed red cheeks and glowing eyes of a fever. Perovskaya was sitting next to the bed, on a chair in front of a small table. Out of the corner of her eye she kept glancing at the patient. In her regard, there was an enormous compassion, silent and delicate, such a tenderness and a desire to relieve the sadness. I did not even recognize in her at all the severe militant that I had met earlier. But when she saw me, a change came over her. Her face hardened, she seemed to return to her former self, fearing to betray her tender feelings.

At one time, Perovskaya had lived in a commune with L. L. sat up in bed, and with a voice punctuated with spasms of coughing, asked her avidly about the trial. Obviously trying to avoid the subject, Perovskaya kept giving one word answers. She kept trying to divert the conversation, bringing up happy or funny episodes from when they had lived together in the commune. L., sensing her diplomatic efforts, seemed to worsen and fade. Seeing this bad reaction, and fearing to have acted maladroitly, Perovskaya quickly began telling him about the trial. She repeated with indignation the closing argument of a defense attorney named Borovinsky (later a poet and a senator), who did not hesitate to declare: 'Here, Honorable Judges, on the bench of the accused, you will see eagles and you will see chickens. My client is part of the second group.' But sensing that she had again caused trouble by telling something she would have rather not said, she fell silent. L. started laughing gently. He said, 'Come on, come on, please continue. I know very well that you take me for a chicken. It is always better to be taken for a peacock, or at least a crow.' The tension broke. Perovskaya's face changed and, smiling, she continued telling L. about the trial.[314]

Chapter 11: Disorganizing

The day after the sentences were handed down in the Trial of the 193, Vera Zasulitch awoke early next to Masha Kolenkina. She rose and neatly laid out a set of nice clothes. They were much different from her usual unkempt attire, which was a shapeless gray linen cloak with holes crudely cut for her head and arms and whose corners doubled as handkerchiefs.[315] Vera carefully packed up a fake application she had prepared the night before, requesting a certificate supposedly necessary to obtain a diploma. It was critical that she arrive at Governor Trepov's office well before 9 a.m., the hour when Trepov regularly began to receive supplications from petitioners. After dressing, she kissed Masha goodbye and set out walking cold streets to catch the train. When she reached Trepov's office there were already around ten people waiting to present their petitions. "Will the Governor be receiving today?" she asked an officer. "Yes, and soon," came the response. Someone in front of her asked, "Will he be receiving in person?" The response again was affirmative.

While waiting, Zasulitch was asked by another waiting woman to read over her petition. Vera corrected an error in it.

She suggested that the woman show the paper to the officer who was looking over other similar papers. The woman did not want to show it by herself, so she asked Vera to talk to him for her. The officer, after speaking briefly with Vera, ushered both of them into an inner room and told them to wait in the corner. Other supplicants lined up behind her. From the other side of the room Trepov, surrounded by staff, entered. He approached Vera first and asked her what she wanted. "A certificate," she replied. Trepov noted something in pencil and turned to her neighbor in the receiving line. Vera quietly withdrew a British Bulldog snub nosed revolver she had been concealing and, after a misfire, exploded a single shot that hit Trepov. As her aim was a bit negligent, the shot struck Trepov somewhere below the belt, inflicting a serious injury to his buttocks that proved not to be fatal.

Zasulitch immediately threw down the gun. She expected to be seized and beaten. And indeed, after a stunned moment of shock, guards grabbed her, threw her on the floor, gouged at her eyes and hit her a few times. She thought it strange that at the time she felt no sensation of pain, although she would later discover bruises. An officer present took command and ordered the guards to stop before they killed her. There needed to be an inquiry to find out who Vera was, and who had sent her.

Zasulitch was removed into another room, much larger, where there were few guards. One of them said to her, "We have to search you." Vera replied, "For that, you need a woman." A scene worthy of Kafka ensued.

> The officer: "Where would we find a woman here?"
>
> Vera: "On every staff, there is a midwife."
>
> Officer: "The time that it would take to find one . . . And you might have another weapon on you!"
>
> Vera: "Nothing will happen. All you have to do is

tie me up if you are worried about it."

Officer: "I am not worried about myself. I know very well you will not shoot me. But I just came back to duty from being sick. What would I have around here to tie you up with?"

Vera: "If you don't have a rope, use a napkin."

The officer looked in the desk and took out a napkin. He did not look very intent on using it. Timidly he looked up at Vera. "Why did you fire at him?"

Vera: "Because of Bogolyubov."

Officer: "Ah." He said it as if it was exactly the response he expected.[316]

Zasulitch's shooting of Trepov marked a definite turning point on the path to terrorism. Typical of terrorist acts, Zasulitch's assassination attempt provoked the Russian government into an overreaction. The lenient decisions that had just been handed down in the Trial of the 193 were immediately quashed, and were replaced with new harsh sentences. Instead of Myshkin being the only defendant exiled to Siberia, now fourteen of the defendants were ordered exiled.[317] The government was sensitive about criticisms that had been leveled at its "show trial" style political handling of the Trial of the 193. As there seemed to be very little risk, given the undisputed and overwhelming nature of the evidence, a decision was made by Alexander himself to try Zasulitch using the jury trial procedure introduced as part of Alexander's great reforms. This procedure had never been used before for a political trial. Jury trials, being new to Russia, were poorly understood. Trouble soon ensued. The judge allowed the defense in effect to put Trepov on trial, by arguing and introducing evidence to highlight Zasulitch's "motive," the unwonted brutality of the punishment of Bogolyubov. Given this latitude, Zasulitch's defense attorney Peter Alexandrov handled the case brilliantly. He presented the jury with a sympathetic version of Zasulitch's entire life story, including her chance introduction to Nechaev, her subsequent imprisonment, and her (supposed) learning of Bogolyubov's beating from reading a small item in the newspaper. All of it was rosily embellished. Trepov, he argued, deserved to be punished, and Zasulitch was justice's angel of vengeance. The prosecutor reacted a bit sheepishly, and was totally unprepared to point out the inaccuracies in Alexandrov's version of Zasulitch's story. The gallery was even allowed to cheer Alexandrov's arguments.

The jury, in response to these tactics, did what juries do. It became inflamed. It rapidly handed down a verdict of "not guilty." Havoc broke loose. Alexander immediately tried to intervene and order Zasulitch re-arrested, but by that time, she had already been released and spirited into hiding. Ultimately she was smuggled out of Russia and into Switzerland.[318]

Dramatic acts by "revolutionaries" now began in earnest. One of the more creative involved three imprisoned "Southerners" who had been caught plotting a violent revolt. The organization devised an ingenuous rescue plan. Mikhail Frolenko, the same who had previously pretended to be the husband of Zasulitch, now presented a fake passport under the name "Fomenko." He succeeded in getting himself hired as a warder at the Kiev prison where the three radicals were held. "Fomenko" showed himself to be an intelligent and reliable prison employee. After several months of diligent performance, he succeeded in getting himself promoted to be a head warder. Then through contrivance, warder "Fomenko" caught Yacob Stefanovich, one of the jailed extremists, red handed in the act of writing a forbidden note. The Governor of Kiev took no action against Stefanovich, but he did acquire great faith in the sleuthing ability and loyalty of "Fomenko." The extremists, on the other hand, pretended to be extremely upset and angry with "Fomenko" due to his successful spying against them.

"Fomenko" fell in line to be promoted to head warder of the "political" wing of the prison. However, the incumbent head warder, one Nikita, was a decent and competent man. No pretext could be found to trigger Nikita's dismissal. The revolutionaries invented all kinds of fictitious offenses against Nikita, of which they complained to the Governor, but to no avail. Nikita maintained his composure and just kept repeating, "Jesus Christ suffered. I will also suffer." Finally Osinski came up with a plan. He went to a tavern frequented by Nikita, found him there and bought him some drinks. Out of delight with the fine fellow, Osinski offered Nikita a very advantageous employment as the bookkeeper for a sugar refinery in the country. The bait was taken. Nikita agreed to accept traveling expenses and a month's pay. He gave notice that he was leaving his position at the prison. In the wake of Nikita's resignation, "Fomenko" was promoted to head warder in charge of the political wing.

By now it was late May, 1878. The terrorists were in a huge hurry to complete the escape. Some of the other political prisoners imprisoned in Kiev knew the real identity of "Fomenko," presenting a serious risk of discovery. The plotters determined that "Fomenko" must free the prisoners right away, although he could find only two fake guard uniforms for them to wear. The third prisoner had to tag along wearing ordinary civilian clothes. To make matters even more difficult, one of the real warders came along just as Frolenko was preparing to unlock the escapees' cells. Thinking quickly, Stefanovich threw an unbound book, really just a collection of loose pages, out the window. "Fomenko" asked the warder to go down to the ground to pick up these sheets. Then, as Frolenko and the escapees made their way out of the hallway, in the complete darkness one of them slipped. To catch himself, he grabbed a rope that turned out to be connected to a loud alarm bell. But once again, "Fomenko" smoothly talked his way out of the desperate situation. He assured the responding guards that it was he who had accidentally tugged the alarm rope. The guards believed him. Obediently, they opened the gates of the prison so that he and his companions could leave. Osinski awaited, a short distance away with a getaway vehicle, to take the escapees down to the Dnieper River. They got away cleanly in a waiting boat. "Fomenko" disappeared. So complete was the belief in his deception, it was assumed by the authorities that the escaped prisoners must have killed him. They spent a great deal of time looking for the body.[319]

In the aftermath of this escape, Perovskaya moved to Kharkov, where many radicals sentenced in the Trial of the 193 were now imprisoned. There she joined up with "Southern" radicals in a plot to free activists imprisoned following the Trial of the 193. She resumed her role as "prison nurse," making friends with and perhaps bribing some guards. A group of nine, including Perovskaya, lived in three apartments in Kharkov while hatching rescue plans. Her first objective was to free Ippolit Myshkin. However, the government got wind that a plot was in the works, and increased the security on Myshkin to the point where no rescue was feasible. After a month and a half, Sonia learned that an older political convict named Porfirio Ivanovich Voinaralsky was about to be transferred to another prison. Prior to his arrest for the Trial of the 193, Voinaralsky had been a member of Chaikovsky and an important regional organizer of "Going to the People." He had donated his entire fortune, some 40,000 rubles, to the cause.[320] Perovskaya decided to rescue Voinaralsky.

The communal residents of the "movement" helped Sonia work out a detailed plan. Three of them, Frolenko, Alexander Barannikov and Alexander Mikhailov, dressed as military officers and staff. They intercepted the wagon transporting Voinaralsky and ordered the sergeant in charge of the transport to turn the prisoner over to them. Other bandits in the group followed separately behind. When the sergeant became suspicious, the confrontation turned violent. Barannikov shot one of the guards driving the wagon, but Frolenko's shot missed the other. The officer riding inside the carriage with Voinaralsky alertly and courageously held his sword to the prisoner's neck to keep him from jumping out. While holding the carriage stopped at gunpoint, the terrorists should have unhitched the wagon's horses, but being inexperienced, they failed to do so. The surviving carriage driver was able to spur the horses to a gallop. The wagon's horses were faster, and better trained, than the terrorists' horses. The horse of Alexander Kviatkovski, one of the conspirators following behind, shied and refused to approach when it heard the gunshots. The transport wagon managed to escape and, ultimately, was able to summon help. As a result, the terrorists themselves were nearly captured, and one of the gang's members was caught shortly afterwards at a nearby train station. When she learned of the failure, Sonia was furious with her comrades. She blamed them for cowardice, masculine incompetence and too much "Russianness."[321]

In the wake of their attack, it was too "hot" for the bandits to remain in Kharkov. Most of them filtered out of the city and went to St. Petersburg, where they soon became involved in planning another terrorist attack. The radical community was incensed because one Ivan Kovalsky had just been sentenced to be executed. Kovalsky, a nihilist, had helped run a clandestine printing press in Odessa for what he called the "social democratic party." When the government detected the printing operation, shortly after the Trepov assassination attempt, Kovalsky was arrested in a nasty violent shootout. His armed resistance to arrest was the reason for his death sentence. To protest Kovalsky's execution, radicals rallied in Odessa. Police fired into the crowd, killing one. On August 2, Kovalsky was shot by a firing squad. The terrorists decided to strike back with, in their words, "a death for a death."[322]

Rightly or wrongly, the radicals held Nikolai Mezentsov,

the imperial police chief, responsible for the new and harsher sentences which had been imposed on Trial of the 193 defendants after Zasulitch's attack on Trepov. They decided to "execute" Mezentsov in retaliation for the execution of Kovalsky. Lessons the terrorists had learned in the failed Voinaralsky rescue were put to use. Alexander Mikhailov masterminded the attack. This time, he made sure to have a good horse. He got hold of an animal named Varvar, a champion trotter. He studied Mezentsov's movements and learned that Mezentsov was in the habit of walking to work accompanied by a single adjutant when the summer weather was pleasant. The attack was, as a result, made boldly in the heart of St. Petersburg, near the corner of Mikhailovsky Square and Italianskaya Street, at around 9 a.m. on August 4, 1878. With Barannikov acting as his lookout, Serge Kravchinsky came up behind Mezentsov and plunged a dagger deep into his body. By firing a revolver, Barannikov delayed the adjutant from giving chase just long enough for the terrorists to reach the getaway vehicle hitched to Varvar. Mezentsov died almost immediately, while Kravchinsky and Barannikov escaped. Mezentsov's murder, boldly carried out in broad daylight on a major city street, was the terrorists' most high profile violent exploit to date.[323]

After the botched Voinaralsky rescue attempt, Perovskaya did not accompany the other radicals to St. Petersburg. Instead, she left Kharkov and traveled to the Crimea to visit her mother and brother Vasily. She was already wanted by the authorities, who (without even knowing anything about her role in the violent Kharkov rescue attempt) had decided to place her under administrative supervision. The morning after her arrival at her mother's home, the police came to place Perovskaya under arrest. She was immediately shipped to her designated place of exile, in far northern Russia in a small town called Povenets, 600 kilometers northeast of St. Petersburg. However, although her demeanor remained meek, Sonia had no intention of accepting exile. [324]

For the first part of the two-day long rail journey, Perovskaya behaved quite well. She was all sugar and smiles with her two police escorts, and they in turn were considerate and respectful of her. When the first guards were replaced with another pair, she was already much more than half way to Povenets. Sonia finally saw her opening. While waiting late at night to change trains at a small station in Volkhov, a transfer point around two hours east of St. Petersburg, the escorting officers let her stretch out on a couch in a waiting room. The policemen stretched out also, one in front of the window, the other in front of the entrance to the room. Sonia, however, noticed that the door opened outward. She lay still, and was very patient. Every time a train was called, the officers jumped up. They kept looking nervously at Sonia, but she always appeared to them to be in a deep sleep. Eventually they too fell asleep. They did not even raise their heads when trains were called. Very softly, Sonia rose. She removed her shoes and very delicately tiptoed over the officer sleeping by the door. Without anyone seeing her, she made her way onto the platform. She crossed over the tracks and hid in some bushes on the other side.

In an hour, a train bound for St. Petersburg arrived. On board, the conductor made a fuss because she did not have a ticket. Perovskaya, with a scarf draped over her head, pretended to be an ignorant peasant who had never traveled by train before. The conductor was taken in. When the police escorts awakened, they were chagrined to find that Sonia had disappeared. Despite telegrams they sent ahead, she got off the train without detection upon its arrival in the capital. She quickly made her way to the house of a sympathizer. [325] The princess would lead the rest of her life from this point on living as an "illegal," meaning, underground with an assumed identity. This clandestine life in itself was a serious criminal offense.

Olga Lyubatovich, with Masha Kolenkina, met Perovskaya right at the time she escaped custody and went underground in St. Petersburg. She presented herself to these women as if they were old friends, even though Olga had never met her previously and knew of Perovskaya only by reputation. Sonia seemed emotional. The other women gathered around to hear her tell of how she had escaped from her police escort. Olga could see that this young girl – a child, almost, in her appearance, according to Lyubatovich – had a close rapport with Kravchinsky, who made haste to come to meet her. This was born of their days and weeks spent together in the Chaikovsky circle. Kravchinsky brought news of humiliations and sufferings being endured by radicals, including Myshkin, now imprisoned in Kharkov. Lyubatovich saw an immediate cloud come over Sonia's demeanor. The vengeance Kravchinsky had inflicted by killing Mezentzov was no consolation to her. She resolved to leave immediately for Kharkov, even though all of her friends tried to convince her to stay longer in St. Petersburg. She wrote to Lev Tikhomirov, her pretend "fiancé," who at that time following the Trial of the 193 was living away from the radicals with his parents at Stavropol. She successfully appealed to Tikhomirov to return to St. Petersburg to take over Kravchinsky's place as the editor of the radical newspaper, Land and Liberty. Kravchinsky was preparing to depart Russia.

With difficulty, Sonia's associates persuaded her to remain in St. Petersburg for just a few days. To "celebrate" her departure, Kravchinsky organized a night at the opera. The young activists were aghast at Kravchinsky's bravado. He rented an entire loge, into which, in small groups, entered eleven men and women radicals, all "illegal." In between acts they giggled and joked, everybody thinking how shocked the government would be to learn of such a nest of "wrong thinkers" in a box at the opera. But the government was not searching for them at the opera. The performance they attended was *Le Prophète* by Giocomo Meyerbeer. The "plot" of this mid-19th century opera (which, itself, is set in the 16th century) includes an uprising by peasants against their feudal rulers. It ends with a gigantic palace explosion in which the hero, his mother, and the villains all are killed. It was an opera much adored in Sonia's revolutionary circle.[326]

When Sonia arrived in Kharkov, she soon found that, as the St. Petersburg group had already predicted, she was not able to make any progress with jail break schemes. She kept very busy nonetheless. She organized a service to smuggle in food and clothing to the politicals in prison. She networked with other Zemlya i Volya adherents in the town. She conducted a midwife course so as to become even better qualified for work among "the people." She was described by friends who knew her in Kharkov as looking very young and girlish for her 25 years, with a small face, prominent large forehead, blonde hair and a pink and white complexion. She was extremely serious and meticulous. She would go to every shop in town to try to get the best value for the money available to be spent on the prisoners. She had a strong will and a low opinion of male intelligence and reliability. But despite her personal effort, due to a lack of funds and help the rescue plans had to be abandoned.

The entire organization was of necessity becoming more hardened. The police were now more knowledgeable and more active. They had succeeded in identifying and arresting some of the important leaders. Radicals like Perovskaya who were living clandestine lives had to be on the alert every minute of every day. [327] Reacting to the constant vigilance of the secret police, they began to excel at deception. One of the subterfuges was that two members of the "illegals," a man and a woman, would be assigned to rent a safe house, posing as a married couple. In this way, less suspicion was generated. The house was then used for meetings, preparations, changes of disguise, and sometimes as a temporary hiding place. On conclusion of the enterprise the residence would be abandoned.[328]

Chapter 12: Terrorists Split Off

In late 1878 and early 1879, philosophical differences began to emerge among Zemlya i Volya activists. In many ways the debate was a replay of what had happened ten years earler when Nechaev insisted on public forms of protest. The moderates opposed assassinations and other acts of terror. They viewed violence as highly counterproductive because it made the radicals look bad in public opinion. Terrorism also inevitably would bring on waves of arrests and government surveillance. The moderates continued to advocate propaganda and education of workers and peasants as the methods most likely to bring about fundamental change.

The extremists within the revolutionary movement were, by now, veterans of this "populist" approach. They felt that it had proven to be frustrating and ineffective. Jail and prison had added to the hardening of their mindset. Vera Figner, who was one of these extremists, would later recall:

> The hopes of many crumbled to dust; the program which had seemed so feasible did not lead to the

expected results; faith in the soundness of its theoretical construction, in one's own strength, wavered. The keener the enthusiasm of those who had gone out among the people to spread propaganda, the more bitter was their disillusionment. [329]

The sensational assassination of Mezentsov, coming as it did on the heels of the sensational shooting of Trepov by Zasulitch, exerted a magnetic force which attracted a select few men and women throughout Russia who had the proclivities to seek to join the cause of the pro-violence faction within the ranks of Zemlya i Volya. This built momentum which fairly soon led to a schism within Zemlya i Volya between the mainstream, who wanted to continue with the program of recruiting support for uprising among the workers and the peasants, and a small but insistent faction that began to argue openly for terrorism. They theorized that violent acts would catalyze deep latent forces of discontent. The most dramatic act of all, for which they increasingly argued, was the assassination of Tsar Alexander II. The revolutionaries held Alexander at fault for the new and harsher sentences that were imposed on the defendants, following Zasulitch's shooting of Trepov, after they had already been given lenient case dispositions at the end of the Trial of the 193.

In the provincial region of Saratov, approximately 850 kilometers southeast of Moscow, Vera Figner was engaged in "Going to the People" as a medical practitioner. She was in most ways a typical female child of the Sixties. One year older than Perovskaya, she was born to a family of prosperous nobles. Her father, a forester, had liberal leanings. He once remarked, "If the serfs had not been freed, and had revolted, I should have led their rebellion." As a peace mediator he would devote much energy to helping resolve conflicts involving peasants that arose from the imperial decree freeing the serfs. However, like Lev Nikolaevitch Perovsky, at home he was hot tempered and stern. Vera was much closer to her mother.

Vera Figner grew to be a student radical, as did several of her siblings. She was profoundly affected by the poetry of Nikolai Nekrasov, founder of *The Contemporary* and Chernyshevsky's mentor. After an arranged marriage, Vera secured permission to study medicine in Switzerland. Once there, she swiftly divorced her husband due to his non-radical political views. In spite of the 1873 decree requiring all female Russian students to return, she remained in the University of Berne working to complete her medical degree. However, in December of 1875, after much agonizing, she responded to a personal appeal from Mark Natanson for her to return to Russia to work among "the people." She quit the program and left the Swiss school even though she was only five to six months short of getting her diploma.

Because of the late timing of her return to Russia, Figner was not jailed in the 1874 arrests of the "populists." She went through a series of "Going to the People" postings. After the Trial of the 193, she relocated to Saratov where she worked alongside her sister Evgenia, also a radical, who had passed the exam to be an assistant surgeon. The two made a sensation with "wonder worker" efforts in a population that was hugely underserved in terms of attention to basic modern medicine. As usual, they soon attracted negative attention from the local authorities. Despite their efforts to avoid appearing as nihilists, everybody in power was well aware that the Figners were present among the villagers not just to provide medical care, but also to incite discontent and rebellion.

In the spring of 1879 the Figners received a visit from 33-year old Alexander Solovyev. Solovyev had been sent to university, and then to law school, at the expense of Alexander's liberal aunt Hélène. His father worked on Hélène's estates as a medical aide. Despite, or perhaps more accurately because of, this generous opportunity, Solovyev became a radical. He abandoned his studies to "go to the people." He then joined Zemlya i Volya.[330] His purpose in visiting the Figners at Saratov was to consult with them and seek their support for his project to kill Tsar Alexander. Solovyev offered Vera his opinion that going to the people was "mere self-gratification when one considered the existing order of things." There was "no chance of success." Therefore, terrorism was required and warranted. Solovyev reflected the growing trend of thought among the radicals. There was a sense that "Going to the People" had failed, that there was no new energy to sustain it, that the radical energy needed to be devoted to sensational acts of violence.

Solovyev extemporized to Figner:

> The death of the Emperor may bring about a turn in social life; the atmosphere will become purified; the intelligentsia will no longer be diffident, but enter upon a broad and fruitful activity among the people.

When Figner wondered if the failure of the attempt might bring about still more serious reaction, Solovyev assured her failure was unthinkable. He was determined to die for the cause, and he would enter the undertaking with every chance for success. Figner later described Solovyev as a "man, who united the courage of a hero with the self-renunciation of an ascetic, and the kindness of a child."[331] She felt it was not in her power to dissuade him, even had she wanted to do so.

Solovyev returned to St. Petersburg where, in March of 1879, he met with Alexander Mikhailov to discuss his mission. Mikhailov was by now one of the important proponents of terror within Zemlya i Volya. Being well organized and disciplined, he was rapidly assuming a role as a sort of "operations" leader. Solovyev actually had two competitors for the job of killing the Tsar. One was Grigory Goldenberg, a "Southerner" who, with help from Osinski, had just finished assassinating the governor-general of Kharkov, Prince Dmitri Kropotkin. Another was a Pole named Kobilianski. Mikhailov decided it was best to go with Solovyev. Assassination by Kobilianski would inevitably be interpreted as Polish nationalism, not revolution. Assassination by Goldenberg, a Jew, would inevitably be interpreted in ethnic and religious terms, and would result in a bloody pogrom. Mikhailov convinced Goldenberg and Kobilianski to relinquish the "honors" to Solovyev. Solovyev was indignant that anyone else was even considered. "Only I satisfy all the conditions," he declared. "I must do it. This is my work. Alexander II is mine and I will not give him up to anybody."

It was decided that the assassination should appear to be an individual effort by Solovyev. Other group members would be on hand merely to have a horse and cart waiting to spirit him away. Solovyev would carry a poison capsule in his mouth to swallow if captured. A controversy arose as to whether the terrorist act should be done in the name of Zemlya i Volya. Mikhailov was in favor of an official group endorsement. But moderates within the organization, especially its founder Georgi Plekhanov, were adamantly opposed.[332] To them, all an assassination would accomplish would be to "add a numeral" (i.e., by replacing Alexander II with his son, Alexander III), and it would bring on a new wave of repression. The moderates threatened to inform authorities about the plot. It was a fundamental fracture within the group. Ultimately, there was no sanction on behalf of Zemlya i Volya. But there also was no betrayal of the attempt.[333]

On the morning of April 2, 1879, Alexander was returning to his Winter Palace from his daily walk. Captain Koch, the head of his personal guard, walked with him but at a respectful distance, in order not to disturb the sovereign's thoughts. A little farther away, there was the usual gathering of curious onlookers. Alexander noticed a tall young man step forward from the crowd. Along with a black cape, he wore a uniform cap adorned with a cockade in the style of a government official. As he looked at the young man, he noticed that he was pointing a pistol at him. With all of his 60-year old reflexes, Alexander leaped to the side just as the trigger was pulled.

Miraculously, the shot missed.

What followed was dark comedy. In full view of his aides and the crowd of gawkers, Alexander took off fleeing at full speed, running away like a boy while Soloviev chased close behind him. The terrorist fired again and again, five shots in all. As he sprinted, Alexander used a technique of evasive action drilled into him decades earlier, in his military training. He kept changing direction, moving first left, then right, desperately zigging and zagging to throw off his pursuer's aim. One of the shots grazed the Tsar's cape. The last shot, fired just as Koch finally managed to tackle Solovyev, went between Alexander's legs. It was a frightful and humiliating experience for one of the world's most powerful rulers.[334]

Alexander carried on with grace before his mistress, the family members, noblemen and ladies who gathered in the palace to cheer his survival of a brush with death. He believed his escape was divinely ordained. While the bells of the city tolled, he dramatically emerged on a balcony. He received a thunderous ten minute ovation. But especially coming, as it did, on the heels of the assassinations of Trepov, Kropotkin, and Mezentsov, Solovyev's attack cast a pall over Alexander. No longer would the ruler feel himself at liberty to stroll. From now on, his travels about St. Petersburg would take place only in heavily guarded vehicles moving at a fast clip. Public perception was shaken. There was a general sense that the nihilists had much more in store for the administration.[335]

The administration, for its part, reacted to the attack in a manner that other governments, including that of the United States, have found tempting when confronted by terrorism. On April 5, 1879 it decreed a broad suspension of ordinary judicial and administrative procedures for any matters that were deemed to involve a threat of terrorism.[336] It was an overreaction. The repression fell on ordinary citizens as well as revolutionaries, and created dissatisfaction among social strata loyal to the government.[337]

Solovyev, immediately after he was grabbed, swallowed potassium cyanide. However, the poison did not act rapidly enough. Perhaps it was too old. Koch heard him crack the capsule with his teeth, and ordered his stomach to be pumped right away. As a result, Solovyev vomited profusely. When he recovered himself, he looked around. His first and widely reported remark was, "Could it be that I did not kill the Tsar?" He then asked for and was given a cigarette, which he puffed nonchalantly. He proceeded to hold forth with an air of importance in a sort of impromptu "press conference." His every word and his every pronouncement were assiduously noted by a gathering of high government officials.

As the moderates within Zemlya i Volya had foreseen, the furor around Solovyev's assassination attempt provoked an immediate harsh government response. Osinski, inventor of the latest proclaimed "Executive Committee," had been arrested in January, and was already being held in custody. He was swiftly placed on trial and sentenced to death. The hanging of Osinski and two other "Southern" revolutionaries was carried out in the Kiev prison on May 14, 1879.[338] Solovyev went to his own death two weeks afterwards, on May 28. He had refused all overtures to beg grace from the tsar. He was transported to the gallows riding backwards through the streets of St. Petersburg wearing a placard with huge letters, "State Criminal." Newspaper reporters were on hand to provide graphic accounts of his last, very public, moments. With firm footsteps he strode up the steps to the scaffold. An assembled crowd estimated at 4,000 looked on with approval as they witnessed Solovyev's death convulsions, the agonized face chastely obscured by a white hood.[339]

Nearby, the terrorists of Zemlya i Volya seethed. The day after the hanging, a broadside proclamation was found scattered about the city. "We are taking off the gloves, we do not fear either the battle or death. At the end of the accounting, we will smash this government to bits, such will be the number of victims we will count." A shivery breeze stirred the air of St. Petersburg.[340]

Believing that revolutionists in the provinces would generally favor their views, Plekhanov and other moderates pushed for a conference of party leaders to resolve the future course of the movement.[341] Mikhailov and the others who had supported Solovyev agreed to hold this conference in late June. It was arranged for the conference to occur in the province of Voronezh, well south of Moscow near the Ukraine border. Voronezh had been one of the more prominent venues for "Going to the People."[342]

The terrorist faction, however, had no intention of relenting. Mikhailov, Frolenko, and others decided to steal a march on the "party congress" by having their own prior organizing meeting. The terrorists' pre-meeting was arranged to occur in Lipetsk, a quiet spa resort town only about 125 kilometers north of Voronezh. No one who was thought to give credence to the "populist" views of Plekhanov was informed of the existence of this pre-meeting. Perovskaya in Kharkov, for example, was carefully screened from learning any news of Lipetsk. Frolenko was dispatched to the "South" to personally invite hand picked attendees. While in Odessa as part of this trip, Frolenko invited a new person to attend. Up until now, this new person had not been particularly noticed or active in the leadership of the revolutionary movement. This new man was Andrei Ivanovitch Zhelyabov (pronounced "Je-LYA-bov").[343]

Zhelyabov was not cut from the usual cloth of a Russian "Sixties" nihilist. His immediate progenitors were serfs. His two grandfathers, Zhelyabov and Frolov, were house serfs who had migrated along with their master from the north of Russia to the Crimea shortly after the Napoleonic wars. His father, Ivan Zhelyabov, received training as a market gardener. Being industrious, he saved money and, with 500 rubles, purchased the right to marry Frolov's daughter from her master. Andrei

Ivanovich was their first son, born in 1850.[344]   Like
Perovskaya, he grew up in the Crimea.

Andrei's grandfather Frolov was highly influential with
him as a boy. He was very tall, very gaunt and very solemn,
with a long, grey beard. Zhelyabov afterwards believed he was
slightly touched. He could read "the old church script" and
possessed half a dozen holy books. He was devoted to Andrei,
and the two became inseparable. Grandfather Frolov busied
himself with young Andrei's education. He taught Andrei to
read archaic church script and Andrei learned to recite the
Book of Psalms by heart.[345] Like his grandfather, Andrei grew
up tall and thin. Frolov's daughter, Andrei's mother, was also
a huge influence. She was scornful of landowners, whom she
dismissed as "beasts and torturers." She was also disdainful of
her frugal husband due to his penchant for taking the line of
least resistance, and willingness to see good points in the
landowners.

An important formative episode for Zhelyabov, according
to his autobiographical account, occurred when he was only 7
or 8 years old. His aunt Lyuba, who was the most attractive
young woman in the family, was dragged off for sex with the
local landowner, Lorentsov.   Grandfather Frolov cursed
Lorentsov's servants who came to take her, but ultimately he
was impotent to do anything to stop the ravishment. Zhelyabov
says in his autobiography that he swore that he would kill
Lorentsov.[346] However, there is no independent confirmation
of this incident, and no way to check on the details. Nor is there
indication that Andrei, as an adult, ever did anything to take
revenge on Lorentsov.[347]   What the reported episode
foreshadows is a trait in Zhelyabov that is highly typical of a
terrorist – a passion for going overboard in support of other
people's causes and injustices.

Andrei's future benefitted greatly from the charity of a
local landowner named Nelidov. After hearing that the young
Zhelyabov was a prodigy of learning, Nelidov made a point of

sending for him. Andrei could, at that time, read only the arcane church script. Nelidov taught him to read regular print. Soon Andrei, aged ten, became an avid reader immersed in Russian literature. Nelidov arranged to send Andrei as a boarder to a junior school in Kerch. He was an above-average student and qualified to attend the faculty of law at Novorossisk University at Odessa. He was enabled to attend there by a grant of thirty rubles per month from a legacy bequeathed by a local merchant to assist needy students. The university accepted Zhelyabov as a student "whose exemption from the payment of university fees is justified by their poverty and their disposition towards study."[348]

Andrei grew up to be tall, handsome, charming, and chivalrous. Not until he reached the age of 21 in 1871 is there any concrete evidence that he was involved in any activity that smacks of being radical. At that time, he became involved in a fairly typical "Sunday School," volunteering to teach free secret classes in subjects that had been deleted from the university curriculum as part of the White Terror. An outstanding public speaker, Andrei became an instant heartthrob for progressive teenage girls who attended these classes. He was also popular with girls he tutored in private homes of the upper classes.

A crucial turning point for Andrei Zhelyabov was his expulsion from the Odessa university. This grew out of a trivial incident in which he was not at all personally concerned. The trouble began on October 16, 1871, in the classroom of Professor Bogishich, a Croat. Bogishich spotted a student, one Baer, lounging and possibly falling asleep in his seat during a lecture. He stopped in the middle of what he was saying and called out, "Do you think you are in a drink-shop? Do you need a pillow? If you can't behave you can get out." When Baer aroused himself and began to mumble an explanation, Bogishich completely lost his temper and physically hustled him out of the room. The lecture proceeded, but other students on hand felt that Bogishich's treatment of Baer had been abusive, out of line, and even worse, un-Russian.

Upon Bogishich's next scheduled lecture four days later, no students appeared in the classroom. Instead, a crowd of them collected in the hallway and jeered as he went by. This impromptu student strike was reported to university authorities. The rector arranged to meet the following day with the students who had protested. He arrived to find a large crowd. He asked the students to appoint a spokesman and disburse, which they did. Zhelyabov was merely one of several delegates whom they appointed. He was not even in the Bogishich class.

After meeting with the rector, and with the rector's approval, the student delegates went to speak with Bogishich. He assured the delegates that the matter had been a misunderstanding. He said he had not realized that using the Russian word *kabak*, or drink shop, had undesirable associations. He assured them he had not intended to hurt anybody's feelings and he was prepared to say as much in his next lecture, on October 23. The students were satisfied. It seemed the incident was at an end.

Evidently, however, the professor was riddled with doubt. Come time for the lecture on October 23, Bogishich failed to appear in the crowded classroom. Instead he sent a message that he was sick. The result was an uproar. The student body quickly assembled and, when the vice-rector arrived, Zhelyabov was at the podium. He was haranguing the crowd and declaring, amid great applause, that it was a matter of principle that satisfaction be obtained from Bogishich. After the assembly disbursed, protest meetings continued to carry on in small groups and private homes. The authorities overreacted, perhaps in part because Tsar Alexander II was soon due to make a visit to Odessa. The university council, an innovation introduced under Alexander's educational reforms, was convened. It ordered a court to try the ringleaders, and cancelled all lectures until the court proceedings were finished. It also made a formal expression of sympathy and regret to Professor Bogishich.

When these events were reported to Alexander's conservative minister of education, Count Dmitri Andreivich Tolstoy, he telegraphed back his approval of the council's actions. He requested "immediate and strictest measures." Specifically, "students expelled from university to be banished immediately from Odessa." The council trial proceeded from October 25 until November 5. At its conclusion, Zhelyabov was ordered expelled and banished from Odessa for one year. There was a great deal of opposition, among other university professors and even among local government officials, to the manifest harshness of this decree. On November 11, Zhelyabov was arrested, to be banished back to his hometown, the village of Sultanovka near Kerch. As he embarked on his forced departure, he was lauded and celebrated by a large crowd of sympathizers who came to see him off. [349] The experience gave him a taste of the thrill of martyrdom. It would prove to be intoxicating.

Zhelyabov is a textbook case to illustrate how a strict government policy aimed at holding down militant elements can backfire. After returning home to his parents, Andrei applied for permission to live and work giving private lessons in nearby Feodosia. University officials helped him by supplying certificates of his progress in school. In August of 1872, he applied for readmission to the Odessa university. The application was granted by the university and forwarded to the ministry of education for approval. The administration, however, denied approval. It decreed that Zhelyabov's sentence of banishment had been for a full year, and a full year had not yet passed. In view of this, "and also of the necessity for preserving the student body from undesirable influences," his readmission could not be approved.

The university council next requested permission to

readmit Zhelyabov as of November 8, exactly one year after his sentence of expulsion. After a month passed, the ministry of education wrote back to pronounce a further ruling that, because the regulations governing universities provided only for the admission of students at the beginning of each scholastic year, no proposal to readmit a student in November could be entertained. This marked the end of Zhelyabov's academic career. [350]

During his time of expulsion, Zhelyabov secured a position as private tutor for a liberal sympathizer and wealthy industrialist named Yahnenko who owned a sugar factory near Kiev. He promptly became enamored of his employer's 20-year old daughter Olga. Olga was a lovely girl, pretty, affectionate, and musically gifted. She also fell deeply in love with Andrei. By the summer of 1873 they were married. That fall, Zhelyabov took a socially responsible post as a teacher at the Odessa Municipal Poor House.

His favorable marriage and consequent improved social standing did not diminish Zhelyabov's restless drive to sacrifice himself. He simply could not remain happy with a normal and faithful domestic life. A friend later wrote of him, "Anything he did or said was always bound up with some deep inner passion."[351] Feelings of discontent smoldered ever more warmly in him. He resumed "Sunday School" activity, holding secret evening classes for working men. He also joined a subversive group based in Odessa, one which was engaged in smuggling and distributing prohibited political literature. The police soon learned of the illegal organization and arrested its ringleaders. Zhelyabov was implicated due to an encoded letter he had sent to Anya Rosenstein Makarevich, the wife of the group's incarcerated leader. She was a nihilist on whom he had developed a crush. Zhelyabov was arrested.[352]

However, the local Odessa chief of police, who was well aware of the unjust treatment Andrei had previously received in the Bogishich affair, recommended that he not be prosecuted. The chief also released him on bail of 2,000 rubles. He pointed out that Zhelyabov should not be regarded as a nihilist, in that he had recently married the daughter of a local luminary. However, the central government by now had made up its mind that Zhelyabov was a dangerous malcontent. A telegram came at once from St. Petersburg requiring that Zhelyabov be re-arrested. He spent four months in jail, lost his job, and, according to his later claim, in this incarceration "became a revolutionary."[353]

In March of 1875, Zhelyabov was released on an increased bail of 3,000 rubles posted by his father-in-law. In a manner similar to Perovskaya, he lived quietly for two and a half years in the Crimea while awaiting his eventual trial, which came as part of the Trial of the 193. He was under constant supervision by the police. Though the two of them maintained a certain degree of mutual loyalty, Yahnenko was beginning to realize that his relatives were right, that his daughter's marriage was a huge mistake, and that his son-in-law, however handsome, was an intractable problem. Andrei acted moody and depressed. He continually experienced fantasies about nihilists such as Anya Makarevich, and about his own death for the "cause." He began to quarrel with his

Anya Rosenstein Makarevich, photographed in Florence, Italy, 1908

photo credit: Mario Nunes Vais

wife Olga. He forbade her to go out in the evenings to entertain friends of the Yahnenkos with her singing. He later wrote that he could not allow her to "delight the ears of plutocrats." Olga tried long and hard to remain obedient to her husband. She bore them a baby son in 1876. But she had secret crying sessions over his behavior and attitude.[354]

In September of 1877, Zhelyabov was summoned to surrender to his bail in preparation for the Trial of the 193. He was incarcerated in the St. Petersburg House of Detention, shortly after the flogging incident involving Trepov and Bogolyubov. In this "dissident academy," as well as the ensuing trial itself, Andrei became acquainted with many leading lights of the revolutionary movement.[355] Like Perovskaya, Zhelyabov took a low profile in the trial proceedings, and he attracted little notice. When the verdicts came out, he was acquitted. In the ensuing celebrations, Andrei and Sonia briefly met for the first time. Zhelyabov promptly returned to Odessa, where he went through the motions of resuming his family life.[356]

What could motivate an intelligent, gifted young man to turn his back on a home with a charming, attractive wife and a young son bearing his name? The persona of the terrorist is a pathology centered around an egocentric form of ascetisicm. No matter how hard Olga might try to tame him with love, no matter how much moral and financial support he might be offered by her wealthy, liberally minded father, Andrei Zhelyabov was determined to throw it all away, in favor of, in its fundamental attractive essence, a martyr's death.

After spending just a short time in the Yahnenko family home with Olga and little Andrei, Zhelyabov left to work all spring and summer of 1878 growing melons in a field rented by a revolutionary named Mitya Zheltonovsky. Mitya's wife, also named Olga, was only 25 years old, but she was dying of tuberculosis contracted while incarcerated for propagandizing in connection with "Going to the People." Mitya and his wife Olga had been part of the Makarevich circle in Odessa, and thus, were very friendly with Andrei's idolized Anya. The ordeal of Olga's slow decline and death, during the course of a long hot summer that Andrei spent toiling 16 hours a day in the melon field, apparently preyed further on Zhelyabov's tormented character. He finally returned to his own wife Olga in Odessa after the harvest. Once again, he did nothing more than go through the motions of family life. His real energies were spent on associating with the Odessa community of underground radicals.

At the end of November or in December, 1878, Zhelyabov "broke it off permanently" with Olga. He left the family home to live separately and apart. He also made sure to announce this "divorce" very publicly. Even one of Zhelyabov's admirers, Pimen Semenyuta, admits "much sympathy was expressed for Olga Semyonovna, who had really loved him and hoped that he was not in earnest."[357] Zhelyabov's sympathetic biographers have tried to spin this heartless desertion as a humane act done from a sense of duty that was intended to avoid enmeshing Olga and young Andrei in the infamy of his martyrdom.[358] A more likely and frank assessment would be that Zhelyabov had no desire to be burdened with a caring wife and family who were not enthralled, as he was, with the vision of a glorious death on the cross for the sake of somebody else's "cause."

After the final separation from Olga, Andrei lived an extremely spartan life. Semenyuta found his dwelling "pitiful," and he came across him on the street in a state of "actual hunger." Zhelyabov was trying to live on a "pittance" earned giving lessons.

Semenyuta explicitly informs us about a key element of Zhelyabov's personality, a recognizable star in the constellation of traits of the terrorist persona. Andrei could not stand to be a follower. During the fall and winter of 1878, Valerian Osinski was the undisputed leader of the revolutionary movement in Odessa. Far more debonair and cultured than Zhelyabov, Osinski was highly charismatic and attractive to women in his own right.[359] Although they traveled in the same radical circles, Zhelyabov made all kinds of excuses, and declined to even meet Osinski. Semenyuta provides an interesting insight. "Andrei Ivanovich, between you and me, was noticeably ambitious and could not bear anybody to be superior to him."[360] Even when he was gaunt with hunger, Zhelyabov could not bring himself to ask for any financial support from Osinski's ample war chest. Semenyuta ultimately had to use a ruse to persuade Andrei to accept even a small amount of cash.

However, at the "very end of 1878, certainly not later than mid-January 1879," Zhelyabov did accept an important piece of help from Osinski. Osinski got Zhelyabov a good false internal passport. It was made out in the name of "Vasily Andreivich Chernyavsky." This was not merely a forgery, but a tested valid passport, something that was very difficult to obtain.[361] It would enable the newly "divorced" Andrei to tunnel permanently underground. By a stroke of luck, the government was able to arrest Osinski just afterwards, in late January of 1879. His departure from the scene left a large void in the organization of the "Southern" terrorists.

When Mikhail Frolenko, himself a "Southerner," visited Odessa in the spring of 1879 in search of committed violent revolutionaries to attend the secret terrorist pre-congress in Lipetsk, Zhelyabov was a mature fruit ripe for the picking. Even though he had never before engaged in any terrorism, and even though he was a near total unknown in St. Petersburg, Frolenko, with his cunning and perceptiveness for people, sought out Zhelyabov and asked "if he was prepared to join us in continuing Solovyev's cause." He guessed right and hit the target. Frolenko later wrote of his star recruit: "From being a little known provincial rebel, or really just a dreamer, he was instantly transformed into an *ataman*, a terrorist leader."[362] Olga Lyubatovich recalled that since the time she had known Zhelyabov several years earlier in Odessa, "He had really matured, physically and intellectually. He was a dark haired man, tall and rangy, with a pale face and a dark thick beard and expressive eyes. His speech was full of flame and passion, his voice pleasant and strong."

Chapter 13: The Formation of Narodnaya Volya

Zhelyabov arrived at Lipetsk, along with Mikhailov, on June 13, 1879. Using their false names and passports, they took a room together. Gradually the other extremists began to filter into town. Eleven in all attended.[363] Among them was Nikolai Morozov, son of a wealthy noble landowner, who was a gifted writer and one of the intellectuals of the movement. Morozov had just published an incendiary article in the newspaper of Zemlya i Volya that stoked the raging controversy between the party's moderates and its terrorists. Entitled "Political Killings," it espoused a sophisticated rationale and justification of terrorism. Morozov wrote:

> Political killing is, above all, an act of vengeance. Only when it has avenged the comrades that have perished can a revolutionary organization look its enemies straight in the eye; only then can it rise to the moral heights that a champion of freedom must attain

to be able to lead the masses. Political killing is the only means of self-defense in the present conditions, and one of the best ways of agitating. By striking at the very center of the government organization it shakes the whole system with terrifying force. The blow radiates instantly throughout the state like an electric current and disrupts all its functions. When the advocates of freedom are few in number, they always shut themselves up in secret societies. This secrecy endows them with tremendous strength. It has given mere handfuls of daring men the ability to fight millions of organized but overt enemies ... But when to this secrecy is added political killing as a systematic means of struggle, such people will become truly terrible to their enemies. The latter will live in constant fear of their lives, never knowing from one minute to the next when or whence vengeance will come. Political killing is the realization of revolution in the present. [364]

At Lipetsk, the budding terrorists pretended to be tourists walking in the woods. Their meetings gave the appearance of chance encounters, in meadows far from any habitations, where spies could be seen hundreds of yards away. In the course of these meetings, they went straight to the Nechaev playbook. They formed themselves into a real life version of the "Executive Committee" which Osinski, and before him Nechaev, had contrived as a terrorist stratagem. Positions were assigned to the members according to their inclination and ability. The glib, charismatic Zhelyabov took the role of the fiery, moving speaker. His code name was "Boris." He would rapidly become the group's perceived leader.

Another key leadership role was assumed by the portly Alexander Mikhailov. He was the organizational wizard and chief of security. Due to his passion for keeping the Committee's operations "clean," his code name was "the

Janitor."

Nikolai Morozov was placed in charge of published propaganda. Slender and willowy, and with a soft, childlike voice,[365] he was nicknamed "Sparrow." Before long, "Sparrow" would come into intellectual conflict over anarchist principles with Perovskaya's erstwhile fictitious fiancé, Lev Tikhomirov. Tikhomirov seemed aged beyond his years. He was known as "Starik" or the "Ancestor." The "Ancestor" was also a writer, and he was named party theoretician. Tikhomirov put a philosophy of terrorism into terms even more simplified than those of Morozov. "Terrorism is a very pernicious idea, absolutely chilling. It is capable of transforming weakness into force."[366] Frolenko, who was not a political philosopher, stated the prevailing argument more crassly. "We're all going to be killed, aren't we? There's no other possibility. We shall die, and that's a fact. But we can die for a mere nothing, or we can die doing something big. So the obvious thing is to do something big."[367]

A test for entrance into the new group was unanimously agreed. The candidate was to be asked: "Are you ready at once to offer your life, your personal freedom and all that you have?" If he or she said "yes," then they could be taken on. Membership of the committee was made irrevocable. Once accepted, a candidate was committed to never resign, to "admit of no ties of friendship, affection or relationship" and to "devote his or her whole self to the service of the party." The conference concluded with an "indictment" of the Tsar for unforgivable sins. The "Janitor" recounted the grounds, from the terrorists' point of view, which consisted mainly of the history of repression culminating in the beating of Bogolyubov, the retraction of lenient sentences after Vera Zasulitch's shooting of Trepov, and the executions of terrorists that had occurred in Kiev and in St. Petersburg.[368] Lipetsk broke up and its enthused participants filtered into Voronezh to carry out the Executive Committee agenda for the "party congress" of Zemlya i Volya.

Voronezh began on a note of evident discord. Plekhanov opened by reading with unconcealed scorn Morozov's essay on "Political Killings." He expected to be joined in general criticism of the article. Instead, his mocking reading was greeted with a stony silence. Sensing that the tide had turned against him, Plekhanov promptly walked out of the conference to return to St. Petersburg, where he would try to muster support among moderates there. But his discomfiture did not end the Voronezh conference.[369]

Sofia Perovskaya, who was admired and respected by both sides for her degree of "moral elevation and boundless devotion,"[370] stepped up into leadership after Plekhanov's departure. She had arrived at Voronezh determined to work for unity within Zemlya i Volya. She felt strongly that the beleaguered party needed every possible ounce of strength. She spoke out in opposition to Zhelyabov's advocacy of a top-down "central committee" structure. This "constitutional" model was not in keeping with Sonia's personal political views, which were strongly influenced by Chernyshevsky's vision of a post-apocalyptic society peopled by anarchist communes.[371] In her statements to the gathering at Voronezh, she criticized the Lipetsk faction for leaving the peasants in the background. With Vera Figner, Sonia was the main force in hammering out a note of accord on which the conference ended. Under this compromise, Zemlya i Volya would continue its propaganda role in rural villages, but would give one third of its total funds to the support of armed revolt.

Impressed with Sonia's prominent, outspoken role in opposing him at Voronezh, Zhelyabov uncharacteristically shut up and stopped making speeches. Instead, he made vigorous efforts behind the scenes to cultivate Sonia, and to win her over to the Executive Committee's side, that is, the path of terrorism. To assuage her concern that the "peasant cause" was being sacrificed and ignored, he constantly reminded her of his own serf parentage, and the difference from her royal antecedents. For several months, Sonia carried on with her efforts at diplomacy and cultivation of the moderates. But the vision of abandoning her life to a final, desperate act of violence in support of an adopted cause struck a sweet spot in Sonia's personality. A more moderate Russian activist who opposed terrorism characterized her as "the most brilliant" of those embraced the path of violence, because she was filled with a sense of indignation and disdain against the "terrorism of the government itself."[372] Inside, Perovskaya was boiling with fury over the fate of those who had been hanged, and over the fate of those such as Myshkin who were rotting in prison.

By the end of summer, although she still claimed formally to be neutral with respect to the party split, Sonia's comments and actions were those of a woman who had thoroughly embraced the idea of terrorism. And, once she finally went over, she would prove to be the most terrible terrorist of them all.[373] It was almost as if she had a dual personality. Kravchinsky wrote: "This woman, with such an innocent appearance and with such a sweet and affectionate disposition, was one of the most dreaded members of the Terrorist party."[374]

At the St. Petersburg suburb of Lesnoi, near the end of August, occurred the final dismantling of Zemlya i Volya. Lesnoi was, at the time, the main location of radical "safe houses" in which the illegals resided. As stated by Figner, the conference at Voronezh had not removed, but only stifled, the dissension within the party. The greatly outnumbered Plekhanov announced his intention of leaving both politics and Russia, to concentrate on Marxist studies. With him went most of the moderate faction, including Vera Zasulitch. Interestingly, upon returning to Russia she had established herself as one of the most prominent opponents of terror. It was agreed that the two factions would henceforth be totally autonomous, and that neither of them would continue to use the old name. The moderates, who were awarded the old organization's printing press, reorganized themselves under the name *Cherny Peredel*, which roughly translates as "Black Partition." The terrorist faction adopted the name *Narodnaya Volya*, meaning the "Will of the People." As one of its first official acts, Narodnaya Volya proclaimed a "death sentence" against Alexander II on August 26, 1879. The Executive Committee decided to abandon attacks on all other military and political leaders and to use all of its energy to go after the Tsar himself.

Still hoping for a reconciliation, Sonia spent much of her time lobbying the moderates, even after Lesnoi. Her political beliefs still inclined to those of the "villagers," as their opponents called them. But her personality was all for fighting back against the administration. She was, according to one of the moderates, "the incarnation of the spirit of revolt. She was determined that official brutalities must not be left unanswered. In a small, almost childish voice she proclaimed the necessity of terror." Sonia was angered when Plekhanov suggested she leave the country in order to avoid arrest. She was determined to stay in Russia and die for the cause. The attraction of martyrdom was, for her, a sucking vortex. To one of her fellow feminists who was supporting Cherny Peredel, she commented, "there's nothing real about your people. We're alive."[375] Sonia eagerly agreed to Mikhailov's request that she go to Moscow to pose as the wife of Lev Hartman in connection with Narodnaya Volya's latest plan to assassinate Alexander. Her actions indicate that she had made up her mind to die for the cause. She wound up her affairs in St. Petersburg, and she handed over "all her money and contacts" to representatives of Cherny Peredel.[376]

The Emperor was far bigger game for the terrorists than the unsuspecting government officials they had previously assassinated. Signs of the cunning Mikhailov are all over their battle plan, which featured a new and dramatic weapon just added to the terrorist arsenal – dynamite.[377] It was decided at Lesnoi to kill Alexander by blowing up his train when he returned to St. Peterburg after spending the fall in the Crimea.

The attack featured three almost wholly independent prongs. Vera Figner headed up the Odessa effort. Nikolai Kibalchich, Narodnaya Volya's home grown explosives expert, posed as her husband. Resort was made to the same stratagem that had worked in the past. Frolenko would take a job in a sensitive position, this time, as a railroad guard. Figner successfully posed as an aristocratic lady, approaching a local official in order to help him obtain the job. The plan worked well once again, with Frolenko handling his sub rosa employment with his usual aplomb. But ultimately, due to windy, rainy cold weather, the Emperor decided not to travel by boat to Odessa, but instead to take a train directly from the Crimea to St. Peterburg. Thus, his travel route would no longer take him through Odessa.[378]

The second attack was headed up by Zhelyabov. Anna Yakimova, a member of the Narodnaya Volya Executive Committee, posed as his wife. Aided by some of his recent recruits, Zhelyabov worked tirelessly for nights on end to dodge police patrols along the tracks and lay lengthy concealed wires leading to two explosive-laden brass cylinders positioned underneath the railroad tracks near Alexandrovsk, a small town outside Kharkov. The work was greatly hindered by cold, rainy weather as well as Zhelyabov's own illness and night blindness. With difficulty, Zhelyabov got the wires and cylinders placed in time. But when the moment of the Tsar's train transit arrived, the charges failed to detonate.[379]

The third, and most successful, attack was the one led by Perovskaya. With 1,000 rubles of "revolutionary" funds, Mikhailov had bought a house in a poor neighborhood near the tracks, approximately 14 kilometers from downtown Moscow. The area was mainly waste land, rubbish heaps, and little market gardens, with here and there a ramshackle one storied cottage. Perovskaya and Lev Hartmann, a member of the Executive Committee, moved in posing as husband and wife under the name of "Sukhorukov." Mikhailov took rooms in town from which to help direct the operation. Two other *narodniki*, Aronchik and Chernyavskaya, in the guise of another young married couple, established themselves in a flat which was to serve as conspiratorial quarters. Other collaborators took rooms, or put up at cheap hotels, and work began.

The plan was to drive a gallery from the cellar of the house to the railway embankment some fifty yards away and there lay a charge under the line. The first main preoccupation was not to arouse the suspicion of the neighbors. The locals in the neighborhood, market gardeners or else day laborers in factories in the town, were mostly Old Believers. They felt it was a sin for a man to shave his beard, thus defacing the image in which man had been created. The Old Believers tended to be suspicious of newcomers. However, the terrorists benefitted because they were equally aloof and suspicious of the police.[380]

Hartmann gave himself out to be a workman employed in the town. It was natural that he was not visible during the day. The main brunt of contact with the outside world thus fell on Perovskaya. In the middle of October, Goldenberg arrived from the South. Mikhailov took him to the house and set him to work. Goldenberg later said, "as I was new to it, I did the simple work. I cleared the earth from the gallery to the hatch and from the hatch to the store house. I used to help Perovskaya with the housework."

None of the terrorists had expertise in tunneling. Although Hartmann had some knowledge of how to construct a mine shaft, there were no skilled manual workers among them. Their tools were primitive. They had a short pointed "English spade" to pick out the dirt at the gallery head, and two shovels to pull it back. They had a cheap compass for keeping the tunnel straight, but as a matter of fact they did not keep it very straight. As the gallery advanced Hartmann fixed up wooden rails along the floor and a little truck on wheels, worked by a rope on a pulley, to get the earth back out of the tunnel.

The tunnel they dug was about one meter high by 78 centimeters across. Its mouth, in the wall of the cellar, was boarded up to prevent discovery in case of a stranger making his way down. There was a hatch in the boarding to let the workers in and out and for the earth to be removed. An iron pipe was installed for ventilation. One man worked at the head of the gallery; another shoveled the earth onto the truck. A third stood at the hatch to receive it. A great problem was the disposal of the earth removed from the tunnel. The capacity of the storehouse was limited. They piled it up in the cellar, they put it under the floor boards of the living room. Finally they had to spread it over the yard at night or dump it in nearby rubbish heaps. It was hard work. The frail "Sparrow" cracked up from the strain and had to return to St. Petersburg.

The terrorists understood that they faced the gallows the moment they were discovered. Almost with gaiety, their entire faith was placed in nitroglycerine. They were determined never to be taken alive. Sonia put out, to be ready for use on a moment's notice, a bottle of nitroglycerine that the terrorists felt sufficient to blow up the whole house. In case they were discovered, everyone knew and agreed that Sonia was the person entrusted to explode the fatal bottle with a pistol shot. Despite this explicit awareness of their own impending death, the "Sukhorukov" household remained in unflagging good spirits. At dinner time, they all talked and joked as if nothing were at stake. "Sonia was the one who most frequently delighted the company with her silvery laugh." Comic verses were composed to make light of the vicissitudes and incidents of the mining work.[381]

Those lodging in town would arrive at the house just before daylight. They worked from six to eight, had tea, then continued until two in the afternoon, which was dinner time. They had a short rest after dinner and then worked on until 10 o'clock at night. When things were going well the diggings progressed at the rate of 30 centimeters per hour of work. There were frequent alarms. They had been working a week when the former occupant came around looking for some jam which she said she had left in the storehouse. By this time the storehouse was full of earth and props for timbering the gallery. Perovskaya said she had lost the key. Later she took the jam to the woman herself.

A few days afterwards, the storehouse caught fire. Neighbors ran to help. It was fatal if they were to see the contents of the storehouse, jammed as it was with soil from the excavation. Thinking very fast, Sonia jumped in front and held out her arms to keep them away. She cried out that God had brought about the fire. If it was His will, he would put it out himself. The sentiment appealed to the Old Believers. With this bit of ingenuity, Sonia managed to keep them away. Time and again the venture was saved by Perovskaya's resourcefulness. She did the shopping. As the quantity of provisions was far more than what two young people could consume, at one point the volume of her purchases elicited the well-meaning interest of gossiping neighboring housewives. She then made use of a cat that had attached itself to the conspirators. She blamed the cat for the amount of food she had to buy, spinning an elaborate yarn around its appetite, ingenuity, and capacity for breaking crockery.[382]

There were other close calls. The laboring terrorists came to the base of a telegraph pole and had to divert the gallery around it. It rained long and hard, the same rain that was causing the Emperor to change his travel plans, and that was hindering Zhelyabov at Alexandrovsk. Water collected in the gallery and began to rise. The conspirators had no pump. Incessant bailing doubled the work and brought them nearer to complete exhaustion. Mikhailov would later describe the situation as being "like working while buried alive, using the last superhuman efforts in the fight against death."[383] Finally, due to continuous rain and faulty timbering, the roof of the gallery fell in. The subsidence from this event formed a big crater on the surface. This crater was right next to a trail alongside the track where railway police patrols regularly passed. But no patrols came by on the afternoon of the collapse, nor did anybody else notice the crater. That night, the conspirators managed to fill the crater. One of the diggers from that point forward carried a dose of poison, so he could commit suicide in case he was buried by another sudden collapse.

When the terrorists reached the railway embankment, progress again became harder. Instead of soft soil, the conspirators now encountered large stones that had been laid within the bed of the tracks. Removing them would bring the risk of another collapse. They decided that they needed a drill to cut a hole in the stones. But there were no more funds on hand for buying one. The conspirators made a bold decision to mortgage the house. Hartmann went into town and found a wealthy widow who was willing to lend money.[384] The lender sent out an official of the housing department and a policeman to inspect the property. This was a very anxious moment. Perovskaya, however, pulled it off smoothly. She also bargained hard. Six hundred rubles were successfully borrowed. The conspirators bought a drill and kept moving.

The use of the drill led to a modification of the plans for the actual mine itself. The terrorists began to fear that they did not have enough dynamite. The frenetic Goldenberg was dispatched to get more dynamite from the abandoned Odessa project. Goldenberg arrived in Odessa and picked up a suitcase full of explosive from Frolenko. Kibalchich, the explosives expert, was then in South Russia. Instead of just concentrating on transporting the dynamite to Moscow, Goldenberg decided to meet Kibalchich to discuss the situation. They exchanged telegrams, but the result was a mixup. On November 12,

Goldenberg wound up waiting at Odessa for Kibalchich, while Kibalchich was waiting at Kharkov for Goldenberg. The two managed to communicate, probably by telegraph, and arranged to meet in Elizavetgrad, closer to Odessa and approximately one fifth of the way to Moscow. Goldenberg's incongruous actions in pretending to be a wealthy traveler, while insisting on carrying his own baggage, generated suspicion. A porter notified the police.[385] When Kibalchich arrived he found a stir at the station. Kibalchich made out that a young man had been arrested with a small but very heavy trunk. It was Goldenberg. He had been caught with the dynamite.

On November 14, the party at the Sukhorukov house heard about Goldenberg's arrest. Three days later, they received a telegram from Simferopol. In crude code, the message indicated that the Emperor was riding in the fourth coach of the second train. "Price of flour two rubles our price four." On that day the conspirators held a final conference. It was decided that Sonia would watch and give the signal for Hartmann to press the lever to trigger the explosion. All the 18th of November, the conspirators hung about waiting for news from Alexandrovsk. None came until evening, when they heard the Emperor had arrived at Kharkov. That meant Alexandrovsk had been a failure.[386]

Chapter 14: Attack Is Made on a Train of Marmalade

On the morning of November 19th, Prince D. D. Obolensky came in from the country to Tula in the hope of getting a lift across the 180 kilometers northward to Moscow in one of the imperial trains. The Emperor's passage had disorganized the time table. Ordinary trains were running up to eight hours late. Obolensky found the police and railway officials at Tula completely exhausted. Rumors circulated that the "nihilists" were up to something. Catching Goldenberg with his trunk full of heavy explosive strongly tended to confirm that something was afoot. A favorite theory was that the revolutionaries would throw a torpedo on the rails as the train passed.   There were patrols, house searches, and precautionary arrests. Prince Obolensky was on friendly terms with court officials. He had little difficulty securing permission to travel in the baggage train. Under the original schedule this train should have been the first. But, due to a mechanical issue, the baggage car locomotive was unable to keep to the time table. It was decided, on the spur of the moment, to alter the order and have the Emperor's train travel ahead of the separate baggage train.

Obolensky found a number of friends on board the baggage train. He chatted with them, had something to eat, and sat back to read a book. At 11 o'clock at night a conductor came through to announce that they were getting close to Moscow. Obolensky started getting his things together. Suddenly there was a crash. He was thrown out of his seat. He scrambled out of the coach and walked up the line. Guards, soldiers, and railway men were running up and down shouting. In the pitch dark, everything was in confusion. Obolensky tripped over a fallen telegraph pole. He noticed a hole in the ground from which emerged a thin trail of smoke. Some 50 meters away was a small house. One of the guards went across to it. There was a light burning in front of the icon, the samovar was boiling and the tea china was on the table, but there was no sign of the occupants. Obolensky walked up to the fourth coach. It was derailed, on its side, a broken mass of iron and timber. No one was hurt. Fortunately, it was solely a baggage car with no one riding in it. The car was full of jam, being brought back from the imperial estates in the Crimea for the palace in St. Petersburg. Marmalade and broken containers were scattered everywhere. A railway engineer appeared and argued that the rain must have loosened the embankment. Obolensky, however, smelled dynamite. He recognized the smell because he had recently been supervising blasting operations on his estate.

Obolensky walked to town and took a cab to the Kremlin. By then it was very late. The official reception was over and the Emperor and his staff had gone to bed. Obolensky insisted on seeing Count Adlerberg. The sleepy count was incredulous. He said the matter should be reported to the governor-general. Obolensky went back to his cab and drove on to the private

Contemporary drawing depicting the aftermath of the Nov. 19, 1879 imperial train explosion and derailment

residence of the governor-general, who was Prince Dolgorukov. The prince was in his dressing gown in the study, drinking a final cup of tea. Obolensky was shown in to him and reported that a mine had been exploded under one of the imperial trains. "Never!" said the governor-general. "Impossible." But Obolensky was firm. At last Dolgorukov broke down and knelt beside the table with the tea to offer up a prayer of thanks that the Emperor was unhurt.[387]

Much as such an event would today, the boldness and unprecedented scale of the November 19 terrorist attack on the Tsar's train set off a huge sensation in Russia and indeed throughout Europe. A new term for the perpetrators emerged. They were no longer just "nihilists," they were now the "new barbarians." People flocked to the site to see the "Sukhorukov House" and the tunnel dug by the new barbarians.[388] Alexander felt unjustly treated. He reportedly lamented, "But what do they have against me, these scoundrels? Why do they track me like a wild animal? I have never tried to do anything but good for my people!" He wavered, as usual, between voices such as that of his brother Konstantin, who urged him to grant a constitution for the 25th anniversary of his accession, and those of his more conservative advisers, who urged a response of no concessions and a renewal of severe repression.[389]

Sofia "Sukhorukov" filtered out of Moscow without detection and returned to St. Petersburg. A week later, when in the private company of other Narodnaya Volya women, she still had moments of being visibly upset and quaking with disappointment over the failure of the Moscow attempt.[390] Her "husband" Lev Hartmann, meanwhile, fled to France to avoid arrest. The Russian government learned of his role in the Moscow explosion due to revelations made by Goldenberg under interrogation. He was arrested by French police at the request of the Russian authorities. However, the attempt to secure Hartmann's extradition became a major international diplomatic flap. The French government, by this time, was a democratic republic. Although there was no sympathy for Hartmann's terrorism per se, there was substantial public support in France for the anti-monarchical cause of Russian civil liberties and a constitution. Victor Hugo, among other prominent personalities, became personally involved in lobbying the French president to deny extradition. The issue rapidly became a *cause célèbre*. Ultimately, Hartmann was released and allowed to remain in France. Russia promptly recalled its French ambassador.[391]

If Narodnaya Volya could be said to have a mastermind, it was the "Janitor," Alexander Mikhailov. He was four years younger than Perovskaya. Even before Narodnaya Volya, Mikhailov had a hand in most of the high profile Russian terrorist attacks of the late 1870's, including the assassination of Mezentsov, the chief of the Third Section, the assassination of Prince Dmitri Kropotkin, the governor general of Kharkov, the unsuccessful attempt against Mezentsov's successor General Drenteln, and Solovyev's unsuccessful attempt on the life of Tsar Alexander. The "Janitor" also ordered the cold blooded murder of a man suspected of informing the government on terrorist activities.[392] He was not in any sense a political theorist, which is why he generally got on well with Narodnaya Volya's "thinkers," Morozov and Tikhomirov (although these two did not get along at all with each other). When Morozov began to publish the "Bulletin" of Zemlya i Volya, some activists objected that it contained unabashed glorification of terror for its own sake. Mikhailov's answer was typical: "What does it matter what is in the paper? The great thing is that it appears clandestinely and that the police are at their wits' end . . . . For me an ideal paper would have no [political] content at all." His first reaction to the nihilists of the Chaikovsky era was that they argued too much over theory, and did not pay attention to "real force."[393]

The "Janitor" was extremely detail oriented. He was always analyzing small streets and by-ways, even in a seemingly insignificant environment such as Odessa. Aware that one of Zhelyabov's weaknesses was night blindness, he insisted that he always draw his curtains, because doing anything and everything to preserve his eyesight was paramount. "Sunlight damages the eyes and for us eyesight is top priority," he remarked.[394] Mikhailov had a knack for spotting and enlisting in the terrorist cause people of unusual and varied backgrounds. He knew how to make use of sexy young women, and of unstable or unsavory characters who could not be fully enlisted as members of the organization.[395]

Mikhailov exemplifies the profile of the terrorist. Being from the gentry, he had an extremely comfortable childhood. When the Narodnaya Volya terrorists were at large, getting prepared for their own impending deaths, they took the time and effort to write up some mini-autobiographies for posterity. The "Janitor's" is highly interesting:

> From the earliest youth a lucky star shone over my head. My childhood was one of the happiest one can have . . . My parental home was like a miraculous world in which ruled harmony and mutual love . . .

There were moments where my child's heart could hardly contain all the happiness and joy with which my surroundings filled me. And up to this day as a mature man I love warmly my kind and wise parents.

Mikhailov concluded the self portrait with an ode to those who shared with him the experience of accepting the inevitability of a near and early death:

> I have never known another man to whom fate has been so generous . . . My fondest hopes have been fulfilled . . . I have lived among the most worthwhile kind of people, and I have always earned their love and friendship. This is the greatest happiness a man can find.[396]

Mikhailov was a mediocre student at best. He found the atmosphere of school oppressive. He rarely spoke in front of groups of people. When he did, he was a stutterer. After three months in the Petersburg Technical Institute, Mikhailov soon gave up the idea of higher education. He decided instead to become a professional terrorist.[397]

At the end of 1879, the "Janitor" had two of his most diabolical projects in full swing. One of them was defense, the other offense.

Nikolai Kletochnikov was a low level civil servant when, at the age of 31, he decided to throw up his job and move to St. Petersburg. In his personal life, he was a loser. With his pallid complexion, stooped manner, and thinning hair, he hardly seemed the ideal candidate to start a new life as a revolutionary hero. However, Nikolai Kletochnikov knew all about the recent wave of assassinations, and he was secretly in sympathy with them. What is more, he was suffering with tuberculosis, as he realized, and he privately resolved to end his life with a bang. Without revealing anything much about himself, he made friends with some short haired St. Petersburg girls who were readers of the illegal underground news sheet, Zemlya i

Volya. They found it amusing that this old fogey wanted anything to do with them. Meekly he asked if they could introduce him to a revolutionary. At first, they pretended not to know what he was talking about. But after one or two outings in which he kept repeating this request, one day the girls unexpectedly came to get Kletochnikov. They brought him back to their room, where he found, waiting in a chair, a fat man named Pyotr Ivanovich. This man, the girls whispered, was a big revolutionary.

In the course of his interview with Ivanovich, Kletochnikov plucked up the courage to burst out with his question. Could the revolutionaries find something for him? Ivanovich surveyed Kletochnikov for quite some time. Then he said, "You know what? I have a little job on hand, only at the moment, it's not really work." He went on to discuss a woman named Anna Petrovna Kutuzova. She was the widow of a colonel, who made a living by letting rooms. There was a suspicion that this Anna was helping the government's spy service, because she rented her rooms to girl students, and a good number of them wound up being called in for police interrogation on minor matters. It was a suspicion. Kletochnikov could cut his teeth as a revolutionary by helping see if the suspicion was correct. Kletochnikov promised Ivanovich that he would try. Of course, the rotund man's name was not really Pyotr Ivanovich. It was the "Janitor," Alexander Mikhailov.

Anna Kutuzova turned out to be a lady who was a bit past middle age. She maintained a nosy and slightly overbearing air with her lodgers, most of whom felt vaguely threatened with eviction if they did not take a part in her evening card games. Anna was a passionate card player, often keeping the action at the table going past midnight. In order to ingratiate himself, Kletochnikov became Anna's steadiest companion at the card table. Anna soon took a liking to this lodger who did not drink or smoke, and who was amiable about her card games, not even minding that he usually lost a ruble or two to her. Eventually, she asked him to become her partner when playing cards with outside friends. This whole time, Anna did not let out a peep about anything at all related to the police.

Kletochnikov broached the subject gingerly. In the inevitable card table chatter, he casually voiced his disdain for the girls one could meet on the streets of St. Petersburg. He made spontaneous comments to the effect that he was not at all happy with their short hair cuts and attitude, that they would be better off locked up in nunneries. These clever remarks still produced no reaction.

Kletochnikov finally resolved to bring his project to an end. He found Anna's unctuous company tiresome and boring. He informed her that he would be leaving the flat. He could not find a job, he was running out of money, and he would soon be broke. St. Petersburg was expensive. He needed to return to the provinces. Anna was startled at the thought of losing her favorite card game companion. After a few moments, she looked at Kletochnikov. "I have a nephew in the Third Section," she said. "Perhaps I could ask him!" Kletochnikov nearly jumped out of his chair. That very evening, Kletochnikov visited the flat of his young girl acquaintances. They arranged for him to meet "Ivanovich" the next day. When Kletochnikov told him the story, the "Janitor's" suspicion about Anna Kutuzova was confirmed. Now Kletochnikov could finally escape his assignment with her. "Escape?" The "Janitor" shook his head. "Not until you are enrolled in the Third Section." Kletochnikov could scarcely believe his ears. But he knew he would comply. He duly met with Anna's "nephew" and, with her help, was soon hired on. The "Janitor" helped add to Kletochnikov's credibility by giving him information to feed the Third Section on a radical who Mikhailov knew was already being watched.

Kletochnikov was an outstanding paper pusher. He soon became a steady, well regarded clerk for the Third Section.

Due to his meticulous, neat handwriting, he was shortly promoted to a position as a copyist for official reports on radical activity and investigations. The geekish Kletochnikov developed a reputation as a workaholic, often staying late and also working on his nominal days off. He was given a pay raise. In April of 1880, for his diligent service he was awarded a medal and admission to the Order of St. Stanislaus.

Little did the government suspect this meek paper pusher had become, by the end of 1879, the number one source of inside information for Narodnaya Volya. Using the contents of detailed reports and lists of names that he carefully committed to memory during his long hours spent at the office, Kletochnikov thoroughly briefed the "Janitor" on all of the investigations, intended raids and arrests being conducted by the Third Section throughout Russia. With Kletochnikov, the "Janitor" was able to learn when the Third Section had identified a terrorist safe house. Through him, Mikhailov also learned that a revolutionary named Reinstein had turned double agent and was responsible for a recent spate of arrests of radical leaders. The "Janitor" promptly dispatched a team of agents to lure Reinstein to a meeting in a Moscow hotel room. Reinstein's throat was cut.

Kletochnikov also reported to Narodnaya Volya on many other important developments in the government's fight against terrorism. He advised the "Janitor" that Goldenberg had finally cracked after months of interrogation, and that he had begun to talk. Goldenberg's information was potentially very damaging, since he had been one of Mikhailov's close associates, and one of only eleven people who had attended the formation meeting of the Executive Committee in Lipetsk.

Mikhailov kept Kletochnikov a closely guarded secret. No one else, even within the organization, was allowed to know the identity of the man who was now referred to by a new code name: the "Guardian Angel."[398]

In July of 1879, Kletochnikov's inside information saved

Stepan Khalturin from almost certain arrest at the hands of his roommate, a trusted boyhood friend and fellow worker who had decided to turn informant. Khalturin was one of the founders and leaders of the Northern Workers' Union, an organization dedicated to galvanizing opposition to the government within workers employed in St. Petersburg industry. While the would-be informant was busy negotiating over the price he would accept for leading police to the group's underground leaders, Khalturin, tipped off based on Kletochnikov's spying, suddenly abandoned his hideout on St. Petersburg's Vasilievsky Island in order to avoid arrest.[399]

Chapter 15: Dynamite in the Winter Palace

Stepan Khalturin is a type we shall revisit in this series of terrorist profiles. He was a highly skilled artisan. Although he could call himself a worker, by no means was he a penniless, oppressed or struggling worker. In point of fact, his skills were very much in demand in the Russia of the 1870's. Born at the end of 1856, he came from a well-to-do, if technically serf, family in a province called Vyatka, deep in the Russian hinterlands some 1,000 kilometers east and north of Moscow. Stepan's father, reputed to be irascible but a good businessman, supplemented his income as a minor local official with profits from selling farm products, especially dried mushrooms and berries. From his mother Stepan absorbed and inherited extremely smooth manners, and what Georgi Plekhanov would later describe as an "almost feminine" personality.[400]

Although his parents sent him to school, Stepan dropped out after finishing the elementary grades to pursue the trade of his grandfather and uncle, woodworking. At age 16 he left home to attend an avant-garde, well equipped technical school designed to train young Russians to become skilled artisans. After one year there, Khalturin earned the nickname "Stepan gold hands" because of his exceptional ability working with wood. At the same time, Stepan also became an avid reader. During his one year in technical school, September 1874 to June of 1875, he made regular visits to the local library and checked out 92 books, most of which were "social" literature by authors such as Dostoyevsky, Honorè di Balzac and Victor Hugo.[401]

In Vyatka there was an ample supply of exiles, former participants in "Going to the People." One local exile whose acquaintance Khalturin made was Florent Pavlenkov, who in his younger days had been a friend of Chernyshevsky and an associate of Karakozov. Stepan quickly expanded his reading to include illegal underground literature. Khalturin became enamored of the vision of *What Is to Be Done?* In the spring of 1875, Khalturin's father died unexpectedly, leaving Stepan an inheritance of 1,000 rubles. Stepan resolved to use it to leave Russia to go to the United States. Khalturin obtained a passport for travel to Germany, from whence he would be able to travel to any other destination of his choice. He was planning to travel with two other young men. At the last minute the group was joined by a fourth traveler, who presented himself as a political exile. However, this fourth man, Fyodor Selantin was, in reality, a convicted bigamist, meaning, in terms of 19th century Russia, that he was a con artist. Once the group reached Moscow, Selantin soon managed to bilk Khalturin out of his passport and his entire 1,000 rubles, thus effectively ending his plan for travel to America.[402]

Undaunted, Khalturin quickly obtained employment working as a mechanic for the national railroad in Moscow. By September, he saved enough to quit the job and travel on to St. Petersburg. Again, he was able to catch on and find work rapidly. He received a new passport from his family in Vyatka, but by now he had lost interest in international travel. The 18-year old Stepan plunged into activism among the workers of St. Petersburg. Here he immediately met and made friends with the leaders of the "worker movement" that was growing in parallel with the "populist" efforts of Chaikovsky participants such as Perovskaya. Khalturin helped organize and operate a sort of radical lending library for workers. He also became active in distributing illegal propaganda literature in factories. Khalturin and his worker associates provided key support for Plekhanov in forming Zemlya i Volya, and in organizing its initial rally in front of Kazan Cathedral in December, 1876. This was the rally in which Bogolyubov and many others were arrested.[403]

Soon after the Kazan Cathedral rally, Khalturin went "underground," discarding his "Stepan Khalturin" identity in favor of a variety of false names. Over the next several years, he continually moved from one industrial establishment to another, always finding success in securing employment. Once his foot was in the door, he devoted himself to propagandizing, instigating unrest, and supporting strikers. When St. Petersburg became too "hot" for him in the aftermath of Vera Zasulitch's shooting of General Trepov, Khalturin left for a time to work in a factory in another Russian industrial city, Nizhny Novgorod. However, later in 1878 he returned to the capital under the false name Stepan Baturin and secured a job working in the government's navy shipyards. Once more Khalturin, with others in his "Northern Workers' Union," became active in the underground, helping Zemlya i Volya in its efforts to proselytize among workers. Penetrating this organization was one of the Third Section's biggest preoccupations in late 1879. Thus, news about informants and investigations aimed at cracking the "Northern Workers' Union" quickly came to the attention of Kletochnikov in his role as the Third Section's copyist.

When Zemlya i Volya split into its "terrorist" (Narodnaya

Volya) and "organizing" (Cherny Peredel) factions in mid-1879, Khalturin initially sided with Plekhanov. His reported sentiments echoed those of the moderate faction regarding the assassination attempt by Solovyev: "As soon as we succeed in getting something working, uh oh. Here the intellectuals go blowing everything up. If only they would give us a little time to gain strength!"[404]

Despite this, Khalturin proved to be cut from a terrorist cloth. He caught the fever at almost the exact same moment as Perovskaya: the end of the summer of 1879. A member of the Northern Workers' Union was offered a post in the Tsar's Winter Palace in St. Petersburg. From him, Khalturin learned that palace officials were looking for qualified carpenters to work on a renovation project. At first, Khalturin joked to others in the organization that it would make a good occasion to get rid of the Tsar. Later, he thought better of his own joke, telling people never to repeat it, and he decided to take the idea seriously.

Stepan Khalturin

In order to get a job in the Winter Palace, Khalturin needed a recommendation. It would be especially helpful to have one from an ex-soldier. Here Khalturin's reputation as an excellent ebony craftsman came into play. Khalturin was able to get an endorsement from another woodworker who was an ex-soldier and a former artisan employed for projects at the Winter Palace. In another embarrassment for the Russian government, nothing was done in the way of a thorough security check. On August 24, 1879, Khalturin was hired to work as a carpenter in the Winter Palace under the false name, "Stepan Batishkov."[405]

Khalturin made his success in securing the Winter Palace position known to Anna Yakimova, of the Narodnaya Volya Executive Committee. Yakimova in turn informed the "Janitor," Mikhailov. Mikhailov was by now used to making the final decision on plots such as this one. He met with Khalturin several times. Stepan was very surprised at the way Mikahilov, while walking with him down a street, would suddenly turn around to admire the rear end of an attractive girl passing in the other direction. But the "Janitor" was not really looking at female anatomy. He was checking to see if the conspirators were being shadowed by the Third Section's ubiquitous spies.

Ultimately, the "Janitor" was convinced of Khalturin's seriousness. He approved of putting into motion a plan to bomb the Winter Palace although, at the time, this was only to serve as a backup to the three pronged dynamite attack, then in full swing, against the Emperor's train on his return voyage from the Crimea. Alexander Kviatkovski, the Executive Committee member who was previously involved in supporting the botched Voinaralsky rescue and the Solovyev assassination attempt, was appointed to be the Narodnaya Volya liaison to Khalturin. Little by little, Kviatkovski began supplying Khalturin with small packets of the homemade explosive, a gelatinous mixture of nitroglycerine and magnesium, to be smuggled into the Winter Palace. Khalturin's project was to be kept in strictest secrecy, even within the organization.

Khalturin played his hand cleverly. His skills as a cabinetry finisher were beyond any question. He did his best to fit in with the somewhat corrupt mores of the Winter Palace workers. He went so far as to pilfer some small tools and food, just to appear to be as normal as everybody else. He succeeded in making friends in every part of the building. Complaining that his quarters were too hot, at the end of September he succeeded in getting his sleeping cot transferred to a room in the basement of the Palace, two floors beneath the Emperor's dining room. Scratching his head and at times picking his nose, he made an effort to give off the body language of an ignorant, unmannered country rube. Like Perovskaya, he seemed to enjoy overacting the role of the peasant. But his youth, good looks and skill as an artisan captured people's attention. Vasily Petrotsky, who was a supervisor in the police guarding the basement of the Palace, took a liking to Khalturin. Petrotsky started talking about setting up a marriage between Khalturin and his daughter. He even brought the daughter into the palace to meet Khalturin. Stepan, who seems never to have had any actual interest in women, played along with Petrotsky in order to curry favor.[406]

As Khalturin was working his way into good graces in the Winter Palace while slowly smuggling in dynamite, the efforts of the Moscow dynamite team led by Perovskaya resulted in the explosion, discussed above, that derailed the imperial baggage car containing jars of marmalade. The "Executive Committee" of Narodnaya Volya wasted no time in circulating an impudent broadside, claiming credit. In part, it stated:

> On November 19th of this year, near Moscow, on the Moscow-Kursk Railway, by decree of the Executive Committee an attempt was made on the life of Alexander II by means of blowing up the royal train. The attempt was unsuccessful. The reasons for the mistake and failure cannot conveniently be published at present.
>
> We are confident that our agents and our whole party will not be discouraged by the failure, but will draw from the present case not only fresh experience,

a lesson in circumspection, and at the same time a new confidence in their strength and the possibility of successful struggle . . . .

[W]e once again assert that Alexander II is the personification of a hypocritical, cravenly bloodthirsty and all-corrupting despotism . . . . This disastrous process of extermination of all independent elements in society is being simplified to the final point, the scaffold. Alexander II is the chief representative of the usurpation of popular rule, the main pillar of reaction, the person who is chiefly to blame for the judicial murders; fourteen executions rest on his conscience, the hundreds of people tortured to death and the thousands now suffering cry out for revenge. He deserves the death penalty for all the blood he has shed, for all the torments he has caused.[407]

Publication of this sensational and seditious flyer caused St. Petersburg authorities to redouble their already vigorous efforts to track Narodnaya Volya literature to its source. As a result, shortly afterwards they succeeded in finding a safe house in which Alexander Kviatkovsky, the liaison to its printing press, was captured. In this safe house, authorities found a stash of dynamite, along with several hand drawn sketches. Investigators were able to identify one of these sketches, marked with a cross and a circle, as being a diagram of the floor plans of the Winter Palace. They could tell by its accuracy that the diagram had been made by someone who had actually been in the Winter Palace.

Security at the Winter Palace was immediately tightened. The basement quarters where Khalturin was sleeping were subjected to a surprise search. But the examination of Khalturin's trunk, supervised as it was by Stepan's would-be father-in-law Petrotsky, did not reveal the dynamite stored on the bottom. All of the Winter Palace staff were issued special medallions to be displayed for entry. Their pockets were searched going in and out. However, this did not stop Khalturin from smuggling in more small packets of dynamite, taped to his chest.

From being just a backup plan, Khalturin's project now became Narodnaya Volya's main focus. Zhelyabov was assigned to act as his contact now, in place of Kviatkovsky. He began meeting with Khalturin and providing him with more of the small packages of nitroglycerine to be smuggled in under his clothing. Khalturin had to be very cautious, because he shared his room in the basement of the Winter Palace with two other workmen. While awaiting the chance to sneak the explosive gel into his trunk, Khalturin had to keep it tucked under his pillow. The mixture emitted fumes that caused him severe headaches.

Khalturin and Zhelyabov, both being handsome and headstrong, soon came into conflict with each other. Khalturin wanted lots more dynamite, to make sure the job would be successful. Zhelyabov, on the other hand, fretted that the plot would be discovered before it was fully hatched. He insisted that the bomb should be set off at once. Zhelyabov induced Kibalchich, the Narodnaya Volya explosives expert, to do a calculation indicating that the 35 kilos of explosive then in Khalturin's possession would be enough to blow up the Tsar's dining room two floors above. This calculation, however, was filled with assumptions about unknowns.[408]

One day, as Khalturin was working on a project on the upper level of the Palace, Tsar Alexander II himself unexpectedly came into the room. The two were all alone. Khalturin could very well have attacked and killed the ruler with his bare hands, but he could not bring himself to do something so savage. It seemed Alexander was regarded as kind and considerate in his encounters with workmen at the Palace. Evidently, however, Khalturin had no similar qualms about blowing up the entire Palace, inevitably killing many unsuspecting people besides the Tsar, with a dynamite explosion.[409] Khalturin's work and demeanor continued to be appreciated in the Palace. At Christmas time in 1879, he received a bonus of 100 rubles.

By mid January Khalturin, although he continued to add more dynamite to the trunk, finally agreed to turn his attention to the detonation. The trunk itself would serve as the bomb. Khalturin rigged up a long, slow burning fuse inside an iron pipe. He calculated the flame, once lit, would take twenty minutes to reach the bomb. He informed Zhelyabov that the plan was ready. The event needed to await the coincidence of two conditions: Khalturin must be alone in his room to set off the fuse, and it must be an evening when the Tsar was dining in the dining room above.

Every evening for two weeks, Khalturin was thwarted by one or the other issue. Finally, on February 5, he saw an opportunity. At 5 p.m., "Batishkov" (as Khalturin was known in the Palace) had tea with another workman, Bogdanov. Oddly, "Batishkov" insisted that the two of them do it while sitting in the dark. Bogdanov finished his tea and left the room. Then another workman, Razumovsky, entered and asked why "Batishkov" was sitting in the dark. "Batishkov" answered that he was just getting ready to leave. Razumovsky needed to find some tools. "Batishkov" lit a candle for long enough for Razumovsky to locate the tools, then blew it out, remaining seated in the dark when Razumovsky left. A short time later, another worker looking through the window into the room saw "Batishkov" bending over a candle and doing something at the far end of the room.

Shortly after 6 p.m., Khalturin emerged from the Palace. By prearrangement, he found Zhelyabov in Admiralty Square, in front of the Winter Palace. The two of them walked across the square to await events. At twenty two minutes past six, there was a huge explosion. All of the lights in the Winter

Winter Palace dining room in the aftermath of the explosion of February 5, 1880

Palace went out. Zhelyabov and Khalturin sought the shelter of a Narodnaya Volya safe house.[410]

Tsar Alexander II, on the evening of February 5, had an engagement to host for dinner Alexander of Hesse-Darmstadt, brother of the Tsar's sick and bedridden wife. The brother-in-law's train to St. Petersburg was delayed by snow, so he was late in reaching the Palace. As a result, the dinner was postponed by a half hour. The royal family was just on its way to the dining room when the explosion went off. It produced a tremendous shaking of the concrete building, reminiscent of an earthquake. When candles were finally lit after the lights went out, it could be discerned in the darkness that everything was covered with a layer of dust. The smell of a dynamite explosion was in the air. Alarms sounded and chaos reigned. The responding firefighters encountered a horrifying scene filled with smoke, dust, bodies of men who had died instantly in the blast, and others injured and crying out for help.[411] People started streaming out of the dark and shaken building. Eventually, the responders began carrying out the many people who had been injured. Eleven people in all were killed; 56 others were injured and maimed.

But the quantity of explosive proved insufficient to bring down the Palace. Although the imperial dining room was damaged, most of the fatalities occurred not in the dining room, but on the floor in between, immediately above Khalturin's basement quarters. Alexander was able to find his way to the quarters of Katia, on the second floor, where she was waiting for him with a lit candle. Upon hearing the news that the Emperor was unhurt, Khalturin went into a nervous state of collapse.[412]

Two days later, Narodnaya Volya published a communiqué claiming "credit" for the bombing.

> In carrying out a decision of the Executive Committee, on February 5, at 6:22 pm, was carried out a new attempt on the life of Alexander the Reactionary, by means of an explosion at the Winter Palace. The explosive charge was correctly calculated, but the Emperor was a half hour late for dinner, and the explosion happened while he was on his way to the dining room. So, unfortunately for the nation, the Emperor survived. With deep regret we have witnessed the death of the poor soldiers who have been forced to protect this crowned scoundrel. But since the army is the stronghold of tyranny and

does not acknowledge its sacred duty to take the side of the people, these tragedies will be inevitable . . . We say to Alexander that we will conduct this fight until he has ceded power to the hands of the People and has given his mandate for the formation of a National Assembly consisting of freely elected representatives. We invite all Russian citizens to help us in this fight against unfeeling, inhuman tyranny, under whose talons the best forces of the nation are dying.[413]

Chapter 16: A Dictator Takes the Helm

The brazen bombing of the Winter Palace captured the full and undivided attention of the imperial government. The Tsar called in all of his cabinet ministers and close family members for conferences. On February 8, three days after the explosion, Tsar Alexander II held a large council of state. While the ministers remained largely silent, his 34-year old son and heir Alexander Alexandrovitch took the floor. After expressing strong opposition to any notion of a constitution, he proposed a very simple idea. Appoint a single supreme commander, as in a time of war! He would be an absolute dictator and that way, could be in a position to do battle with the enemies of the state. The vision of the "success" of the White Terror of the 1860s was invoked.[414]

These proposals were not Alexander Alexandrovitch's own ideas. Over time, the younger Alexander had became a tool of the St. Petersburg reactionary faction entrenched in the Anichkov Palace, where the heir had his headquarters. One of the arch-conservatives, Konstantin Pobedonostsev, had been his head instructor. Pobedonostsev continued to be the heir's mentor after he reached adulthood. Alexander Alexandrovitch grew into a large bear of a man, but he was not a mental giant, to put it charitably. He had not been groomed for the throne. That honor had gone to his older brother Nicholas, who then died unexpectedly in 1865. Alexander Alexandrovitch was a tippler, a habit whose extent he tried to conceal from his wife Maria Feodorovna, the former Princess Dagmar of Denmark. His big pleasures in life were fishing, hunting, and drinking. His idea of fun was to have his aide carry a concealed flask of cognac while on expeditions with Dagmar. When she took a moment's leave, he would have the flask brought out in a flash for a quick swig, then concealed again by the aide before her return. Unlike his father, Alexander Alexandrovitch was not at all tempted by Western liberal thought. He was a staunch advocate of what we would today call "family values." He was very moral and religious. He was outraged and bitterly offended by his father's long running and scarcely concealed affair with Katia Dolgorukov.[415]

The reactionary party that mentored Alexander Alexandrovitch issued a sort of manifesto of counter-reform. In opposition to the idea of a constitution, the conservatives presented the model of a "living popular autocrat." The tsar must remain an autocrat, and never devolve into a mere "chief executive." They denounced the idea of a "bureaucracy contaminated by nihilism."

When Alexander the son proposed appointing a single military commander to serve as absolute dictator, his father responded that he was not in agreement with the idea. He would think about it. But that night, Alexander the father hardly slept. The next day, at a reconvened council of state, Tsar Alexander II once again heard out the proposition of his son and his advisors for setting up a dictatorship. Alexander, to everyone's surprise, now reversed course and announced that he was accepting the concept. But when they heard who he had in mind to fill the job, they were even more stupefied. Alexander announced that he was appointing Mikhail Loris-Melikov.[416]

This unexpected selection was actually a shrewd decision on the part of the Emperor. The naming of the 56-year old Loris-Melikov shocked the right wingers because he was by no means a conservative, and because he was a total St. Petersburg outsider. He was not even a Russian, he was an Armenian. Although he had noble antecedents, Loris-Melikov's father had been a successful merchant. Loris-Melikov had had a fine military career, working his way into a position as a general, fighting against the Turks in the Balkans, and fighting against nasty rebels in what remains today a hotbed of terrorism, the mountainous area of Chechnya and Georgia. He had distinguished himself during the Russo-Turkish war, not only by besieging Turkish outposts until they surrendered, but also because while doing so, he persuaded the local populations to accept the billeting of Russian soldiers. He had actually managed to return part of his budget to the state treasury, a virtually unheard-of accomplishment. He had also proved to be an excellent civil administrator. He had helped fight off an outbreak of the plague in Astrakhan province, on the Caspian Sea. He had been perceived as a success fighting terrorists while serving as governor-general of Kharkov, his current position when Alexander called upon him to become the dictator. Loris-Melikov had proved capable of taking a hard line on terror while, at the same time, managing public opinion and avoiding mindless excesses of repression.[417]

A sense of anticipation mixed with apprehension hung over the date of February 19, 1880. Ceremonies were scheduled to commemorate both the 25th anniversary of Alexander's coronation, and the 19th anniversary of his decree freeing the serfs. It was feared that the terrorists would strike again. However, the event went off without a hitch as the Emperor was cheered by large crowds.

But when Loris-Melikov returned to his home the next day shortly after 2 pm, as he dismounted from his carriage a young man came out of nowhere and ambushed him, firing a revolver. The shot penetrated Loris-Melikov's overcoat and his uniform, but missed his body. With a reaction born of years of combat, Loris-Melikov hit the ground before the attacker could fire a second shot. Then, just as quickly, he sprang back up to his feet and pounced on the assailant, knocking him to the ground. By the time his stunned Cossack guards could reach the fight, Loris-Melikov had already disarmed the assassin.

Loris-Melikov's personal courage and audacity fighting off the attack made him a hero with the public.[418] None but the most sensitive seemed to be upset when a military tribunal convened at Loris-Melikov's behest condemned the terrorist, one Hippolyte Mlodetski, to be publicly hanged the following day. Even Narodnaya Volya distanced itself from Mlodetski. Two days after the attack, when Mlodetski was already dead, the Executive Committee issued a communiqué which rather egotistically stated:

> With reference to the attempt of February 20, the Executive Committee find it necessary to state that its inception and execution were due solely to private initiative. It is a fact that Mlodetski offered his services to the committee for some terrorist act. But he was unwilling to await a decision and he proceeded to carry through his attempt without knowledge and without the assistance of the Executive Committee.[419]

Loris-Melikov as dictator rapidly showed himself to be every bit the capable administrator and reformer he had promised to be, given his earlier career filled with successes. He took the initiative to force the reactionary Dmitri Tolstoy into involuntary retirement as minister of education. He abolished the Third Section, reassigning its security functions to the ministry of the interior. Loris-Melikov flirted with Russian students, granting them long suppressed demands such as the right to organize their own independent study groups and to create mutual aid societies to help poorer students. He eased censorship restrictions on the press.[420] He avoided overreacting to a published humor piece that placed him on the same dance floor with such figures as Vera Zasulitch, Lev Hartmann (Perovskaya's fictitious husband from Moscow, whom Russia was then trying unsuccessfully to extradite from France), and Nikolai Chernyshevsky. The conservatives were appalled.[421] By August 1880, Loris-Melikov was able to announce that his measures had been a success, and that there was no more need for him to hold plenary emergency powers as head of a Supreme Administrative Commission. In short, his dictatorship was at an end. He would become minister of the interior and chief of police.[422]

Under Loris-Melikov the Russian government made meaningful strides in confronting the terrorist threat. Following his capture in November of 1879, the authorities in Odessa had used bullying, torture and strong arm tactics to try to get Grigory Goldenberg to talk. None of it worked. They were facing a determined radical.

Then the interrogation of Goldenberg was taken over by a young Odessa assistant prosecutor named Alexander Dobrzhinsky. Dobrzhinsky intuitively understood something many others in the Russian law enforcement structure (similar to those in the United States and elsewhere today) had failed to grasp. Rather than trying to torture, intimidate, or overpower the prisoner, Dobrzhinsky applied a fundamental insight into the persona of the terrorist. The best and, perhaps the only, way to obtain meaningful communications from a terrorist is to suspend the normal framework of reality. One must enter into the delusional alternative universe of the terrorist. Dobrzhinsky did just that. Not only did he treat the person being interviewed with sympathy, he actually accepted without reservation, at least for purposes of the interview, the viewpoint of the interviewee. An account by Olga Lyubatovich of her

1882 interview by Dobrzhinsky reveals how skillful and perceptive he was as an investigator speaking with terrorists. He accepted their world view for the purpose of finding out much more about its details. One of his favorite techniques was to propose that the terrorist write a letter to the Tsar, expounding on and trying to convince the Emperor of his or her point of view.

As part of his insight, Dobrzhinsky also understood that the terrorist has an enlarged ego. The terrorist thirsts after legacy and glory. He thus becomes easily deluded into uncritical belief in his own plans of action. Dobrzhinsky exploited these characteristics in Goldenberg.

A "Southern" radical turned informant named Feodor "Fedka" Kuritsyn was placed with Goldenberg as a cell mate. He had already been incarcerated for three years. Fedka had been a talented, cheerful youth, an amateur musician and singer, and had studied at the Kharkov Veterinary Institute. But by now he was a cowed and broken man. His eyes were sunken, his voice trembled. He told Goldenberg he was going out of his mind. He begged Goldenberg to relieve him of his loneliness.

Slowly, Goldenberg began to talk to Fedka. Fedka was getting ready to be put on trial. Fedka's only joy was whispering, so that nothing could be overheard, to Goldenberg. Fedka praised him for not giving in to the swine. When he learned that Goldenberg had executed Kropotkin, the "butcher of the Kharkov students," Fedka's admiration knew no bounds. He kept repeating how happy he was to be in the same cell as such a heroic person after three years of isolation. "You are doing such splendid things!" He spoke of how much it mattered to him and helped him, and added to his strength. So, Goldenberg kept on bragging about his exploits and those of the terrorists. He told him all about the Moscow tunnel, and about the planting of the mine in Alexandrovsk. Fedka and three of his fellow Odessa rebels were tried. Kuritsyn's co-defendants were sent to the scaffold and, on December 7, they were all hanged. Kuritsyn's sentence was commuted to penal servitude. In view of his three years in prison, Kuritsyn was given exile.

Goldenberg's tortures were abandoned. He seemed to have been forgotten by the jailers. He spent his time "preparing" Fedka for his exile. Kuritsyn would be going to Kharkov and from there to Siberia. Goldenberg bragged to Fedka that he knew of safe havens where Fedka could go in Kharkov. He generously shared his knowledge about the contacts and safe houses there. Among his statements to Fedka: "And the very warmest greetings to Sonia Perovskaya, if she has returned from Moscow to Kharkov." At the beginning of January, Fedka left prison. His goodbye to Goldenberg was a sad parting, with Fedka nearly breaking down in tears.[423]

Two days later, on January 15, Goldenberg was summoned for his new official interrogation. Everything was different now. Dobrzhinsky behaved extremely politely, almost benevolently, toward Goldenberg. He asked very few questions, and he did most of the talking himself. From what he said it appeared that the investigators knew absolutely everything. Goldenberg's comrades, captured recently in various places, were confessing and giving frank evidence. Many were honestly repenting, many were writing long and very substantial explanations, giving names, dates and addresses. They were young and still hoped by means of honest confession to start afresh. A huge, nationwide process of disintegration of the revolutionary party was taking place. Goldenberg asked who these young people were. Names did not matter, Dobrzhinsky replied.

Dobrzhinsky went on talking, about the Lipetsk congress, reeling off names and aliases. He described the meetings in St. Petersburg taverns that went on before Solovyev's attempt. He talked about the Moscow tunnel, and the plans to mine Malaya

Sadovaya street in St. Petersburg. This upset Goldenberg badly. It was a top secret plan, which the "Janitor" had only mentioned in passing. Could the jailer have overheard him whispering about this to Fedka? This caused something to snap in Goldenberg, as if he had lost his base of support. Eventually, in the face of more confrontation with details, Goldenberg came to a cold and depressing realization. He himself was the source of the information. He had given it away through Fedka.

Dobrzhinsky played to Goldenberg's ego. He praised the extremists of the Sixties as being the true "best people we have" and "the flower of the nation." They were perishing for no good reason. "Russia must be saved!" he declared. He portrayed the fate of the nation as a tremendous drama, in which Goldenberg could take the lead role. "We must stop this orgy of executions, deaths, spite and mutual distrust. You think everything at the top is calm and unanimous? I know some very highly placed persons who rage when they hear of new arrests and court martials. What an unfortunate country this is!" He pointed out that the Bulgarians, the Romanians and the Finns all had constitutional or representative government in some form, because the Russians had granted it to them. And yet, the Russians did not.

"There is no one who could do more than you, Mr. Goldenberg, to help Russia." In the nights which followed, Goldenberg experienced delusions of grandeur. He appeared from heaven like the Messiah, like Jesus. In these visions he was appealing to the government and to the revolutionaries alike. He became convinced that it was his fate, his destiny, to save thousands of lives and stop the bloodshed. And in the wake of this vision, he began his confessions. Dobrzhinsky kept on with massaging Goldenberg's ego. Goldenberg was asked to describe the revolutionaries he knew. And he knew a great deal. After giving a written deposition Dobrzhinsky personally brought him to St. Petersburg and had him meet with Loris-Melikov. Loris-Melikov talked the same line as Dobrzhinsky, calling Goldenberg a Moses, leading his people out of the desert to the promised land, to peace and repose. Goldenberg was thrilled. And Goldenberg kept talking. Eventually he would write "descriptions" of 143 people involved with the radical movement, including the leaders of Narodnaya Volya.

Tsar Alexander II read with great interest Loris-Melikov's report on the interviews with Goldenberg. Goldenberg's identification of Kviatkovsky was regarded as a particularly important turning point. He made a note, "I consider this a most important discovery."[424]

On the night of May 21, 1880, the long suffering Empress Marie finally died. The Tsar allowed just 40 days of mourning to pass before he announced to his ministers his intention to marry Katia Dolgorukov. Alexander obstinately rebuffed every criticism of this intention. The marriage ceremony was performed, behind closed doors with only a few selected witnesses, on July 6, 1880. This formalized and legitimized an affair that had already been going on for 15 years, and that had already produced three children. The next day, when word of the secret marriage was announced, there was profound indignation in Alexander's court. Nevertheless, Alexander signed a proclamation making Katia and her children royal highnesses. From that point forward, Katia frequently sat in on meetings between Alexander and Loris-Melikov. Loris-Melikov also engaged, on occasion, in private conferences with Katia. The Tsar was pleased that he did so.[425] When Alexander Alexandrovitch returned to the capital and learned of his father's remarriage, he was shocked.

Alexander, the father, was revitalized by insisting on bringing his relationship with Katia and the three children out into the open and by insisting, in the face of substantial behind-the-scenes intrigues against her, that Katia be accorded the dignity and respect due his spouse. With Katia and Loris-

Melikov supporting him, Alexander at long last freed himself from the yoke of domination by conservative advisors. Katia and her three children immensely enjoyed their new status, being freed from the shadows. Katia now insisted on going everywhere with her new husband. She personally accompanied him on his annual trip to Livadia, in the Crimea, in August 1880. Alexander Alexandrovitch also traveled to Livadia along with his wife Dagmar and their children. There he was deeply disconcerted to find Katia and her children basking in the suites that had formerly belonged to Alexander Alexandrovitch's mother. In a snit, he and his wife threatened to leave the Crimea for a vacation in Denmark (Dagmar's native country). Alexander, the father, told Alexander, the son, he would cease to be the heir, if he acted that way. Alexander Alexandrovitch stayed on in the Crimea, but continued to be unhappy. Finally he got permission to return to St. Petersburg.

Loris-Melikov also accompanied Tsar Alexander II to the Crimea. He was tasked with working on Alexander's newest reform project – a preliminary step in the direction of a potential constitution for Russia.[426] Ever the diligent administrator, Loris-Melikov presented Alexander with a series of options. The centerpiece of the proposal, which Alexander ultimately endorsed, was the addition of certain delegates – members of a locally elected body, the zemstvo -- to the Council of State, the group responsible for advising the Tsar on law and policy. It was not a parliament, but it was a step in the direction of a more republican form of government than anything imperial Russia had ever seen.[427]

Two commonly shared traits of terrorists are their loose overall grip on reality, and their political beliefs which are typically imbued with fantasy and a total lack of any practicality. These traits were amply demonstrated by Perovskaya in the aftermath of the Winter Palace bombing. Tsar Alexander II's public and pronounced shift to the left, with the guidance of Loris-Melikov, sapped Narodnaya Volya of much of the support for its terrorist tactics among the liberals of Russian society. Cash donations from "legals" dried up, straining the group's finances.[428] The notion that the assassination of Alexander would by itself trigger some spontaneous mass uprising that would vindicate the position of the terrorists was pure wishful thinking. Eliminating Alexander, in view of the reactionary element of the St. Petersburg power structure for whom the heir Alexander Alexandrovitch was in essence a puppet, was now an extremely foolish course of action from a political point of view. Alexander was already heading in policy directions Narodnaya Volya had publicly requested, liberalizing press restrictions and granting an increased role in lawmaking to elected local representatives in the face of opposition from conservatives. But Sonia steadfastly refused to allow her compatriots to relent in their efforts to assassinate Alexander.[429]

In late March of 1880, Sonia and the others on the Executive Committee learned, through Kletochnikov, of Goldenberg's revelations. Soon afterwards, Sonia traveled under her false passport to Odessa. There, Vera Figner was in charge of Narodnaya Volya operations. Figner was busy plotting the assassination of S. F. Panyutin, chief of staff of Count Totleben, the governor-general. Perovskaya countermanded this project. Pointedly, she reminded Figner that the Executive Committee had resolved to devote all of its attention and resources to killing Alexander. Lesser officials were to be attacked only if it did not in any way prejudice the attack on the Tsar. Sonia redirected the Odessa effort to be a plan to assassinate the Tsar. The method would be to dig a tunnel under the street, in which a mine would explode while he was passing overhead in the process of transferring from the train station to the steamboat wharf. Perovskaya expected the Tsar to pass through Odessa to make this transfer in May. This tunneling scheme obviously had much in common with the earlier Moscow efforts coordinated by Sonia. Once again she posed as a wife, this time, the spouse of a shopkeeper. Figner raised the sum of 1,000 rubles to open a grocery shop on Italianskaya Street, where the Tsar was expected to pass. Narodnaya Volya members were assigned to work daily shifts digging a tunnel from the shop to the street.

Perovskaya wanted Grigory Isaev as part of her team. He had proven his superior merit as a tunneler during the Moscow attempt. Isaev arrived shortly after Perovskaya, together with Anna Yakimova. The tunneling, although very arduous, was successful in reaching the middle of Italianskaya Street, where the Tsar's route would pass, but the terrorists encountered other problems. Isaev blew off three of his fingers in an experiment with the explosives. Then it was learned that the Tsar had changed his plans and was no longer intending to visit Odessa. The Odessa mine project was declared a failure and abandoned, with the hole refilled.[430]

Although Perovskaya was posing as Isaev's fictitious shopkeeping spouse, in fact, Isaev and Anna Yakimova, code named "Baska," became lovers. When Isaev suffered the explosion accident, Yakimova risked her life to take him to the hospital and to stay by his side during his emergency treatment. Being an outlaw living underground without a passport, for "Baska" every moment visiting in the hospital was precarious.

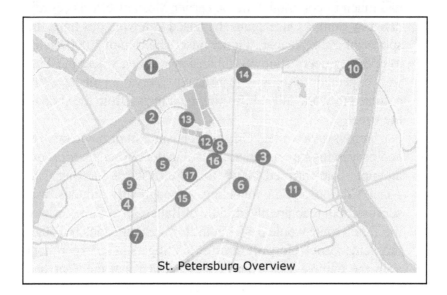

St. Petersburg Overview

St. Petersburg Overview Map

Key to Locations:
(1) St. Peter and Paul Fortress
(2) Palace Square (in front of Winter Palace)
(3) Narodnaya Volya safehouse – Kibalchich residence
(4) Narodnaya Volya safehouse – Khalturin stayed here after WP explosion
(5) Kamenni Bridge
(6) Narodnaya Volya apartment – Kolodkevitch residence
(7) Rot Ismailovsky Polk – residence of Perovskaya and Zhelyabov
(8) Trigoni apartment – site of Zhelyabov arrest
(9) Voznesensky Ave. "headquarters" of the Narodnaya Volya
(10) Smolny Monastery grounds – where bombers practiced Feb. 28, 1881
(11) 5 Telezhnaya St. – residence of Helfman
(12) Cheese shop location in the Malaya Sadovaya
(13) Ekaterinsky Canal embankment, site of the assassination
(14) Preliminary House of Detention – Perovskaya's last night spent here
(15) Semyonovsky Square – site of the execution
(16) Nevsky Prospect in front of Anichkov Palace – site of Perovskaya arrest
(17) Apraxin Dvor

Chapter 17: The Narodnaya Volya Love Affairs

In virtually the same time frame when a small fraction of the former "Going to the People" radicals evolved a tactical philosophy of terrorism, falling emotionally and physically in love with the opposite sex also came to be a hot trend amongst them. And as we have already seen, there was a pronounced tendency among the Generation of the Sixties to follow trends set by peers. Many of those who plunged with abandon into the fanaticism of terrorism, and made peace with the notion of glorious suicide that goes along with it, also abandoned their former sexual abstinence. In fact, many went overboard in the opposite direction, displaying an almost hedonistic resolve to relish the pleasures of sexual intercourse before the expected agony of imprisonment and death. It was a bizarre, ephemeral and ultimately painful twist.

In short order, numerous radical feminists in the movement coupled themselves up with male terrorists. The trend may have originated with a previously married radical named Maria Oshanina, who also went by her maiden name of Olovennikova. Olovennikova had a distinguished terrorist pedigree. She had attended Lipetsk, had been an early and ardent proponent of terror, and had been an original Narodnaya Volya Executive Committee member. She took for her lover the "Janitor's" boyhood friend, Alexander Barannikov. Barannikov was as dashing, tall and handsome as Mikhailov was stumpy and fat. His good looks were attributed, in large part, to his mother, who was Persian. Barannikov had been attending military academy with the ambition of becoming a general when he suddenly decided to quit school, change his life and become an underground revolutionary. When he quit, his uniform was found alongside a river, next to a suicide note.[431] It was a scene cut straight from What Is to Be Done.

The romance bandwagon also took momentum from a woman named Fanny Litchkous. She had an affair with Serge Kravchinsky. Fanny was a non-underground, "legal" student who was in sympathy with the radical movement. She was 23 years old, very pretty and with a pleasant personality. She was already pregnant by Kravchinsky when he stabbed Mezentsov, and then fled Russia in November 1878 to avoid arrest. By means of a stressful journey, Fanny managed with great difficulty to smuggle herself out of Russia in order to join her lover in Switzerland. She arrived feeling very ill. Her baby was born prematurely in the spring of 1879 and died two days later.[432]

Another romantic event involved Valerian Osinski. During the long night while they were awaiting his hanging at dawn on May 14, 1879, a thrilling scene unfolded involving Osinski and Perovskaya's old friend and housemate, Sofia Leshern. In the early morning hours before the guards came to take Osinski to the scaffold, the sound of their voices echoed back and forth across the yard between the men's and women's cell blocks in the Kiev prison. Over and over, they called out to each other, "Valerian!" . . . "Sonia!" Other "politicals" housed in the same cell blocks overheard them. After Osinski's execution, accounts of his haunting last duet with Leshern rapidly made the rounds of the terrorists living in the underground.[433]

Chain smoking Olga Lyubatovich, a former flaming nihilist turned terrorist, fell deeply in love with the man who was, at the time, the leading writer of propaganda in support of Russian terrorism. This was the boyish, skinny Nikolai "Sparrow" Morozov. The attraction was immediate as soon as she was introduced to "Sparrow" by Kravchinsky. Lyubatovich found herself irresistibly attracted to his poetic character, his love of nature, and his renunciation of the wealth to which he had been born. By the winter of 1879-80, the two of them were living together, first in a St. Petersburg underground safe house apartment, and then while on the run after the safe house was busted. During this time, Morozov was one of the main editors of the Narodnaya Volya newspaper. Lyubatovich became pregnant. Morozov split with Tikhomirov over party doctrine, with Morozov continuing to advocate the anarchism of Bakhunin, while Tikhomirov urged a "centralist" approach, also called "Jacobin" because it was reminiscent of the French Revolution, whereby the terrorists would seek to take the reins of power and exercise total control. Morozov became angered at the support Tikhomirov's "Jacobin" views received from Zhelyabov and others, and as a result, he and Lyubatovich left Russia to go to Switzerland. In Switzerland, Lyubatovich gave birth to a daughter.[434]

The terrorist leadership dabbled in matchmaking. Sofia Ivanova, an early adherent of the terrorist faction of Zemlya i Volya that developed into Narodnaya Volya, was stationed in a safe house in Lesnoi as the fictitious "wife" of Alexander Kviatkovski after her escape from exile in early 1879. The two of them were supposed to pose as tourists. Kviatkovski was already in a "real" marriage. In fact, he already had a son with a "Sixties woman" who had declined to go underground. But Ivanova developed a thing for her pretend spouse, whom the conspirators affectionately nicknamed "Alexander the First." She, too, rapidly became pregnant. Kviatkovski and Ivanova lived together in the Lesnoi flat until September 1879, when Ivanova was reassigned by the Narodnaya Volya Executive Committee to act as the fictitious spouse of Nikolai Bukh. Her job, and that of Bukh, was running the Narodnaya Volya printing press. However, in that capacity she continued to work intimately with "Alexander the First," who acted as the sole liaison between the writers and the printing operation. This went on until Kviatkovski was captured on November 24, 1879. Not long after his capture, Ivanova gave birth to a boy. Ivanova was captured two months later at the Narodnaya Volya printing press safe house. The arrest came after a bloody gun battle in which terrorists held off police officers by firing from within the flat that housed the Narodnaya Volya printing press, while Ivanova frantically burned incriminating evidence. The boy was allowed to stay with Ivanova in jail until her trial, but then he wound up being raised by Kviatkovski's sister. He died at the age of four.[435]

Tatiana "Tanya" Lebedeva was upset with Mikhail Frolenko because Frolenko did not invite her to attend the proto-terrorist gathering at Lipetsk in June 1879. She felt she was every bit as hard core a terrorist as Frolenko and the other future Narodnaya Volya Executive Committee members. She was still miffed with him in the fall of that year, when the two of them were assigned by the Executive Committee to act as each other's fictitious spouses in connection with the Odessa prong of the attack on the Tsar's train. While playing her role as his wife in the small town of Gnilyakov, Tanya found herself warming to the clever Frolenko. The two of them became passionate lovers. After this first Odessa attempt was aborted and Frolenko gave up his position as a railroad guard, Tanya traveled with Frolenko to Tula, south of Moscow, where they got married "for real." The couple returned to St. Petersburg where they continued living together and working for Narodnaya Volya.[436]

Nikolai Kolodkevitch was one of the original Lipetsk conspirators in Narodnaya Volya. His code name within the organization was the "Purring Cat." The "Purring Cat" had a great thick beard, black hair and flashing deep blue eyes. Gessia "Jessy" Helfman, herself an attractive young Jewish woman and a devoted servant of Narodnaya Volya, fell in love with the "Purring Cat." She became pregnant sometime around the beginning of 1881.[437]

We cannot say for sure exactly when Sofia Perovskaya finally abandoned her celibacy, for which she was justly famed within the radical movement. However, after she became a terrorist, she, too, climbed aboard the "couples" bandwagon. When she finally chose a sex partner, it was the unquestioned alpha male within Narodnaya Volya: the giant, strikingly handsome[438] and articulate Andrei Zhelyabov. Zhelyabov, as mentioned, had a wife and son whom he had abandoned when he decided to go underground. There are hints that he womanized to a degree even before this "divorce." But whereas the old Sonia had looked upon any such promiscuous behavior with a piercing disapproval, now she poured her enormous energy into her own sexual and emotional relationship with "Boris." By the time she returned to St. Petersburg after the unsuccessful grocery shop tunneling attempt against the Tsar in Odessa in April of 1880, she allowed others within Narodnaya Volya to learn that she was deeply in love with him.

Sonia moved into a flat in St. Petersburg with Rina Epstein, a young woman who was in sympathy with the radical "movement" but who remained within its broader non-terrorist group. Rina refused to become personally involved in terrorism beyond helping smuggle illegals across the border into and out of Russia. In September of 1880, Epstein moved out of the flat. Zhelyabov moved in inconspicuously as Sonia's "brother."[439] Sofia had the false identity papers of a widow who had moved away, "Sofia Andreyevna Voinova," while Zhelyabov was stealing the identity of an actual "Ivan Ivanovich Slotvinsky." "Slotvinsky" claimed to be retired from military service.[440]

The details of the relationship between Perovskaya and Zhelyabov remain shrouded.[441] Was it an enactment of Vera Pavlovna and Dmitri Lopukhov? Or was it Vera and Sasha Kirsanov? No writing survives from either of them discussing their love life. Thus some, such as Sonia's real brother Vasily, could doubt that there was ever a sexual relationship at all. "Sonia's view on marriage was that it was not for her, although she did not condemn it for everyone. She did not see how she could be happily married while friends were being hung and killed and while the population was suffering under the rule of an autocracy."[442] Vasily acknowledges, however, that Sonia had feelings for Zhelyabov. Vasily's last contact with Sonia, from which he reported this discussion, was in the fall of 1879, before the Moscow train bombing. So it is most likely that the reported conversation with Sonia came at a time when she was still struggling within herself, and had not yet given herself up to a complete physical liaison with "Boris."

Sonia, in her dealings with other "revolutionaries" who lived and worked around the two of them in 1880 and 1881, always spoke calmly and without the slightest trace of sentimentality. However, her fellow devotees of Narodnaya Volya were sure that Zhelyabov was Sonia's "great, one and only love."[443] Figner, who herself remained celibate, wrote that Zhelyabov awoke Perovskaya's "warmest admiration and enthusiasm."[444] The most direct account of the dimensions of the love affair between Sonia and Boris is that of Tikhomirov. However, his voice is inconsistent and not entirely credible. For Perovskaya he retained a twinge of the bittersweet sentiments of a rejected suitor who had settled for marrying a second choice. In some of his memoirs Tikhomirov would speak disparagingly of Sonia, as well as Olga Schleisner, the wife of Mark Natanson, by calling them: "Typical women! Not very smart, but what fanaticism, self-assurance and willpower, the latter to be sure in its lowest denominator: obstinacy. Something will get into their heads and you will not dig it out even with a scalpel." And for Sonia, he injected into his discussion a strong palliative dose of egoism. "With her character, she needed a man who would make her his slave, and I was not the type."[445]

Regardless, Tikhomirov's memoirs describe Sonia's life, from the beginning of 1880, as her "year of love." He comments that, "if he is not mistaken," Zhelyabov was the one person, and the only person, with whom she ever fell in love. His depiction of Sonia's love affair with Zhelyabov is actually found in his narrative on "Boris," one of the few former Narodnaya Volya comrades towards whom he was complimentary.

> Sofia was for Zhelyabov his 'wife' in the sense in which he understood the term. . . It meant a great deal to him. He valued her intelligence and character, and as a colleague in the cause she was incomparable. Of course one can't talk of 'happiness.' There was constant anxiety – not for themselves but for each other – continual preoccupations, an increasing flood of work which meant that they could scarcely ever be alone, the certainty that sooner or later there was bound to come a tragic ending. And yet there were times, when work was going well, when they were able to forget for a while, and then it was a joy to see them, especially her. Her feelings were so overwhelming that in any but Sofia it would have crowded out all thoughts of her work.

He added,

She had always been a strong feminist and maintained that men were the inferior sex. She had real respect for very few of them. But Zhelyabov was up to her caliber. She was utterly in love with him, in a way I never thought could happen to her with any other man.[446]

Sonia would not hear of any relenting in the face of the political moderation now being shown by the Tsar's government. She already had been exposed to Loris-Melikov while he was serving as governor-general of Odessa. She scorned his reputation as a liberal. Perovskaya was well aware that Loris-Melikov, whatever his political beliefs, was a hard-nosed, implacable enemy of terrorism. Her haste to proceed with the decreed "execution" of Alexander before he could return to his "tsar-liberator" persona under the guidance of Loris-Melikov actually became even more urgent. She did not want sympathizers to "fall on their knees" before such an initiative. Under pressure from Sonia, "Boris" organized a new assassination of Alexander to occur in August, 1880. The plan this time was to explode two sunken waterproof bombs underneath a stone bridge when the Tsar's horse carriage crossed over it while he was on his way out of the city. As had happened with Zhelyabov's attempt before, the bombs did not go off. Zhelyabov blamed the failure on one of the Narodnaya Volya co-conspirators, Makar Teterka, showing up late.[447] After crossing the bridge, Alexander left St. Petersburg with Katia for the stay in the Crimea already discussed above, making any immediate further efforts at his assassination impossible.

Narodnaya Volya, with Zhelyabov and Perovskaya now working intimately as partners in its innermost leadership circle, attained success of real substance in infiltrating important constituencies in Russian society. These feats were leveraged on the repute that the Executive Committee had attained due to its two high profile attacks on the Tsar. This added to their credibility among the disaffected. In part, the successes became possible because the government under Loris-Melikov had loosened the previous prohibitions on things like worker meetings. With the approval of the Executive Committee, "Boris" and Sonia started a new "Worker's Section," emulating the model formerly used by Khalturin. The city of St. Petersburg was divided into three districts, one of which was personally headed by Perovskaya. In each district they started by identifying workers who would commit to the cause. These were then sent into the factories to form cells of other disaffected workers. Zhelyabov played the role of an inspirational speaker, appearing unexpectedly at worker events and whipping the attendees into a frenzy of faith and fury with his impassioned, eloquent speeches.

Kamenni Bridge, which Narodnaya Volya planned to blow up underneath the Emperor in August 1880.
photo by the author

By the end of 1880, Zhelyabov and Perovskaya had identified a core of twenty leaders among the workers, who were willing to take on the role of group leaders, and they claimed to have

250 "members" of the Worker's Section in total among St. Petersburg's factories. A new underground worker's gazette was started which, in contrast to Tikhomirov's intellectual Narodnaya Volya, concentrated on printing propaganda aimed at workers.[448]

What is more, the Executive Committee led by Perovskaya and Zhelyabov penetrated deep inside the Russian armed forces. In this they were greatly aided by the "Janitor's" recruitment of Nikolai Sukhonov. The same age as Sonia, Sukhonov was the son of a doctor and a graduate of the Russian Naval Academy. By 1880 he had become a capable and experienced naval officer who was promoted to lieutenant and placed in charge of the Naval Electrical Institute in St. Petersburg. However, he manifested the temperament of a "revolutionary." The "Janitor" introduced Sukhonov into the Executive Committee, and he rapidly showed himself to be just as dedicated as its other fanatical members. Sukhonov undertook to identify other officers in the Russian armed forces who were "reliable" enough to be approached on behalf of the terrorist cause.

Shortly after Zhelyabov's failed bridge bombing assassination attempt, Sukhonov arranged for a group of 20 officers, whom he felt that he could identify as "safe," to attend a secret meeting in his quarters. Zhelyabov made a surprise appearance in this meeting. "Boris" went on to make one of the more stirring speeches of his career. He painted a dire picture of the sufferings of workmen and peasants. He described the alleged official indifference to any attempt to ameliorate their situation. He then rhetorically asked if the officers were prepared to see the Russian people exposed to this maltreatment without making any effort to improve it.

Some of the officers in attendance for Zhelyabov's speech went on to help form the "Fighting Services Section" of Narodnaya Volya. This was a web of sleeper cells. Groups of disloyal officers were formed in the garrison towns of the

Empire. These groups reported solely to a "central military group" formed by Sukhonov's secret cell of officers in St. Petersburg. The "central military group," in turn, was solely in touch with Zhelyabov, Perovskaya, and the "Purring Cat," Kolodkevitch. No one else knew the identity of any of the traitors. They were instructed not to propagandize in any way. Their sole duty was to identify other officers, as well as men in the ranks, who were potentially disloyal. To prevent the organization from being compromised, a rule was decreed that none of the officers could participate at all in any of Narodnaya Volya's terrorist acts.[449]

Narodnaya Volya was now at the apex of its political power. It had before it a very rational and effective strategy of continuing to build strength within the workers and military, while waiting to see what would happen with Loris-Melikov's reforms. If Alexander vacillated by failing to follow through, or by repealing liberties he had granted at the recommendation of Loris-Melikov, and if he instead turned back in the direction of the reactionary faction, then the "revolutionaries" could utilize their strength to call for an uprising, and in doing so could expect to receive the financial backing and sympathy of a significant portion of the Russian intelligentsia and the more liberal elements of the Russian ruling class. Many on the Executive Committee favored this strategy. But the key Narodnaya Volya leader who would stubbornly reject any strategy of survival and prolonged confrontation, the key force who would instead insist on keeping the terrorist vow of an impassioned embrace with the Lady in Black, was Sofia Perovskaya.

The Russian government intended to conduct a prosecution of the revolutionaries it had in custody, centered around Goldenberg as its star witness. But, because of Kletochnikov, the terrorists knew Goldenberg was providing very damaging information to his interrogators. Aron Zundelevich, a sort of business manager for Narodnaya Volya, had been captured in December of 1879. He was incarcerated in the Peter and Paul Fortress along with Goldenberg in the early summer of 1880. He received an order to silence Goldenberg. He managed to pass a coded message to Goldenberg, stating "Death to the Traitor." Goldenberg had worked personally with Zundelevich, and the two shared a bond within the revolutionary movement because of their common Jewish heritage. When Goldenberg received the message, he reacted strongly. He insisted on being allowed to meet with Zundelevich. He promised the prosecutors that he would influence Zundelevich in the effort to negotiate an end to terrorism. Nothing of the sort ever happened. His meetings with Zundelevich had a far more profound influence on Goldenberg. On July 15, 1880, after his second meeting with Zundelevich, Goldenberg fashioned a rope from strips of a towel and hung himself from a bar of his cell.[450]

Prosecutors nevertheless possessed 500 invaluable pages of detailed deposition testimony from Goldenberg. They determined to use them to put the terrorists on trial. On October 25, 1880, the trial of 16 defendants finally commenced. The most high profile defendant was Alexander Kviatkovski, because of his membership on Narodnaya Volya's Executive Committee, because of his direct support of the Solovyev assassination attempt, and because of his role in planning the Winter Palace bombing. Kviatkovski used the forum that the trial provided to deliver a long speech over the course of two days, explaining and justifying the terrorist position. The remainder of the defendants generally acted defiantly, some in a more vocal manner than others. Given their admitted involvement in murder, as well as their hostile attitude, there could be little doubt about the outcome. Andrei Presnyakov, another member of Narodnaya Volya who had carried out the murder of a police informant, said in court, as his last statement, that he "admitted his solidarity with Narodnaya Volya and shared in its ideals."[451]

The actual sentences were not quite as harsh as they could have been. The two most high profile terrorists, Kviatkovski and Presnyakov, were sentenced to die by hanging.[452] However, the hangings would not be carried out in public, but within the penal facility with only selected witnesses in attendance. Despite the fact, proved by Goldenberg's deposition and essentially admitted, that most of the remaining 14 defendants were also willing participants in the terrorist conspiracy to assassinate the Tsar and other high government officials, they were sentenced only to terms of imprisonment. Sofia Ivanova was denied her plea to die alongside Kviatkovski. Instead, she was sentenced to four years of hard labor.[453] Kviatkovski and Presnyakov died shortly after dawn on November 5, 1880.[454] Although they had lived several years in open expectation of the noose,[455] the actual moment still proved an emotional wrench. A Russian general in attendance wrote in his journal:[456]

> They took communion, having held the priest in their arms. Then, their hands tied, they bowed and saluted the troops. When Kviatkovsky was dangling at the end of his cord, Presnyakov shed some tears. The same fate awaited him, one minute later. It was a chilling impression! I had not one bit of sympathy for the nihilists, but the punishment was atrocious.

Chapter 18: "Our Girls Are Fiercer Than Our Men"

For Sofia Perovskaya, news of the executions behind prison walls bolstered her determination to sacrifice all else to carry out a dramatic killing of the Tsar. At a meeting of the full Narodnaya Volya Executive Committee, Sonia took the lead in stifling a renewed push by her lover Zhelyabov, and others, for "postponement." Maria Olovennikova, who was in attendance, left the following account.[457]

> There was a good deal of argument over the renewal of terrorist activity. It was clear that it would mean that our other activities would suffer: we would have to devote all our resources to terrorism. Mikhailov took pains to emphasize the importance of the other sides of our work. So did Zhelyabov. He realized the difficulties we were up against better than anyone else. Tikhomirov as usual agreed with the

majority. Perovskaya was all out for terrorism, whatever the cost.

Nikolai Kibalchich, who was also in attendance in this meeting, later summed up the role of Perovskaya and Yakimova in a phrase. "Our girls are fiercer than our men."[458] He added some more comments which shed light on Perovskaya's character. "Perovskaya has the same kind of hatred as Mikhailov, only with a different nuance, more befitting a woman. But she does not show it as clearly as he does. This feeling is noticeable in her movements, in the attention with which she follows the Tsar's movements. In Mikhailov it is strong and steady, in Perovskaya it is sharper, deeper and more vehement."[459]

A former Sixties radical writing in 1906 amplified the terms in which Perovskaya, during this period, had explained her thought process relative to what would be by terrorism.

> I asked her about the seizure of power. She clapped her hands in comic amazement, since this question was raised only by those who did not belong to the organization. Her own personal view was that no program could dictate what would happen. Not to seize control would be to concede to the enemy. But the seizure of power, though desirable, was not a fundamental point in their program. Their opponents would claim that they were 'Jacobins,' but 'our motto, "The People's Will," is not a mere phrase, it actually expresses the essence of our ideas, since in everything we are prepared to submit to the will of the people, expressed freely and clearly. But in the name of this, another problem arises for a revolutionary party, quite apart from the present direct battle with the contemporary political structure; that is to create, after the downfall of this structure, the social conditions in which the people would have the opportunity of expressing freely their will and realizing it . . . .

The conversation then touched on political terror, and the causes that had forced it to play such an important part in Narodnaya Volya. 'Revenge is a personal issue here,' she said. 'One can justify it, and with some difficulty, as a terrorist act committed on the individual initiative of separate people, but not by an organized party. Our revolutionary history does not recognize these acts, apart from situations of self-defense. It would be impossible to organize a party around the banner of revenge – or to attract any public sympathy, something that we must make use of. That first shot fired by Vera Zasulitch was not revenge, but an act of retaliation against an insult to human dignity. That is how it was understood by everybody, and that is also how it was understood at her trial by the representatives of the public conscience.'

'The political history of nations presents eloquent evidence that everywhere where the agents of the government are not answerable to the law for their actions, people will take the law into their own hands to counteract this, and at certain periods a revolutionary administration of justice will arise. But we cannot use this formula of retaliation to justify the aims and methods of Russian revolutionary terror. By elevating it into a systematic method of struggle, the Party uses it as a powerful means of agitation, and as the most effective way of throwing the government into confusion, holding it under the sword of Damocles, and forcing it to make important concessions. All other paths are prohibited to us – prohibited by the government itself.'[460]

Even Olovennikova, a stalwart Sixties radical, was stunned at the degree to which it appeared Perovskaya and those who shared her views within Narodnaya Volya had lost touch with any semblance of political reality. "All they can talk about now is dynamite." She saw the party as bent on a suicidal course.[461]

Upon the Tsar's return to the capital from Livadia five days after Kviatkovski's hanging, Sonia personally assumed command of scouting Alexander to see exactly how, and when, he might be vulnerable to attack. She assembled a squad of six volunteers, acting under her supervision. Each day they went out in pairs to watch for the Emperor's appearances in town, to follow his routes, and to understand his tendencies.[462]

The "Janitor," Mikhailov, determined to carry on with the revolutionaries' practice of publicizing their dead fellow terrorists as martyred heroes. He took snapshot photos of Kviatkovski and Presnyakov to a photo store to get them printed. Mikhailov was unable to enlist a "legal," so he decided to handle the photo reproductions himself. This was a blunder, one especially unusual for the shrewd "Janitor." Understanding the terrorists' propensities, the police had notified all of the photo shops in St. Petersburg to be on the alert. When Mikhailov returned to pick up the photo prints, he fell into a police trap and was captured. This was the strongest blow yet that the Government had registered in its fight against Narodnaya Volya.[463] The cool, calculating Mikhailov, who controlled Kletochnikov, and who coordinated the overall "security," financing and planning of the terrorist operations, could not easily be replaced.

Sonia tried to bolster the ranks by asking Morozov, who had left St. Petersburg right before the Winter Palace bombing to join the radical community in Switzerland after losing what amounted to a power struggle with Tikhomirov, to return to Russia to rejoin Narodnaya Volya. Morozov felt close to Sonia. The two had sat together when they were co-defendants during the Trial of the 193. Sonia's political beliefs also leaned more toward Morozov's anarchist political philosophy than toward Tikhomirov's more "centralist" theories. Morozov responded to her appeal. In January 1881, Morozov left behind Olga Lyubatovich and their newborn daughter in order to make the journey back to Russia. A few days after his departure, Lyubatovich received word that her lover had been been arrested at the border. She was stunned and anguished. Her nursing baby cried all night. The next morning Serge Kravchinsky volunteered to go to Russia and figure out how to free Morozov. Olga refused this. Instead, she vowed to go personally, leaving the baby behind. It was arranged to leave the girl with Serge Podolinsky, a radical doctor who already had three children under his care. When Lyubatovich walked out on her daughter asleep in a crib, her heart was "petrified with sadness." She later wrote, "It is a sin for a revolutionary to start a family."

Olga's return to Russia to follow Morozov was a pitiful and abject failure. While Olga was aboard the train headed to Russia, her milk kept emerging in her breasts and she had no way to release it. The liquid buildup caused her pain, inflammation and fever. The little girl she had left behind quickly contracted meningitis. She died within two weeks after her mother's departure.[464]

The loss of Mikhailov left Perovskaya and Zhelyabov in an even more central role within the ranks of Narodnaya Volya. The group badly needed new blood for their next project. They sought new recruits from the ranks of the "Workers Section." However, Zhelyabov was far less astute than Mikhailov. Many of the new people he brought in turned out to be less dependable and reliable than their incarcerated or deceased predecessors. For instance, Zhelyabov recruited an Odessa carpenter named Vasily Merkulov, who assisted with the tunneling plot there, led by Perovskaya and Figner, in the spring of 1880. Merkulov turned out to be difficult. He was prone to complaining and finding fault, making him irritating for others to work with. He resented the role of intellectuals, as opposed to workers, in controlling the "movement."[465]

In December of 1880, Merkulov was sent on a mission to Kishinev, 200 kilometers northwest of Odessa in territory that is now part of Moldavia. There he was assigned to assist Frolenko and Lebedeva. Using the fake name "Mironenko," the Narodnaya Volya couple had rented a house together that was adjacent to the state treasury. The intent was to tunnel from their cellar into the treasury cellar in order to steal cash stored there. However, for reasons we do not know, the plan did not succeed and had to be abandoned. In January 1881 the "Mironenkos" cleared out and, with Merkulov, made their way back to St. Petersburg. Upon their return, Lebedeva blamed Merkulov for the plan's failure, while Merkulov blamed Frolenko.[466]

Kishinev marked Narodnaya Volya's latest attempt to address an increasingly urgent problem, the need to raise money to finance its many and varied nefarious activities. As is typical for terrorists, their plots had became far too intricate, and their identities had become far too clandestine, to permit them to hold down paying jobs. For several years, Zemlya i Volya derived a large proportion of its funding from the personal fortune of Dmitri Lizogub. Lizogub was a scion of a wealthy landowning family in Cernigov, located in northern Ukraine near the border with Belarus. His father, in addition to being a multi-millionaire, had been a liberal who worked for the abolition of serfdom. Lizogub became a member of Chaikovsky circle in 1873-74. He was not handsome. He was tall, pale and somewhat slim. He had long eyebrows, from underneath which there peered large blue eyes. His smile had something infantile about it. His voice was somewhat slow in utterance and always pitched in the same key. Kravchinsky describes him as "very poorly clad," wearing a linen jacket with large wooden buttons, which "from much wear and tear seemed a mere rag." A "worn-out black cloth waistcoat covered his chest to the throat." From his appearance one would never have guessed that he was a millionaire.[467]

Lizogub was intimately associated with Valerian Osinski, and became a principal financier for the Osinski's "disorganizing" exploits. Although he did not personally engage in any terrorist acts, his connection to the "Southern" terrorists became known to the authorities, and he was placed under tight surveillance. Lizogub came up with a plan to liquidate his assets and dispense the proceeds through an attorney friend named Vladimir Drigo.

On July 30, 1878, Lizogub was arrested in an Odessa brewery while in the company of two other revolutionaries. After Lizogub's arrest, Drigo stopped further disbursements of Lizogub's fortune. The "Janitor," in response, pursued bringing Drigo to heel. Drigo schemed with the police to set a trap for the "Janitor," but Mikhailov smelled it out. Drigo himself wound up being arrested and incarcerated. Eventually, he was, rather ironically, put on trial as one of the November 1880 "Kviatkovski" group of 16 defendants. Meanwhile, as a result of information from Drigo and from Feodor Kuritsyn, who had been placed as Lizogub's cell mate similar to the way he was later placed with Goldenberg, the authorities confirmed everything they needed to know about the enormity of Lizogub's financial support for the terrorist movement. Lizogub was surprised to learn that a noose awaited his neck. He was hanged publicly in Odessa on August 10, 1879.[468]

After Mikhailov's arrest at the end of November 1880, Narodnaya Volya's finances became extremely tight. The group enjoyed a great deal of prestige among elements of society, such as students and workers, who were not in a position to provide any significant degree of financial support. Additionally, Zhelyabov lacked the deftness of Alexander Mikhailov. His methods of fund raising were focused on a small scale, and they were heavy handed. Zhelyabov recruited a 19-year old apprentice named Nikolai Rysakov into the movement. Young Rysakov was "completely dazzled" by the charismatic Zhelyabov, who now went by a new nickname among his admirers – they called him "Taras," after a mythical hero. "Taras" insistently exacted from Rysakov the meager funds that Rysakov's rather poor and hard-working family had scraped together to send him to support his apprenticeship in the capital. Zhelyabov required Rysakov to take out an advance of 90 rubles – three months' allowance – from his father's employer, and to hand 50 rubles of that sum over to Narodnaya Volya.[469]

Using her scouts, Sonia observed that the government had become very security oriented in the wake of the three known assassination attempts against the Tsar during the last two years. The Tsar's daily schedule was constantly changed. Everywhere he went, he traveled at top speed in a carriage drawn by a team of horses. The carriage was also escorted by five to seven mounted Cossack guards. He was, in short, a protected and difficult target. However, on Sunday, Alexander almost always visited the Mikhailovsky Manège, a St. Petersburg cavalry parade ground, for the changing of the guard which occurred at noon. His normal route for traveling the ten or so city blocks to get to the Manège from the Winter Palace took him along a street called Malaya Sadovaya.

Narodnaya Volya's "Executive Committee," led by Perovskaya, decided on a new plan for attacking the Tsar. Sonia's fingerprints are all over the plan from its inception. In its essentials, it was a replay of the same mine attack she had already spearheaded twice before, at Moscow and at Odessa. The terrorists would open a phony "cheese shop" in Malaya Sadovaya; they would then tunnel from its basement beneath the street to place a bomb where it could be exploded under Alexander as he passed overhead on a Sunday.

Yuri Nikolaevitch Bogdanovich, a friend of Figner, was selected for the part of the cheese merchant. Bogdanovich, typical of the Narodnaya Volya extremist, was from a noble landowning family in Pskov. But he relished playing the role of the peasant shopkeeper, and he made sure to look and talk the part. Perovskaya nominated herself to serve as his fictitious shopkeeper wife, the same role she had played previously in

Moscow and Odessa. But she was overruled by the group. Instead, this time "Baska" Yakimova was selected to play the role of the shopkeeper's wife. She and Bogdanovich assumed the family name of "Kobozev," and got in touch with the landlord's agent. After some negotiation they agreed to take the partially subterranean space at an annual rent of 1,200 rubles. They were unable to move in at once, as two of the rooms had been damaged by recent floods and were being repaired, but they signed the lease and paid a deposit of fifty rubles. The landlord's agent reported the curious nature and behavior of the "Kobozevs" to the police. The police checked with Voronezh, the place of their passport's issue. But the terrorists had become very sophisticated in their handling of falsified identity documents. The confirmation came back that Yovdokim Yermolayev Kobozev, a lower middle class citizen, had indeed received this document. The plasterers finished the repairs, and the couple moved into their new premises shortly after January 1, 1881.[470] Tunneling underneath the street swiftly got under way. All of the available Narodnaya Volya men who were in St. Petersburg, except Tikhomirov, participated. They worked around the clock in shifts. The dirt extracted from the mine was hidden inside empty cheese barrels. When Frolenko, Lebedeva and Merkulov returned to St. Petersburg from the Kishinev expedition, they too were pressed into service as diggers. However, Merkulov proved so difficult and resistant to taking orders that Bogdanovich ultimately had to get rid of him as a worker.[471]

Yuri and "Baska" were convincing in their subterfuge of pretending to be a country couple. "But," according to Figner, "from a commercial point of view they were both incompetent, and the neighboring tradesmen at once decided that the newcomers could not be dangerous rivals." In addition to this, Narodnaya Volya's supply of money remained so low during January and February, the terrorists could buy few cheeses with which to stock the "store." So meager were their funds for this purpose, when Vera Figner secured from wealthy sympathizers 300 rubles with which to purchase stock, it was regarded by the conspirators as a stroke of great fortune.[472]

Narodnaya Volya was now experienced with digging tunnels. The work progressed fairly swiftly, but ran against two obstacles underneath the Malaya Sadovaya. The first was a cast iron water pipe, which the terrorists successfully manuevered around, but the second was a larger wooden box-like structure. They could not go over it, because it was too close to the surface, and they could not go under it, because the St. Petersburg water table was too high. They reluctantly decided to cut through it. They were rapidly overcome by the stench that emerged, for the wooden box was in fact a sewer. Undeterred, the digging crew managed to seal off the bottom half of the box, in which the sewage was flowing, covering it with a fabric cover, and proceeded with digging the hole through the top half. The entire cheese shop was permeated with the smell. The diggers began wearing improvised respirators fashioned out of cotton soaked with a chemical.[473]

In the midst of work on the Malaya Sadovaya mine, Narodnaya Volya received an unexpected message from a ghost. On a frigid January night Isaev, who was then posing as Vera Figner's fictitious husband, walked into the apartment where she and two other Executive Committee members were sitting and placed before them a 2.5 centimeter wide scroll of paper. He said to them unemotionally, as if there was nothing extraordinary in it: "From Nechaev, from the Ravelin."

Sergei Nechaev had not been heard of by anyone on the outside for eight long years. For Perovskaya, Figner and the others, who had been in their teens at the time, Nechaev's name evoked mainly the grisly memory of his infamous murder of Ivanov. In the intervening years, however, these former Chaikovsky participants had come full circle. The Narodnaya Volya "Executive Committee" now embraced an outlook and ruthless methodology very reminiscent of that advocated in

Nechaev's *Catechism of a Revolutionary*. For instance, the third edition of the underground bulletin of Narodnaya Volya had published a set of "program guidelines" that was taken directly from Nechaev's *Catechism*.[474] The new terrorists jumped to attention with respect the moment they received the old terrorist's message.

This whole time, Nechaev had been held principally in secret solitary confinement in the Alexei Ravelin, a maximum security wing of the Peter and Paul Fortress. There he was bound with chains. But even though locked down within Russia's most impenetrable dungeon, he proved able to use his strange snake charming personality to perfection. Even in chains, he retained a sinister capacity to bend weaker minds to his will. For the prison staff it was strictly forbidden to say even one word to the unmentionable Nechaev. But with stubborn will, persistence and determination, Nechaev slowly induced many of the officers in his unit, one by one, to bend this rule. Once started on the road to hell, they moved on to speaking with him in full-fledged conversation. Sergei probed and catalogued each guard's personality and weaknesses. He also capitalized on awe for Narodnaya Volya's high profile terror strikes, and the resulting public notoriety. Even high government officials, including Loris-Melikov, paid him occasional visits in an attempt to win him over to assist in fighting the terrorist contagion. Nechaev used the buzz surrounding these visits to impress the officers with his aura of importance. To those he sensed to be wavering in his favor, he whispered that he was a martyr suffering for them, for their fathers and brothers, for truth and justice. Very slowly, always dealing with them separately, always keeping them ignorant of the progress he might be making in turning others, Nechaev cultivated his own "staff" of followers among the prison guards. The "staff" called him by a nickname -- "the Eagle." This was the same title Chernyshevsky in *What Is to Be Done?* gave to his mysterious strong man, Rakhmetov.

Even as he was cultivating his "staff," the Eagle also engaged the prison wardens. Loudly and constantly he protested his degree of isolation. He went on hunger strikes. He threatened suicide. Eventually the prison commanders, too, relented, and began providing Nechaev with access to some of his requested reading materials.[475]

Stepan Shiraev was a member of Narodnaya Volya's Executive Committee who had served as one of Perovskaya's workers in digging the Moscow tunnel and in arming the mine for the resultant train explosion. Following his conviction and sentence of imprisonment in the Trial of the 16 in October 1880, Shiraev was transferred to solitary confinement in the Alexei Ravelin. "The Eagle" soon learned of Shiraev's presence in the unit. Using Nechaev's "staff," the two men were able to communicate. Through contact information gleaned from Shiraev, Nechaev for the first time figured out a way to arrange to smuggle messages to the Executive Committee of Narodnaya Volya in the person of Grigory Isaev.[476]

Nechaev's first message to the Executive Committee was very straightforward. Basically, it was a simple "help me get out of here." When it was received, the Executive Committee was deeply moved and impressed. With "unusual emotion" all of its members unanimously resolved at once that "he must be freed." Detailed messages were exchanged in which Nechaev set forth several scenarios for helping him escape from the Peter and Paul Fortress. At least one plan, involving Nechaev's escape through a sewer pipe, was investigated to the point that Zhelyabov actually went to observe the outlet of the pipe in question. But Zhelyabov concluded the plan would not work because the pipe was too long and anyone trying to get through it would suffocate. Other possibilities were considered. But the ultimate response Narodnaya Volya gave to "the Eagle" was that it was busy devoting all of its energy and resources to its terror attack on Tsar Alexander II. Freeing Nechaev would have to be the next order of business, as soon as the assassination was carried out.

Once the line of communication was open, many more intricately coded messages were received from "the Eagle." Nechaev described in hieroglyphics the methods he had used to acquire his influence. He transmitted detailed information about the fortress in which he was held. He told lurid stories of brutality within its walls. Above all, Nechaev sent detailed directives on matters such as how to handle his "staff," and how to bring about and conduct the revolutionary dictatorship after Alexander's death. Some of the advice for his protégés can only be described as classic Nechaev. For instance, he urged Narodnaya Volya to publicly exaggerate its numbers by a factor of at least two orders of magnitude – i.e., to represent itself at not less than one hundred times its true strength. He advocated a variety of plots for sowing deception. One was to distribute fake news – reporting an imperial *ukase* decreeing that all serfs should be returned to their former masters. For Zhelyabov, he professed his utmost admiration. He suggested that Zhelyabov should become the revolutionary dictator.[477] This cleverly appealed to Zhelyabov's own fantasies.[478]

On January 28, 1881, Loris-Melikov presented Alexander with an official memorandum detailing his accomplishments to date, as well as his planned reforms. In this memorandum he covered his abolition of the Third Section and his abolition of the highly regressive salt tax. [479] The number of peasant disturbances during the period of his stewardship, in 1880, had declined substantially, he noted. The time was right, he went on, to proceed with a new set of reforms. He proposed to involve representatives of local society in formulating the details of new laws. The reforms would be carried out under the authority of "His Majesty's will," and certainly would not amount to a full-fledged Western style democracy, but the initiative would nevertheless be a diligent effort to secure participation and input from concerned citizens. From the citizens, there would be drawn one committee on administrative reforms, and a second commission on financial reforms. The memorandum was discussed in Alexander's high council of state, the equivalent of his cabinet, on February 5. Despite the private reservations of conservatives, the meeting ended with general approval of Loris-Melikov's proposals.[480]

Loris-Melikov could also point with pride to the progress that had been made by his administration in catching terrorists. The authorities had wisely refrained from engaging in a mass execution of the defendants in the Trial of the 16. Instead, they commuted three of the five death sentences to life imprisonment with hard labor. One of the convicts thus spared was Ivan Fedorovich Okladsky. Okladsky was not a quintessential terrorist. Rather, he was more in the profile of what, in the post 9-11 world, we can recognize under the rubric of a "muscle hijacker." He was basically a workingman who was recruited into the ranks of terrorist schemes by Andrei Zhelyabov and then remained under the influence of Zhelyabov's magnetic personality. Okladsky enthusiastically participated in numerous Narodnaya Volya exploits, in which he made himself very useful. But he differed from the typical terrorist profile in that he was not frought with class guilt, he was not an ascetic, and he was not suicidal. Throughout the Trial of the 16, he remained just as defiant as the other defendants. But in the trial's aftermath, in December 1880, he agreed to cooperate with the authorities. At first he declined to give any names (and, it is possible that he did not know any of the real names), but he did agree to assist in identifying the safe houses of the remaining outlaws.[481] He also helped immensely by acting as an eyewitness to verify the identities of suspected terrorists, including Mikhailov, once they were captured.

As a result of information provided by Okladsky, on January 25, 1881, the St. Petersburg police captured Mikhailov's longtime friend, Alexander Barannikov. Other important terrorists fell like dominoes. Barannikov was found to have a false passport that revealed his underground residence address. This turned out to be a seven room flat on Kuznechny Lane. It happened to be in the same building where Fyodor Dostoyevsky lived. The flat was placed under surveillance, which promptly bore fruit when the "Purring Cat," Nikolai Kolodkevitch, was spotted and captured there the following day. After Mikhailov's arrest, Kolodkevitch had been assigned the role of Kletochnikov's "handler," meeting with him for debriefings in Kolodkevitch's residence. Now, Kolodkevitch's residence was also discovered and placed under surveillance. Kletochnikov, hurrying to warn Kolodkevitch of Barannikov's capture, walked into an ambush there and was captured on January 28, 1881. This was on the same day when Loris-Melikov was giving his report to Alexander. Narodnaya Volya's "Guardian Angel" was now in custody.[482]

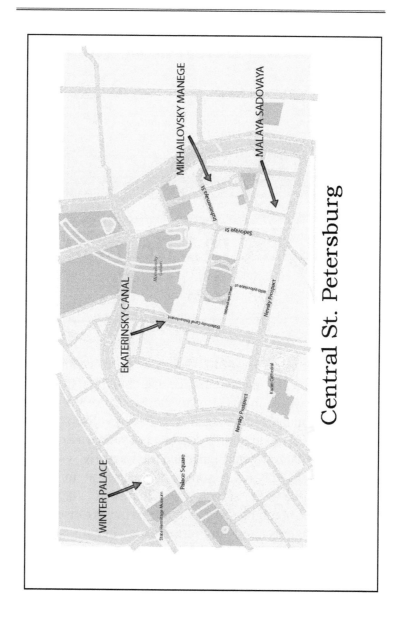

Chapter 19: Death of a Tsar

On February 15, 1881, Alexander followed his normal Sunday routine, taking his carriage and entourage through the Malaya Sadovaya on his way to the Mikhailovsky Manège. There, the tunnel underneath the Malaya Sadovaya was complete and awaited him. But, it had not yet been loaded with a dynamite charge. Vera Figner and the Executive Committee of Narodnaya Volya felt some indignation at this missed opportunity due to the slowness of Kibalchich. As when the Winter Palace bombing was in the works, the terrorists became extremely anxious about any further delay in carrying off the attack.[483] However, Kibalchich was very busy working on a new weapon of destruction, one that would ultimately prove decisive.

Kibalchich was sort of an eccentric "mad scientist." He was constantly trying to improve upon the explosive devices that he was making for terrorist purposes. In early 1881, he modified his prior recipe by producing a new version of his nitroglycerin gel. To this amber colored explosive gel, Kibalchich now added a detonation mechanism that was adapted from one used by the Russian navy. Fleet Lieutenant F. I. Zavalshin, who was studying at the Russian naval mine school at Kronstadt, was also secretly a member of the "Fighting Services" section of Narodnaya Volya. Zavalshin provided Kibalchich with samples of the navy's acid-based detonators. Kibalchich studied and reverse engineered them to suit his purpose, which was a new kind of bomb that would reliably explode when thrown to the ground from a modest height. Grenades had been used in warfare for centuries, but typically they needed to either be equipped with a fuse that had to be lighted, or else fired from large bore ordinance in order to detonate on impact. Neither method would be practical for the sneak attacks typical of terrorists.

Kibalchich combined the military's impact detonator with the extremely volatile nitroglycerine substance to create a new and very powerful bomb that would explode upon hitting the ground. His end product invention would be an oval egg-like shape, weighing about five pounds. Inside would be two needle-like glass tubes filled with fulminate of mercury. Upon the bomb striking a hard object, one or both of the tubes would break. The liquid thus released would set off an immediate chemical reaction that would rapidly ignite the detonator. It sounded like a science fair experiment, which is probably why the Executive Committee declined a request by Zhelyabov to switch to these new bombs as the primary mode of attack on the Tsar. They authorized Kibalchich's new grenades to be used strictly as a backup to the real plan, which remained the dynamite charge to be exploded beneath the Malaya Sadovaya with an electric signal. [484]

In spite of the group's doubts, Perovskaya and Zhelyabov incorporated Kibalchich's new grenade design into their plan for the Malaya Sadovaya attack on Alexander. After the prior experiences with mines and bombs, Perovskaya recognized that the explosion of the mine beneath the Emperor's carriage might not prove fatal. She and Zhelyabov decided to train four of the men in Sofia's squad of "observers" to use Kibalchich's grenades. Two of them would be stationed at each end of the Malaya Sadovaya plaza where the cheese shop was located, prior to the Emperor's passage. After the tunnel explosion, these bomb throwers would rush in and attack the Tsar with the grenades. As the last resort, if all else failed, Zhelyabov would enter the scene and use his size and strength to fight his way into the imperial carriage, where he would personally finish the Tsar with a dagger.

On Friday, February 20 Perovskaya and Zhelyabov for the first time assembled their squad of four "bombers." They met with them in a new Narodnaya Volya safehouse, one run by Nikolai Sablin and Gessia Helfman, posing as a married couple, at number 5 Telezhnaya Street. This apartment had been hastily rented to serve as the command center for the Malaya Sadovaya attack after it was realized that their prior safehouse which was being used for that purpose had been compromised as a result of the January arrests. The four bombers were relative newcomers to Narodnaya Volya, adherents of the "Workers' Section" who had been recruited into the terrorist organization primarily on the strength of Zhelyabov's personal charisma. Perovskaya had used them all as observers, reporting on the Tsar's movements. One of the four was Nikolai Rysakov, the apprentice whom Zhelyabov had previously recruited as discussed above. Timofei Mikhailov was a large, somewhat dim witted young man who had been enlisted out of the ranks of St. Petersburg industrial workers to take the place of Presnyakov in acting as an enforcer for the outlaw group. He did not mind jobs like stabbing spies and beating up people. Ivan Emilianov, tall and lanky, was a technical school student, aged 19. Ignaty Grinevitsky, the fourth, was the only one of the bomb throwers who fit the usual profile of the Narodnaya Volya member. He was 24 years old, the son of a noble Polish landowner. Perovskaya called Grinevitsky by his underground nickname of "Kotik," which means Kitten.[485] The next day, on February 21, Zhelyabov and Kibalchich took the bombers out to a park in the northern part of the city to practice throwing dummy bombs.

Kibalchich was ready to test a prototype of his new grenade by the morning of Saturday, February 28. He arranged to meet Zhelyabov and the four bombers at the corner of Nevsky Prospect and Mikhailovskaya Street to catch a tram to take them to the grounds of a monastery on the eastern outskirts of the city. There they would again practice throwing dummy bombs, as well as a test version of the new grenade. Zhelyabov did not appear for the appointment. After waiting an hour, Kibalchich decided to leave without him. After the bombers took turns practicing throwing the five pound dummy bombs, Timofei Mikhailov volunteered to throw the test grenade. It did explode, but the result was extremely unimpressive. Nevertheless, Kibalchich was satisfied with the experiment. He decided to supervise the assembly of four larger bombs for use in the attack planned for the following day, Sunday, March 1.[486]

The St. Petersburg police had spies of their own, who were capable of reporting news of developments within Narodnaya Volya. One piece of intelligence they received in February of 1881 was that an important revolutionary, whose code name was "Milord," was going to be arriving shortly, or, had already arrived, in the city. The source did not know who "Milord" was, but had heard that he was dandified and had the manners of an aristocrat. Using all of their resources, including Ivan Okladsky who was now cooperating, the detectives realized that the new arrival may well be Nihail Nikolaevitch Trigoni. Trigoni was another typical Narodnaya Volya adherent. He was born in the Crimea and was the son of a general. He had gone to school with Zhelyabov both at Kerch in the Crimea, and at Odessa.[487] Apparently the two were friends. Trigoni was placed in charge of the Narodnaya Volya operations in Odessa. But, when Narodnaya Volya grew desperate for reinforcements in the wake of the arrests at the end of January 1881, Trigoni was summoned to St. Petersburg by the Executive Committee.

In a major mistake by the terrorists (who now lacked their previous security chief, Alexander Mikhailov), Trigoni registered at an apartment under his actual name, rather than using an underground fake persona. The police placed the apartment, and Trigoni himself, under surveillance. One night he was shadowed to a block of flats in the 1 Rot Ismailovski Polk, where Zhelyabov and Perovskaya were living under false names. The police were not immediately able to determine which flat he had visited. Another afternoon, on the Nevsky Prospect, Trigoni was observed by a police agent to stop and speak to "a young woman with a big forehead," who was in all likelihood Perovskaya. The agent followed this girl, but she eluded his pursuit. Later, Trigoni was also followed to the cheese shop in the Malaya Sadovaya.

By Wednesday, February 25, Trigoni realized perhaps he was being watched. A neighbor in his apartment building, a retired naval captain, was so effusively friendly as to be suspicious. However, Trigoni either did not report these suspicions to Zhelyabov, or else, Zhelyabov did not take any special precautions because of them. The retired naval captain was able to inform police that Trigoni was expecting a visitor at his apartment on the evening of Friday, February 27.

At 4 p.m. on the afternoon of Friday the 27th, Zhelyabov and Perovskaya left their home on the Ismailovsky Polk and took a cab together to the state library which is at the corner of Nevsky Prospect and Sadovaya Street (one block to the east of the Malaya Sadovaya). There they parted. Zhelyabov walked west on Nevsky, in the direction of Trigoni's apartment which was about six blocks away, next to the bridge where the Nevsky crosses the Fontanka River. Zhelyabov realized he was being shadowed by a police agent. He made a detour to elude the pursuit. He did two or three other errands and then arrived at Trigoni's apartment at around 7 p.m. Trigoni had been waiting for him there for half an hour.

Zhelyabov came into the apartment and commented, "I

The Malaya Sadovaya, looking south (in March 2016). Note basement shops at left.
photo by author

think you have the police here somewhere." Trigoni went out into the hallway to look. Not seeing anyone, he called for a servant girl in the building to bring a samovar. Just as he did, police came out of the retired captain's flat and grabbed him. When Trigoni did not return, Zhelyabov became nervous and after 20 minutes decided to leave the building. He went down to the main entrance, but it was locked. As Zhelyabov was fumbling with the handle, police came up from behind and caught him. He had a revolver on him, but the police seized him quickly and he was unable to use it. Then they brought down Trigoni and the whole party headed off to the police station. There, it happened that the officer on duty had been involved with the Trial of the 193. He immediately recognized the detainee who had just been brought in as Zhelyabov.[488]

News of the arrest of Zhelyabov spread rapidly. By the following morning, Loris-Melikov, who was recovering from a brief bout of illness that had caused him to cancel his in-person meeting with Alexander, wrote a note to the ruler about the capture. The note was delivered to the Tsar immediately after he attended Saturday morning mass with Katia and his immediate family:

> You know that my first thought was to share with you this news; because no one else besides you can take to heart everything that concerns me.

Alexander wrote in his diary entry for the day that he was "particularly happy and satisfied" with the news about the long-sought terrorist chief. Katia, however, remained wary due to rumors of further possible attacks. She had successfully persuaded Alexander to drop his regular review of the troops in Mikhailovsky Manège the previous week. When Alexander made it clear to her that he did intend to resume his usual Sunday outing this weekend, she pleaded with him not to take his normal route through the relatively small and public street, the Malaya Sadovaya.[489]

The police were aware of suspicions about the Malaya Sadovaya and, in particular, about the new cheese shop there. The police officer in charge of the district noticed "the large number of young men and women seen going in and out." He requested an inspection of the cheese shop by General K. I. Mravinsky of the Corps of Engineers. On the morning of Saturday, February 28, the general entered the below-ground level shop under the guise of a municipal surveyor. He looked in all three rooms. There was an obvious odor, the telltale sign of sewer gas. The "Kobozevs" blamed it on strong cheeses being stored. Mravinsky asked why the front wall of the living room had been boarded up. The "Kobozevs" explained that the boards were placed to keep the dampness from coming through the cement. Mravinsky tugged at these boards, but they did not move and he seemed satisfied. Seeing a pile of coal in a corner of the store room, Mravinsky kicked at it, but he did not ask that it be moved. He also asked about a pile of straw and was told it was used for packing cheese barrels. Both were major clues to what was really going on – the straw and coal were used for covering the soil brought out of the tunnel, as a more thorough examination would have revealed immediately.

The botched "inspection" of the cheese shop was an enormous blunder, even worse than allowing Chernyshevsky to write *What Is to Be Done?* There was a barrel in the store room that Mravinsky noticed to be oozing liquid. "Mr. Kobozev" told him an elaborate story about how it was filled with sour cream. During a carnival, he spun, they had dropped that particular barrel and some of the sour cream had leaked out. Mravinsky did not ask that it be opened. A pregnant cat came into the shop and rubbed herself against his legs. "Mrs. Kobozev" (probably remembering the success of Perovskaya's similar tactic in Moscow) started telling him of how this cat had acted when in heat, and how they kept wondering which animal was the father. Mravinsky appeared to be amused, and the atmosphere of the inspection thawed. Soon he left with the policemen he had brought. He reported to Loris-Melikov that there was no overtly suspicious activity going on in the shop, but that he would keep on eye on it.[490]

Perovskaya was the first among the terrorists to realize that something had gone wrong with Zhelyabov when he failed to return to their shared safehouse during the night of February 27. We have no direct record of the feelings she experienced that night. However, those who worked with her the next day reported that Sonia appeared weak and ill. Sonia's sickness remains a mystery unexplained by historians and biographers. There are clear indications that she was already feeling symptoms of long-term illness well prior to Zhelyabov's arrest. As we have seen, in her youth and as a young woman Sonia was noted for her robust health, hardiness and strength.[491] But her brother Vasily, who last met with Sonia in September of 1879, wrote that even then, a year and a half before the events of February 28, 1881, she was ill. He reports that their mother was upset during this meeting because Sonia was "coughing all the time." She complained about "her chest." These symptoms suggest that perhaps she suffered from tuberculosis, a common urban disease in Russia at that time and one that afflicted royalty, revolutionaries and peasants alike.[492]

When Narodnaya Volya propagandist Lev Tikhomirov was married in St. Petersburg in early January 1881, Sonia did not attend the event with Zhelyabov, pleading that she was not feeling well, according to Yuri Trifonov. Trifonov, who unfortunately does not footnote his sources, also confidently reports that during the time while she was scouting the Tsar's movements, late in 1880 and early 1881, Sonia felt "sick" and "feverish." In early 1881, she had "pain." These indicia of illness are significant because they date from before Sonia's live-in lover Andrei Zhelyabov was arrested. Although Sonia no doubt felt shock, loss and distress at the fate of her boyfriend and fellow hard core Narodnaya Volya leader, these reactions are neither a complete nor an adequate explanation for the numerous vivid eyewitness reports of her seriously sick and weak demeanor after that arrest. "She could hardly walk," a young revolutionary who had an unrequited crush on Sonia, and who accompanied her as her escort, recalled of the first week of March. Vera Figner tells us explicitly that Sonia approached her in early March with a request for a loan because she had spent her last 15 rubles "to buy medicine." This is a telltale sign that Perovskaya herself, with her medical training and experience, was well aware that she suffered from a malady that required treatment.[493] It is a testament to her strength of will and determination that on the fateful day of the attack on March 1, she would betray no sign of sickness or weakness.

We do not know exactly what Perovskaya did the morning after Zhelyabov failed to return to her. She was not the person who brought the news of Zhelyabov's arrest to the headquarters of the Narodnaya Volya Executive Committee on Voznesensky Avenue on the morning of Saturday, February 28. That news was brought to them by Nikolai Sukhanov, the Executive Committee member who was also an officer in the Russian navy. Soon afterwards, Bogdanovich arrived to report the events of the cheese shop "inspection."

By 3 p.m., most of the key leaders of Narodnaya Volya who remained at large gathered at the safehouse they called their "headquarters" to review the situation. These persons, in addition to Sukhonov, were Sofia Perovskaya, Vera Figner, Grigory Isaev, Mikhail Grachevsky, Mikhail Frolenko, Anna Korba, and Tatiana Lebedeva. Sonia took the lead in the discussion. Isaev, Sonia's longtime colleague in tunneling plots, would go to the cheese shop to lay the mine. Frolenko volunteered to be the man to remain behind in the cheese shop to connect the wires that would set off the massive explosion when the Emperor passed. They reviewed that Kibalchich had predicted that the force of the explosion would be likely to also kill the person setting it off inside the cheese shop. Frolenko assured them he was resolved to accept that fate.[494]

Sonia raised the question, if the Emperor should not pass through the Malaya Sadovaya the following day, should the attack proceed anyway, just using Kibalcich's new hand grenades? The others answered her with a resounding and unanimous, "Yes!" Five o'clock, only a short time later, was established as the time when the Narodnaya Volya would begin the assembly of Kibalchich's grenades. This work would be done at the Executive Committee headquarters.

Sukhanov, with some other adherents of the "Fighting Services" section, went to the Perovskaya – Zhelyabov safe house in the Ismailovsky Polk to clean out its contents, as a police raid was anticipated. [495] The police had, in fact, figured out that Perovskaya's safe house in the Izmailovsky Polk was somehow connected to Trigoni. Trigoni had been trailed there by officers during the surveillance prior to his arrest. However, they apparently did not obtain any evidence on Zhelyabov linking him to the Izmailovsky Polk apartment, and thus did not realize that this was his residence. The morning after the arrest, police asked the building's porter to alert them when the male occupant arrived. Of course, the only occupant who returned on Saturday was Perovskaya. She came back soon after Sukhonov and his crew were finished moving her items out of the apartment. The porter came up to the apartment and asked "Voinova" where her brother was. "He is working," she lied. "I must know as soon as he comes in," replied the porter. "I have a form from the police for him to sign." Sonia hurriedly departed, leaving behind traces of explosive materials and cheese labels. She then returned to the "headquarters" on Voznesensky, about a ten minute walk. She arrived at around 8 p.m. By then, Figner, Kibalchich, Sukonov and Grachevski were busy assembling bombs. Perovskaya was visibly weak with exhaustion. Figner convinced her to lie down and let the others carry on with putting together the explosives.[496]

The bombs were basically kerosene cans filled with Kibalchich's nitroglycerine mixture. Apparently, they had to be cut and constructed intricately due to the detonator mechanisms. The four Narodnaya Volya leaders worked on them until 2 a.m., at which point, Figner joined Perovskaya in bed. The three men continued working. When Vera and Sonia awoke at 7 a.m. Sunday morning, two of the four bombs had been completed, and the other two were nearly finished. Perovskaya brought both of the completed grenades with her and took the equivalent of a taxi, a horse drawn carriage, to the Telezhnaya Flat. (Today, the former site of the Telezhnaya safe house is three metro stops away from the Voznesensky "headquarters".) Cradling her charges in a paper bag on her lap, Sonia handled them with as much love and care as the babies she would never have.[497]

"Kotik" Grinevitsky also woke up early Sunday morning. He wrote out a manifesto to explain his terroristic state of mind.

> Alexander II must die. His days are numbered . . . The near future will show whether it is for me or another to strike the final blow. But he will die and with him we shall die, his enemies and executioners. What of the future? I, with one foot already in the grave, am afflicted by the thought that after me there will be many further victims. It will not be my lot to take part in the final battle. Fate has allotted me an early death. I shall not see one day, not one hour of our triumph. But I believe that by my death I am doing all that I have in my power to do, and that no one on earth can demand more of me.[498]

By the time Perovskaya arrived with her cargo at the Telezhnaya flat, "Kotik" and the other three bombers were already present and waiting. Sonia wasted no time getting down to business. She showed them the bombs she had brought for them to throw. She also told them of Zhelyabov's arrest. In a calm, matter of fact way, she informed them she would now be taking over the lead of their attack squad. Zhelyabov had earlier reviewed with them a map of the city. But to be sure to get across exactly where she wanted them to wait with their grenades, Sonia made her own, larger, diagram.

From her months of scouting, Sonia was confident that the Tsar would make his way to the Manège right around 1 p.m. She was well aware that prior failures had been brought on by what she considered to be male incompetence, things like failing to be on time for the Tsar's passage. The four bombers were instructed by her to be waiting at the Malaya Sadovaya, each with their bombs, no later than noon, which was an hour early. "Kotik" and Mikhailov were to stand at the north end of the Malaya Sadovaya where it opened into Italianskaya Street. The other two, Rysakov and Emilianov, were to stand at the south end of the Malaya Sadovaya, where it intersects the Nevsky Prospect (the largest street, the "Broadway" as it were, of St. Petersburg). "Kotik" was the only one of the four to whom Sonia and Zhelyabov had previously revealed the secret of the mine being dug underneath Malaya Sadovaya. Now, she informed the rest of them about the tunnel and the planned explosion. Kibalchich arrived at the Telezhnaya Street flat with the other two bombs at around 10 a.m. Sonia and the four bombers, each one carrying his bomb, journeyed from Telezhnaya to the vicinity of the Malaya Sadovaya. [Today, this trip is around a 15 minute bus ride, or else two metro stops plus a substantial walk.] She went with Grinevitsky and Rysakov to have some coffee and cakes at a café on the opposite side of Nevsky Prospect.[499]

After attending a Sunday morning church service, Alexander received Loris-Melikov at the Winter Palace. The Minister's key order of business was to secure the ruler's final approval and signature on an important new decree. This was to put in effect the new advisory commissions that would incorporate local representatives. It was not, to be sure, a Western-style republican form of government, but for Russia it was an unprecedented step in the direction of a constitutional monarchy. Brushing aside the opposition of conservatives led by Pobedonostev, Alexander approved Loris-Melikov's work, which had been under development for months. A council of Alexander's ministers was scheduled for March 4 to publish the decree and to begin the work of putting the decree into effect.[500]

When his meeting with Loris-Melikov was finished, Alexander returned upstairs to Katia and their children. They were already having lunch. Proudly, he announced to her, "I have just come from signing a paper which, I hope, will make a good impression and prove to all of Russia that I have given her everything that is possible." Alexander stayed with them just five minutes. He wanted to be on time for the Sunday review at the Manège. Katia worried about her partner, this sensitive soul who had at long last become her husband. "I hope you will not go there by Nevsky Prospect. Please take the Ekaterinsky Canal," she nagged at him. She did not need to explain it any more, because they had had prior discussions in which she complained that she felt a sense of danger about his passage through large public streets such as the Nevsky and the Malaya Sadovaya. The canal route she considered safer, because it was protected on one side by a railing and the canal itself, and on the other side, by a walled garden. It was a fairly short ride, only around seven or eight city blocks, for a horse drawn vehicle. "Very well, I will go that way," he promised her. Alexander left the Winter Palace at five minutes before 1 p.m.[501] He was riding in a closed carriage that was accompanied by six mounted Cossacks and two police sleds. Police and guards were also posted along his expected routes of travel.

At 1 p.m., Sonia was waiting near the north end of the Malaya Sadovaya. When Alexander's convoy did not materialize and she could hear the band striking up the music announcing the Tsar's arrival, Perovskaya quickly realized that what she had anticipated had occurred -- Alexander had gone to the Manège by another route. Perovskaya walked three blocks east along Italianskaya Street to the corner of Mikhailovsky Square. From that vantage point she could tell what direction the Emperor would take when he left the Manège when he came out less than an hour later. Indeed, instead of heading for the Malaya Sadovaya, Alexander's cortege left in the opposite direction, exiting the north end of the Manège and making a left turn on Inzhenernaya Street. Seeing this, Perovskaya gave a pre-arranged signal for the bombers by waving her white handkerchief. They knew from her prior detailed instructions that they were to re-deploy themselves on the embankment of the Ekaterinsky Canal.[502]

Sonia had this manuever carefully planned out in advance with the bomb squad. She was aware that there would not be enough time after the Tsar left the Manège to give any new

The embankment of the Ekaterinsky Canal, on March 13, 2016 (135 years after the assassination).
photo by author

detailed instructions to all of the bombers. Besides, her very act of meeting and speaking with them was likely to generate unwanted attention from the many security guards patrolling the area. It took the bombers approximately ten minutes to move from where they had been, at the ends of the Malaya Sadovaya, to the Ekaterinsky Canal embankment. To carry out her plan, Sonia herself needed to take a much more roundabout route, crossing the Canal on Nevsky Prospect at what was then called the "Kazan Bridge" because it is near the Kazan Cathedral. From there she would need to walk 300 meters north along the east side embankment of the Ekaterinsky Canal to reach her own planned position opposite her conspirators.

All of this movement had to be done rapidly yet calmly and deliberately enough not to attract any attention from the onlookers.

Sonia's plan was benefitted critically by the fact that the Tsar stopped off for a visit with his royal cousin, Katerina Mikhailovna. It was another of his regular Sunday habits, one of which Perovskaya had became aware during her lengthy period spent shadowing him. Taking advantage of her upbringing within the aristocracy, Sonia correctly anticipated that if the Tsar did not return to the Winter Palace from the Manège through the Malaya Sadovaya, he would most likely stop off to see Katerina. Katerina lived in the mammoth Mikhailovsky Palace that occupies virtually an entire block along Inzhenernaya Street. (Today, it houses the Russian Museum.) She and Alexander had a cup of tea and a brief conversation that lasted around fifteen minutes. When 2 o'clock came, Alexander prepared to leave the Mikhailovsky Palace.[503]

At just about the same time, the Narodnaya Volya bombers were arriving on foot on what is called the embankment of the Ekaterinsky Canal. In reality, this "embankment" is just a cobblestone-paved road that runs above and adjacent to the canal on its western side. There was a narrow sidewalk with a railing that separates the road from the canal below. Because of a combination of walls and structures along the "inner" edge of the embankment (the side of the road away from the Canal), it was impossible to see around the corner from the embankment onto Inzhenernaya Street, the street that opens into the embankment two blocks east of the Mikhailovsky Palace. Similarly, a vehicle coming down Inzhenernaya also could not see around the corner what was happening on the canal embankment. Sonia counted on this minor element of surprise. She had observed from prior occasions that the Tsar's procession would need to slow down considerably as it rounded the corner at the north end of the embankment. She had instructed the bombers to space themselves out along the segment of the embankment north of Inzhenernaya, with the intent being to hurl the bombs when the vehicle reduced its speed.

Perovskaya covered her path of travel in time to study the face of Grinevitsky as he walked slowly up the embankment toward his assigned position, across the canal from where she was standing. She would later tell one of her confederates that she saw a "barely detectable smile" on his face. She said he "did not show any shadow of fear or emotion, marching to his death. His soul was absolutely tranquil."[504] Her vantage point was directly across the canal from the end of Inzhenernaya. From this spot she could easily keep one eye on the bombers, as they waited along the embankment, and the other on the approach of the Emperor's party. She had arranged a second signal with her followers. When the Tsar's carriage approached the embankment intersection, she would blow her nose with the handkerchief. This would alert the conspirators to get ready for the Tsar's carriage to turn the corner.

At around 2:15 p.m., Perovskaya gave this signal as the Tsar's entourage suddenly arrived at the end of Inzhenernaya and turned right onto the embankment of the Ekaterinsky Canal. Mikhailov, who was the first bomber, positioned near the corner, failed to do anything. No one can say exactly why not. Some have speculated that he lost his nerve and changed his mind about participating in the attack, but given everything else we know about his willing involvement in Narodnaya Volya violence, this seems very unlikely. More plausible is that he either missed the sign from Perovskaya, or else he did see it but still failed to anticipate the speed at which the Tsar's carriage and its escorts would pass by. Whatever the reason, he did nothing. But Sonia's tactic of spacing out the bombers was effective. Rysakov, standing about 50 to 60 meters down the embankment from the corner, saw her signal. He was ready to pitch his bomb, but the swiftness of the procession still surprised and overtook him. He was only able to throw it from behind, after the Tsar's vehicle had already passed him. The grenade landed underneath the rear axle of the carriage. After a very brief delay, it went off with a tremendous deafening explosion that produced a shower of stone fragments and snow. The force of the blast shattered windows across the street, and it threw Rysakov backwards against the sidewalk railing.[505] A Cossack escorting the Tsar's carriage was killed instantly. The horse that this Cossack was riding was severely injured, and it collapsed to the ground. A young boy, who had been standing on the embankment with his mother watching the procession roll by, was also badly hurt and started screaming.

The Tsar's carriage was lifted slightly off the pavement by the explosion, but it held together. The horses pulling the carriage felt the blast and were terrified. They instinctively took off down the embankment at top speed. Alexander yelled at the coachman, Frol Sergeev, to stop them. Sergeev was able to get them stopped only after they had run about 100 meters. One of the two sleighs that had been trailing the Tsar caught up to the imperial carriage. A Colonel A. I. Dvorzhitsky, who was commanding this sleigh, got out, went over to the coach and opened the left side door. The Tsar emerged, then stepped down on the frozen pavement. He appeared to be walking with a limp as he stepped out to speak with Dvorzhitsky. He was apparently injured slightly by splinters from the floor of the carriage. Afterwards some blood was found inside the compartment where he had been riding.

Dvorzhitsky suggested that Alexander should go immediately to the Winter Palace. But the Tsar had other ideas. He wanted to walk back to the blast site to see what had happened and to check on those who had been hurt. A crowd had gathered on the embankment. Onlookers followed along with the Tsar as he walked back down the embankment toward the carnage from the explosion. The two year old boy who had been injured was screaming and crying with pain. Soon he would die. His mother was screaming also. The remaining Cossack guards were gathered around their dead comrade. His horse was writhing and squealing in agony. It was a pitiful scene.

Captain Koch, the commander of the other trailing sleigh, was holding the man who had thrown the bomb. Rysakov had tried to escape by running away after the blast. After about 20 meters, he had been seized by bystanders. A revolver was found in his pocket. The Tsar walked up to the soldiers holding Rysakov and asked, "Is this the one?" Koch said yes. "Who is he?" Alexander asked. Koch replied that the man arrested had identified himself as "Glazov," an artisan. Alexander seemed relieved that at least his latest attacker was not from the nobility. In the ongoing melee and confusion, a shot rang out as an officer put the writhing horse out of its misery. A young man's voice was heard to call, "Where is the Emperor?" "I am safe, Thank God," Alexander spoke up in reply. This was the sixth assassination attempt on his life of which Alexander was aware, and he had survived all of them. He had often expressed to others, including Katia, the sentiment that his survival in these attempts was the result of divine will. The prosecution would later claim that the nearby Rysakov at this point exclaimed, "Don't thank God yet!" Rysakov himself denied having said any such thing.

Alexander wanted to go to see the crater where the bomb had exploded. The Tsar had taken only two or three steps along the embankment in that direction when a man, who had been leaning against the railing along the sidewalk, suddenly straightened up and dropped a package on the pavement right in between the two of them. It was Grinevitsky, throwing his bomb. A second huge explosion occurred that was equal to the first. When the shower of debris and smoke cleared, Alexander was lying on the ground covered with shards of ice and his own flesh. The whole area was full of blood, bits of flesh, bits of stones, clothing and other debris. Twenty or so people surrounding the Tsar were either killed or badly wounded. Alexander himself had severe injuries to both his legs, in addition to his face and abdomen. His left leg, in particular, was shattered from the knee down. He was gushing blood. Alexander was heard to say, "I'm cold, so cold. Take me home quickly." Dvorzhitsky and Koch directed onlookers in lifting the Tsar onto one of the police sleighs. Strangely, one of the men who assisted in lifting him was Emilianov, the fourth bomber. The Tsar was rapidly transported to the Winter Palace, where he continued to bleed as he was carried up the stairs. By the time a doctor reached him, his pulse was almost imperceptible. He was soon pronounced dead. [506]

Grinevitsky, too, was mortally wounded by the bomb he exploded. He was taken, along with many others killed and injured by the blast, to a local hospital. There he briefly regained consciousness that night around 9 p.m. Asked who he was, he responded, "I don't know." Soon afterwards he relapsed into unconsciousness and died.[507] He thus became history's first suicide bomber.

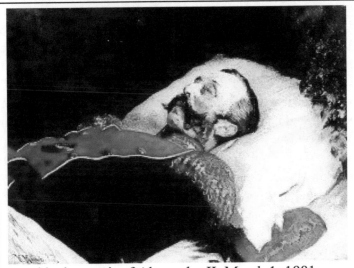

Deathbed portrait of Alexander II, March 1, 1881

Painting by K. E. Makovsky

Chapter 20: "Sonia Has Lost Her Head"

Immediately after the assassination, Perovskaya retraced her steps back south along the Ekaterinsky Canal to Nevsky Prospect. She then walked east along Nevsky approximately 1.5 kilometers to Vladimir Prospect, where she had arranged a post attack meeting with Arkady Tyrkov. Tyrkov had been a member of her scouting crew. He later recalled:

> [T]he door opened and she came in with quiet, noiseless steps. Her face could be seen to be agitated, as though she had come straight from the crash site. As always, it was strictly focused, with a tinge of sadness. We sat at a table and because there were some people in the darkened room, we had to be careful. Her first words were, "I think it was a success. Well, if he was not killed, he was seriously wounded." To my question: "How, who did it?" - She said, "Nikolai dropped the first bomb, then Kotik (Grinevitsky). Nikolai was arrested. Kotik seems to have been killed …"[508]

By late evening, Sonia's mood had changed. She entered a gathering of officers in the so-called Fighting Services Section of the Narodnaya Volya. Everyone now knew about the assassination. The rebellious officers were aglow with triumph and hope. When Perovskaya entered, however, they immediately saw that her face was drawn and white and her eyes were streaming with tears. The officers rose and crowded around to congratulate her. But she would not listen. She could only repeat, over and over, that the party must now devote all of its resources to rescuing Zhelyabov.[509]

The next day after the assassination, Narodnaya Volya issued a manifesto in which it claimed responsibility for the Tsar's murder. Prepared ahead of time, probably at the direction of Zhelyabov and Perovskaya, it was replete with terrorist world view:

> Workers of Russia!
>
> Today, March 1st, Alexander the Tyrant has been killed by us, Socialists. He was killed because he did not care for his people. He burdened them with taxes. He deprived the peasant of his land; he handed over the workers to plunderers and exploiters. He did not give the people freedom. He did not heed the people's tears. He cared only for the rich. He himself lived in luxury. The police maltreated the people and he rewarded them instead of punishing them. He hanged or exiled any who stood out on behalf of the people or on behalf of justice. That is why he was killed. A Tsar should be a good shepherd, ready to devote his life to his sheep. Alexander II was a ravening wolf and a terrible death overtook him.[510]

This viewpoint was not accepted by anything outside of a tiny minority. Russians went into a state of shock, grief and mourning for their fallen Emperor. The terrorist act of blowing up human beings, including bystanders, in a cold blooded sneak attack, generally is disturbing and hateful to normal people in a civilized society no matter what the cause. An intense manhunt, and womanhunt, got under way in the capital. Thousands of Cossacks were sent into the city, and roadblocks were set up.[511]

Unbeknownst to Perovskaya, Rysakov, after an initial period of resistance, cracked under police interrogation by the day after the assassination. Little by little, in an effort to save himself he started giving them bits and pieces of accurate information. One of his disclosures was the location of the flat on Telezhnaya Street where he and the other bombers had met the "blonde" in charge of the bomb squad on the morning of March 1. (If Rysakov knew Perovskaya's real identity, as seems likely given that they had worked together for several months, he did not choose to betray it.) The intelligence led to a police visit to the flat, which occurred in the very early morning hours of Tuesday, March 3. When the investigating officers knocked, two shots were fired through the door from inside the apartment. While the officers took cover to await reinforcements, they heard a woman's screams for help, and for a doctor, coming from inside the apartment. They broke the door down and found a disheveled sobbing Helfman. Nikolai Sablin, Helfman's fictitious husband, had killed himself with a bullet through his own forehead rather than face capture.

The police hauled away Sablin's body, took Helfman to jail and awaited further developments at the flat. While searching the place, they found the other two grenades that had not been exploded in the attack on Alexander. They found a map of St. Petersburg with marks on both sides of the Malaya Sadovaya, as well as along the Ekaterinsky Canal. They also found the enlarged diagram that Perovskaya had made on the back of an envelope. At 11 a.m., Timofei Mikhailov came to Telezhnaya Street. When he reached the apartment he found himself surrounded by police. They asked him what he wanted. He said he was looking for a cab driver, a friend of his, who had told him he lived there. The police told him to sit down and wait. After a short time he got up to leave. When the police moved to stop him, Mikhailov drew a revolver and started shooting, firing a total of six shots. Two policemen were wounded before Mikhailov could be disarmed.[512]

The next morning, Wednesday, March 4, police finally unearthed the tunnel associated with the cheese shop in the Malaya Sadovaya. The fake cheese shop proprietors were already gone, however, having left the day before to travel separately by train to Moscow. Bulletins describing the "Kobozevs" were telegraphed throughout Russia. Anna Yakimova would later find it amusing that she had been described in these bulletins as being extremely beautiful. Although people in her train compartment were talking about the news of the outlaws, none of them suspected her of being Madame Kobozev.

Terrorists who successfully pull off surprise attacks, if they survive the event itself without being captured, often turn out to appear almost stunned and surprised themselves, and seem disoriented and confused about what to do next. This was certainly true of Sofia Perovskaya and the other leaders of Narodnaya Volya. Their dramatic killing of Alexander II had sowed a great deal of panic in government officials and among the public generally. The new Emperor, Alexander's son Alexander III, was for the time being unwilling to even set foot in St. Petersburg. He holed up under armed guard on an imperial estate in Gatchina, 50 kilometers south of the city. But apart from publishing their March 2 manifesto claiming credit for the assassination, Perovskaya and her conspirators strangely lacked in taking any initiative. They seemed to have lost their former exuberance and sense of purpose that had characterized the assassination campaign.[513]

What now obsessed Sonia was the freeing of Zhelyabov. This was particularly true after she read in the newspaper that

Zhelyabov, in jail, had openly claimed the credit for being a leader of the attackers. Tyrkov wrote:

> She kept talking about rescuing Zhelyabov. Of course, the idea was impossible. But she could not or would not see that; she could not keep still, she had to try every possibility. She was anxious to establish some contact in the district court where we thought the trial was going to be. Then we went around together looking for empty flats near the Third Section in the Panteleimonovsky; her idea was to establish a lookout post there, and when they brought Zhelyabov out to make an organized mass attack on the guards and carry him off. She had all sorts of other plans. It would have been hopeless to try and discourage her. She would only have tried to go through with it by herself. She seemed to have lost all sense of realities.

Tyrkov summed up: "People said, 'Sonia has lost her head.'"[514]

Rina Epstein traveled to St. Petersburg during the week after the assassination occurred. In letters written to Serge Kravchinsky, she described the city as being covered everywhere – "the lamps, the houses, the balconies, the windows" -- with "mournful stripes of black and white." A lady she knew, who ran a boarding house where many radicals stayed, criticized her for coming into the city at this time, while security forces were watchful everywhere. But a few days afterwards, while she was at the boarding house, the lady's sister came in with the surprising news that Sofia Perovskaya was looking for Rina. Epstein, who specialized in smuggling "illegals" out of Russia, was very happy at the news. She assumed that Sonia wanted help in getting out of the country. Rina, who avoided involvement with the activities of Narodnaya Volya, was unaware of Sonia's role in the assassination itself. However, she knew Goldenberg had previously told authorities of Perovskaya's role in the

November 1879 Moscow train explosion. This sensational revelation had been discussed in the papers. There was, in Rina's opinion, more than sufficient reason for Sonia to leave St. Petersburg, given the tense atmosphere there.

But when she came into the room and expressed to Perovskaya an expression of pleasure at her determination to go abroad, Sonia "started as though she had heard something utterly incomprehensible." She quickly cut short all of Rina's entreaties to leave. She explained that she had sent for Rina because she wanted to know something about the impending trial of the assassins. She asked Rina to go to a highly placed person, a sort of "Deep Throat" connected with the imperial police, who would be able to provide some information even though all of the investigations were being carried on with utmost secrecy. Perovskaya was aware that Rina had a personal connection to this man, who was not otherwise connected with the "Nihilists." It was arranged that Rina would see "His Excellency" at 10 a.m. the next day. Then, Rina would report back to Perovskaya, whose time was thoroughly booked with multiple appointments throughout the city, at 6 p.m.

"His Excellency" received Rina much more politely than she had expected. He informed her fully on what was happening with the trial of the assassins. The fate of Zhelyabov was already sealed after his confession. At Loris-Melikov's urging, Alexander III had determined initially to hold a short trial on March 3, two days after the assassination, and to execute Rysakov the next day. But after Zhelyabov had given the authorities a detailed statement attesting to his role in plotting the assassination, Loris-Melikov then recommended that both Zhelyabov and Rysakov be tried March 4 and executed March 5. Then the capture of Helfman and Mikhailov, followed closely by the discovery of the Malaya Sadovaya mine, intervened. These events caused the trial to be postponed until after Tsar Alexander II's public funeral on

March 7. Likely, this was the state of affairs that was reported to Epstein by "His Excellency." Regardless, any trial would be strictly pro forma with the executions to follow rapidly.[515]

Sonia did not arrive at her appointment with Epstein until 9 p.m. When she came in, Perovskaya did not look well.

> I communicated to her at once the information I had received. I did not see her face, for her eyes were cast down. When she raised them I saw that she was trembling all over. Then she grasped my hands, sank down, and buried her face in my lap. She remained thus for several minutes; she did not weep, but trembled all over. Then she arose and sat down, endeavoring to compose herself. But with a sudden movement she again grasped my hands, and pressed them so hard as to hurt me.

According to Epstein, Sonia "was so worn out that she could scarcely stand." When Rina related how "His Excellency" had been astonished that Zhelyabov had declared that he was the organizer of the assassination plot, Perovskaya replied, "It could not be otherwise. The trial of Rysakov alone would have been too colorless." The two agreed to meet again the next afternoon. However, by the time Rina arrived, Perovskaya had already come and gone. [516]

Tyrkov gave a similar account of Perovskaya's demeanor during the week after the assassination. He recalled that Perovskaya was "ill." "Sometimes she could hardly walk." She was visibly affected over the enormity of Zhelyabov's impending execution. One of Sonia's friends wrote that after Zhelyabov's arrest, Sonia had the demeanor of a sick person "with hell in her soul," a Russian expression roughly translated as being in severe emotional pain. However, whatever was wrong with her went beyond just grief over her lover's fate. She told Figner she had spent fifteen rubles for "medicine." Despite how she felt, Perovskaya roamed from place to place, now staying with one Narodnaya Volya member or sympathizer, now with another. She never stayed with one host for more than a night. She asked permission for lodging with great trepidation, knowing that if she were found, the host or hostess would most likely be hanged with her.[517]

Sofia Perovskaya, 1881

source: V. Perovsky memoir,
National Library of Russia

On March 7 and March 8, which were in all likelihood the days of the meetings described by Epstein, Perovskaya took an active part in lengthy sessions with the remaining members of Narodnaya Volya's "Executive Committee." The main point of business was to craft an ultimatum to be presented to Alexander III. This "Letter of the Executive Committee to

Alexander III" was drafted largely by Tikhomirov and was published under the date of March 10 (OS), 1881. It was a rather flowery effort to argue that the government should yield to the inevitable, declare a general amnesty for all political crimes, and convene an "assembly of representatives of the Russian people" with elected delegates. Although it was widely read in Russia and abroad, and although it drew praise from the likes of Marx and Engels, the "Letter of the Executive Committee" had no effect on reality whatsoever. Not even the Executive Committee members themselves harbored anything more than the slightest hope that it would have an effect. By the time it was published, the forces of reaction led by Alexander III's longtime mentor Pobedonostsev were already ascendant. Loris-Melikov, who had been the main advocate and champion of liberal reform within the government up until the assassination, soon lost favor with the new monarch.[518]

Perovskaya's thoughts ran feverishly in the direction of making an attempt to assassinate the new Emperor. She began spending much of her days in early March watching near the Anichkov Palace, where she knew Alexander III dwelt when in St. Petersburg. Appearing to her fellow conspirators to be engulfed by a mania that made her forget her better judgment, Sonia made various inquiries, sought out laundry ladies and others who worked for Palace households, and tried to collect information from people who might chance to meet members of the new Tsar's family. But the new Tsar did not venture into his capital city.[519]

Meanwhile, the womanhunt continued, not necessarily for Perovskaya, for the authorities still did not realize that Perovskaya was the "blonde" responsible for carrying out the assassination, but for "Voinova," the woman who had lived with Zhelyabov in the Ismailovsky Polk flat. Police detectives found a shopkeeper, Louise Sundberg, who had often sold milk to "Voinova" and was capable of recognizing her. They kept Sundberg with them as they patrolled up and down Nevsky

Prospect. Finally, at 5 p.m. on March 10, the same day the "Letter to Alexander III" was dated, Sundberg spotted "Voinova" as she exited a cab and started "walking quickly" on Nevsky near the Anichkov Palace. A detective named Feodor Shirokov ran after her and chased her down. It was reported that she offered him a bribe of 30 rubles to let her go. He declined. His prize, a place in history, was far more valuable.[520]

"Voinova" was taken to police headquarters, where a search of her garments revealed printed pages from the Executive Committee of Narodnaya Volya concerning the assassination, a copy of the "Program of the Executive Committee," two copies of the "Worker's Program" of Narodnaya Volya, and some "working papers" that included an epigraph from Jesus Christ: "There is no greater love than this, that a man lay down his life for his friends." She at first refused to give the detectives any information, but after several hours of interrogation, and after being confronted with evidence from Goldenberg, Rysakov, and Zhelyabov, she finally admitted, at around midnight, to her real identity as Perovskaya.[521]

A second, more thorough, police interview occurred the next day. Perovskaya did not conceal her role in either the November 19, 1879 train explosion or the March 1, 1881 assassination. The questioning detectives already knew about these events, but her statements to them fleshed out many more particulars of her actions in connection with those attacks. Her basic attitude under questioning remained one of a righteous spirit of "sacrifice for humanity." She did not incriminate any new suspects, for instance never revealing the identity of the fourth bomber Emelianov, whose real name was apparently not known to Rysakov. Regarding Zhelyabov, she told the detectives that he had come to live with her the previous September. Nothing else. In an apt turn of phrase of one biographer, she "tried to give as much information as possible to the future historian and as little as possible to the investigation."[522] Her outlook was not affected in the least by the prospect of her imminent death.

If Perovskaya felt any degree of remorse, it was only due to the grief and sorrow of her mother Varvara Stepanovna. Loris-Melikov personally asked Varvara Stepanovna to meet with him. He tried to enlist her assistance in securing more information from Sonia. Varvara, in declining the request, assured the minister that it was a futile effort. According to her son Vasily, she recalled telling him, "My daughter, from a young age, found such independence that it was impossible to make her do anything by demand. The only way to get her to do things was with kindness and persuasion. She is a mature person, her views are formed, and therefore no demands or pleas on my end would be able to influence her."[523]

Despite this rebuff, Varvara Stepanovna was permitted several visits with Sonia in the House of Detention during the days following her arrest. The prosecutor and guards sat next to them during these meetings. Sonia did not say much. She mainly just reclined on the floor with her head on her mother's knee, "like a sick, tired child" according to a prison matron who witnessed the visits.[524] Sonia expressed more of her thoughts for her mother in the last letter that she wrote to her.

> My dear, priceless mother, -- the thought of you oppresses and torments me always. My darling, I implore you to be calm, and not to grieve for me; for my fate does not afflict me in the least, and I shall meet it with complete tranquillity, for I have long expected it, and known that sooner or later it must come. And I assure you, dear mother, that my fate is not such a very mournful one. I have lived as my convictions dictated, and it would have been impossible for me to have acted otherwise. I await my fate, therefore, with a tranquil conscience, whatever it may be. The only thing which oppresses me is the thought of your grief,

oh, my priceless mother! It is that which rends my heart; and what would I not give to be able to alleviate it? My dear, dear mother, remember that you still have a large family, so many grown up, and so many little ones, all of whom have need of you, have need of your great moral strength. The thought that I have been unable to raise myself to your moral height has always grieved me to the heart. Whenever, however, I felt myself wavering, it was always the thought of you which sustained me. I will not speak to you of my devotion to you; you know that from my infancy you were always the object of my deepest and fondest love. Anxiety for you was the greatest of my sufferings. I hope that you will be calm, that you will pardon me the grief I have caused you, and not blame me too much; your reproof is the only one that would grieve my heart.

In fancy I kiss your hands again and again, and on my knees I implore you not to be angry with me.

Remember me most affectionately to all my relatives.

And I have a little commission for you, my dear mother. Buy me some cuffs and collars; the collars rather narrow, and the cuffs with buttons, for studs are not allowed to be worn here. Before appearing at the trial, I must mend my dress a little, for it has become much worn here. Good-bye till we meet again, my dear mother. Once more I implore you not to grieve, and not to afflict yourself for me. My fate is not such a sad one after all, and you must not grieve about it.

Your own Sonia

March 22, 1881[525]

The investigation into the assassination conspiracy was headed by Alexander Dobrzhinsky, the detective who had successfully gained the cooperation of Goldenberg. Aided by the turning of Rysakov, the roundup gathered momentum as police under Dobrzhinsky's direction continued to identify and capture Narodnaya Volya members and associates. On March 14, Tyrkov was arrested. On the same day, Natalia Olovennikova, sister of Maria, was arrested. On March 17, with Okladsky pointing him out from a screened vantage point as he was reading foreign language newspapers in a library, the police identified Nikolai Kibalchich as the strange bearded "technician" of Narodnaya Volya, of whom they had been told by Rysakov, Okladsky, and Merkulov. The police followed Kibalchich to his safe house apartment, where they arrested him without resistance. They then nabbed Mikhail Frolenko when he came by to visit Kibalchich later that day.[526]

From the time of the assassination forward, the Russian government was confronted with the question of what to do about the trial of the terrorist assassins. The "trial" of terrorists is a problem that has severely perplexed modern governments – including that of the United States – and continues to do so right down to the present day.[527] It is a built-in problem inherent in terrorism. The terrorist utterly rejects the society that is judging him or her, and thus, regards the trial primarily as a step on the path to martyrdom. Typically, the terrorist admits the elements of "criminal behavior" involved in the charged offense. Thus, in reality, there is very little to try in the conventional sense of the criminal law. The terrorist's core point of view, which he hopes to present before as public a forum as possible, is that the government needs to be overthrown and the fabric of society needs to be torn apart and remade, that an entirely different set of laws and standards should be applied. The terrorist and his criminal actions should be applauded, not condemned, as a means to bringing about that necessary end. Under English criminal law doctrines, in a broad brush the only relevant and pertinent legal defense is the concept of "justification." It is a concept that the court is far more likely to punish with enhanced severity than to allow as a defense.[528]

Perhaps the wisest counsel for dealing with the terrorists was a letter written by author Leo Tolstoy to Alexander III. Tolstoy summed up the situation:

> About 20 years ago emerged a nest of people, mostly young, who hate the existing order of things and the government. These people imagine a full different order of things, or even have no idea of it, and all the godless, inhuman means, fires, looting, killing, destroy the existing order of society. There have been 20 years of fighting with this nest. As ascetic, the nest is constantly emerging new leaders, and still the nest is not only not destroyed, but it is growing, and these people came to the worst, with cruelty and insolence in actions that violate the course of public life.

Tolstoy acknowledged that the new tsar would be propelled to punish harshly, not only because of the violence of the assassination itself, but also because of a public expectation that vengeance was due. "A more awful situation it is impossible to imagine," he wrote, "a more horrible one because it is impossible to imagine a more powerful temptation to evil. Enemies of the Fatherland, the people despise these youth, these godless creatures, disturbing the peace and the life entrusted to millions, and murderers of your father. What more can we do with them, how can we clear from this contagion the Russian land, and crush them like nasty reptiles?" But, relying on Christian concepts, Tolstoy urged the tsar to make a stunning, miraculous gesture of rejecting further violence in the form of executions. His ultimate advice to the tsar was taken from the words of Jesus. It was a direct antecedent of the philosophy of non-violence later developed by Mohandas Gandhi:

> "Give good for evil, do not resist evil, forgive all."[529]

Alexander III and his advisors, although they received Tolstoy's letter, would have none of it. Loris-Melikov's instinct, as we have seen, was to deny the terrorists a pulpit by condemning them to swift death in a summary military tribunal. However, in the wake of Perovskaya's arrest the government decided to conduct a full fledged trial of the assassination conspirators, rather than use the summary military tribunal procedure envisioned by Loris-Melikov. Part of the reason likely may have been a realization that the terrorists were not following up with any new attacks, or any other new initiatives following their stunning killing of the tsar. Another part of the reason may have been that holding a regular trial was a bit of an indirect slap at Loris-Melikov. Alexander Alexandrovitch was rapidly rejecting Loris-Melikov, who had been his father's man, in favor of his own conservative advisors led by Pobedonostsev. But ultimately, at bottom the decision to hold a "real" trial rested on a philosophical approach. The hatefulness and immorality of terrorist methods, and of the terrorists themselves, would be attacked and confronted, head on.

On March 9 an indictment was prepared against the four known conspirators then in custody (Zhelyabov, Rysakov, Timofei Mikhailov and Gessia Helfman), but the arrest of Perovskaya on March 10 provided a good new reason to postpone the trial. A new indictment was written, and the date for starting the trial was moved to March 26. When Kibalchich was arrested on March 17, he was added rapidly into the indictment, without changing the trial date. There were two main and common charges against all six defendants – belonging to a secret revolutionary organization and participating in the regicide – that under Articles 241, 242, 243 and 249 of the Penal Code of the Russian Empire carried the death penalty.[530]

The trial was to be, in a formal sense, a special session of the Russian "Senate." There could be no repeat of nullification by a runaway jury, as had happened in the case of Zasulitch. Nevertheless, a conscious effort was made to frame the proceedings as a "real" criminal trial in the modern sense. International reporters and many other observers were allowed to attend. To accommodate them, the largest available courtroom was used. Edward Yakovlovitch Fuchs, an attorney, was designated to sit as the presiding Judge. Nine "senators" were appointed to hear and decide the case. They included three members who were to serve as "representatives" of various social classes. The mayor of Moscow was designated as a representative of the "merchant class," there was a peasant named Khelker, and service workers were represented by a bureaucrat from Kiev. Legally the "senators" constituted the equivalent of a jury, all of whose members had been hand picked for reliability.[531] Experienced, respected attorneys were appointed to represent five of the six defendants. The exception was Zhelyabov, who opted to represent himself. He did this, of course, to assure that he would be able to speak out personally throughout the trial.

Zhelyabov launched the defense with a pretrial motion which highlighted the fundamental absurdity of "judicial proceedings" for terrorists. The day before trial was set to begin, Zhelyabov submitted this written argument to the Court:

> As our activities have been directed solely against the government, the court of the Senate, being composed of members of the government administration, is an interested party and therefore not competent to judge the issue. The special session of the Senate, as it consists of government officials, is obliged to act in the interests of the government, guided by the instructions without any exercise of conscience, and in obedience to the government orders, which are arbitrarily referred to as "laws." This is outside the jurisdiction of a special session of the Senate.

Secondly, our actions must be regarded as the manifestations of the public, all the recognized struggle which the Russian social revolutionary party for many years has led for the people and for human rights law against the Russian government that has forcibly possessed power and has forcibly confined the people in its hands to this day. The sole tribunal competent to adjudicate is the nation, acting by means of a national plebiscite or referendum, or else through a freely elected constitutent assembly.

And thirdly, because this form of trial (i.e., by constituent assembly) against us personally is not feasible, trial should occur by jury, since the jury largely represents a social conscience and is not bound by the constraints of their oath of faithful service to one of the interested parties in the case.

Based on the foregoing, I object to the jurisdiction of our trial by special session of the Senate and demand a jury trial in a deep confidence that the jury as the public expression of conscience, not only will grant us an acquittal as with Vera Zasulitch, but also will express gratitude to us for our particularly useful activity for the benefit of the Fatherland.[532]

Modern society's concepts of justice are not about to be bent by the terrorist's fundamentally warped perceptions of reality and legitimacy of institutions. Upon convening for the start of trial the following morning, the "Senate" wasted little time in rejecting Zhelyabov's jurisdictional challenge. The court proceedings would have three main dramatic figures: Presiding Judge Fuchs, the prosecutor Nikolai Muraviev, and the self-represented defendant Andrei Zhelyabov.

Judge Fuchs did his best to run a fair semblance of a criminal trial, with witnesses, rules of evidence and cross-examination. However, in doing so he was on a rather short leash. Pobedonostsev and other conservatives went ahead of time to Alexander Alexandrovitch to request that Zhelyabov, as an admitted assassin, not be permitted to use the trial as a pulpit for preaching the views of Narodnaya Volya. Of course, Zhelyabov intended to do exactly that – i.e., to argue Narodnaya Volya's world view at every opportunity. Judge Fuchs was explicitly warned that if this aspect of the proceedings got out of hand, the trial would be stopped and converted to a military tribunal. Under this constraint, Judge Fuchs repeatedly, throughout the trial, admonished Zhelyabov to "confine his statements to his own case" and not to try to argue the Narodnaya Volya point of view.[533]

Nevertheless, Zhelyabov pushed the envelope as deftly as any trial attorney. He swiftly managed to put on record his viewpoint and those of his fellow defendants. At the outset of the proceedings, he was asked to state his "religion." He responded with:

> I was baptised into the Orthodox Church but am no longer a member. At the same time I admit the teaching of Christ to be the basis of my moral convictions. I believe in truth and justice. I hold religion without deeds to be of no value. I hold it to be the duty of a sincere Christian to fight on behalf of the weak and oppressed; and, if need be, to suffer for them. That is my faith.[534]

The prosecution called 19 witnesses, all of whom were government officials or military officers, to testify to the actual attack on the embankment of the Ekatarinsky Canal. Zhelyabov attempted to harry the prosecution with cross-examination on small details. Helfman and Mikhailov, who were represented by attorneys, simply responded to the questions that were addressed to them. Perovskaya admitted that she was a member of Narodnaya Volya and that she had participated in Alexander II's assassination. Perovskaya's only apparent concern during the course of the trial was to misrepresent that Mikhailov was not involved as a bomber.

She and Zhelyabov hoped to save him from the gallows.[535]

Muraviev was an extremely earnest young prosecutor, no older than Zhelyabov and only a couple of years older then Perovskaya. By an odd coincidence of history, which many writers have hastened to point out, Nikolai Muraviev was the exact same person who, as a boy called Kolya some 23 years earlier, played with Sonia when she was five years old, Kolya's father was governor of Pskov, and Sonia's father living next door was vice-governor. Supposedly, Sonia and her older siblings had once rescued young Kolya from drowning.[536] But both Sonia and Kolya kept their personal connection entirely out of the proceedings. The fact that they had once been playmates was never mentioned on the record at trial. One thing that did become apparent was that Nikolai Muraviev, the son of a governor, would demonstrate just as much passion in his attack on the evil character of terrorism as Sofia Perovskaya, the daughter of a governor, had demonstrated in her use of such tactics.

The morning of the third day of trial opened with the closing argument of Muraviev. "Gentlemen, as I am destined to undertake the trial prosecution in this most appalling of crimes ever commited in the history of the Russian land," he began, "I feel overwhelmed by the immensity of my task. Before the freshly filled grave of our beloved monarch, amid the universal tears of a great empire mourning the unexpected and terrible end of its father and reformer, I fear lest my weak powers will not suffice." But his argument would at least be very thorough, lasting five hours. It covered not only the key events in the history of the terrorist phase of Narodnaya Volya, all the way back to its founding conference at Lipetsk, but also, the Nechaev-like exaggeration of the size and power of the so-called "Executive Committee" of the organization, and the evidence in the assassination conspiracy case.

Muraviev in his argument tried to head off any appeal to sentiment to spare Perovskaya's life because of her sex.

We can imagine a political conspiracy; we can imagine that this conspiracy uses the most cruel, amazing means; we can imagine that a woman should be part of this conspiracy. But that a woman should lead a conspiracy, that she should take on herself all the details of the murder, that she should with cynical coldness place the bomb throwers, draw a plan and show them where to stand, that she should stand a few steps away from the place of the crime and admire the work of her own hands – any normal feelings of morality can have no place of understanding of such a role for a woman.[537]

The argument was recognized as brilliant by the majority of his Russian hearers who were in sympathy with him. It was filled with emotions and evocative imagery. With real feeling, he compared the terrorist exploits of the defendants and their fellow conspirators to acts of the devil. He blasted terrorists as "people without moral principles," their core sin being "arrogance of thought." Several hours into the harangue, he referred to "that bloody fog that hovers over the Calvary of the Ekaterinsky Canal, where there loom the grim figures of the tsaricides . . ." At this point, Zhelyabov burst out with a loud laugh, interrupting him. Muraviev paused for a moment as if taken aback. He continued:

Here, I am interrupted by Zhelyabov's laugh. That amused or ironic mirth that has been his attitude throughout the whole course of the proceedings, the mirth with which he greets the shattering picture of the first of March. . . . . But I shall not hesitate to once more expose the mourning of a nation to that mockery. For so should it be. When men weep, then a Zhelyabov laughs.

Zhelyabov's laugh in the prosecutor's face was a defining moment in the trial.[538]

The trial unfolded on a schedule that was very unusual from an Anglo-American point of view. There was a mid-day session, from 11 a.m. to 2:30 p.m., and a night session, from 8 p.m. until midnight. The first two days, Thursday, March 26, and Friday, March 27, were taken up with testimony from percipient witnesses. Court continued with closing arguments on a Saturday, March 28, and to allow sufficient time, this third and final session started "early," at 10 a.m.[539] The defendants were placed in an order such that the least likely to make troublesome arguments would speak first. This was intended to avoid a repetition of earlier mass terrorist trials where relatively stolid defendants took inspiration when they heard speeches by more articulate co-defendants. The order was memorialized in artist sketches: Rysakov, Mikhailov, Helfman, Kibalchich, Perovskaya and then Zhelyabov.

Rysakov had cracked under interrogation and thus faced the wrath of his co-defendants. He was a basket case. In his final statement he disclaimed having belonged to the "terrorist section," and he denied approving of terrorism as a "method of struggle." The real argument made later by his attorney in the penalty phase was that because he was under the age of 21, he was ineligible for the death penalty.

Mikhailov said little, being basically content to rely on the efforts of Perovskaya and Zhelyabov to exonerate him. He was quoted as saying, "I have not the education to explain myself." He admitted being a member of the Social Revolutionary Party, but thought it was "a party for protecting the workers." Helfman took issue solely with some details of the prosecution's account of her history. She sealed her fate by professing her devotion to Narodnaya Volya. Thus, "I wish to point out," she said, "that when I came back to St. Petersburg [i.e., to live underground as an illegal], it was not in order to escape the police, but because I had devoted myself to the service of that cause which I had been and have been serving."[540]

Kibalchich convincingly played the part of the eccentric "mad scientist." For instance, he voiced an objection to the testimony of government witness that the explosives used in the assassination had been imported from abroad. "I must protest the allegation that any substance was imported," he interjected indignantly. "It was all made in our own laboratory." He also objected to testimony that the amount of explosives used for the mine in the Malaya Sadovaya endangered the lives of nearby residents. Kibalchich insisted his calculations proved otherwise. "Taking the diameter of the intended crater as 20 feet, the effective zone of the explosion would have been very localized. In view of the appreciable distance between the edge of the crater and the edge of the pavement, there would in my opinion have been no danger even to passing pedestrians." However, in response to a question posed to him by Judge Fuchs, he did nothing whatever to help his chances in the case. "The court finds it necessary to know, in preparing the dynamite and the grenades, if you knew the purpose to which they would be applied?" Kibalchich responded, "Yes, of course, I knew."[541]

The chief concern articulated by Kibalchich was that the design for his latest invention, a rocket-propelled flying machine, should be preserved for posterity. In custody after his arrest, he relentlessly scratched the walls of his cell with sketches and figures, until finally he was given pencil and paper to write on. He used his final opportunity to address the court to address the fate of his flying machine. "I am of the opinion that the design is practicable," he said. "My draft contains full details, and the necessary designs and calculations are attached. It now appears unlikely that I shall have the opportunity of discussing my invention with qualified experts, and, as the possibility exists of my plans being exploited by unauthorized persons, I now publicly declare that my project and sketch are to pass into the sole possession of my counsel, Mr. Girard." Such was the extent of his disconnection from reality.[542]

Throughout the trial, Perovskaya left the talking to the bearded Zhelyabov, that "wiry type of the fierce and unyielding demagogue," as the Times of London correspondent who was covering the trial described him. She also left entirely to "Boris" the role of the defiant, hissing cat, snarling in the face of the inevitable judgment and sentence. Zhelyabov turned and glared around the courtroom on several occasions when he was interrupted by the judge, or when some in the audience murmured disapprovingly at his remarks.[543] Zhelyabov managed to lay out Narodnaya Volya's point of view on the history of its evolution from "Going to the People" to terrorism, even as Judge Fuchs repeatedly ordered him to stick to "his own case." Zhelyabov in his colloquy with the court scored points based on the argument that the breadth of Muraviev's argument had opened the door to a rebuttal exposition of the merits of the Narodnaya Volya cause.

Sonia appeared satisfied with Zhelyabov's performance. She whispered to him during testimony and argument, and she also spoke with him during breaks until Judge Fuchs, under pressure from Pobedonostsev, ordered that the defendants must be taken back to their cells immediately any time the court stood in recess. In response to questions posed to her at the outset, she admitted her participation in all the acts of which she and her co-defendants were accused.[544] She spoke again in court only at the end of the trial, when all the defendants were given the opportunity for a final statement. What she chose to address in a very few words was the accusation of immorality that had been argued at length by her childhood companion, Nikolai Muraviev:

> The prosecutor has made a number of charges against us. With regard to his statements of fact I have dealt with these in my preliminary examination. But I and my friends are also accused of immorality, brutality, and contempt for public opinion. I wish to

say that no one who knows our lives and the circumstances in which we have had to work will accuse us of either immorality or brutality.[545]

Chapter 21: Resolute to the End

It was now midnight on Saturday. The "Senate" went into session to consider its verdict, and the defendants were taken back to their cells. At 3 a.m. they were brought back in to hear the decision. It was no surprise. They were found guilty, on all charges, except that Rysakov, Mikhailov, and Helfman were found not guilty of participating in the Malaya Sadovaya tunnel plot. The prosecutor requested the death penalty for all defendants, and the "senators" again retired to consider the sentence. Dawn had broken by the time they returned at 6:30 a.m. Regarding Rysakov, they decided that while the penalty for minors from 14 to 21 years old was mitigated with respect to the length of penal servitude and some other types of punishments, this did not apply to the death penalty, which was to be applied the same as for adults to minors from 14 to 21. All six prisoners were condemned to be hanged. The sentence would be carried out on Friday, April 3.[546]

The terrorists had thus been afforded a lengthy legal process. Now it was time for them to be utterly crushed, equally by due process of law. Out of all the defendants, Perovskaya alone, as a member of the high nobility, was afforded the right to have her sentence confirmed by the Tsar personally. She disdained any appeal to him. Varvara Stepanovna requested permission to visit Sonia for one last time. This was denied, on the ground that all of the defendants including Perovskaya were considered by law to be already "dead." They were not allowed to meet with anyone other than an Orthodox priest.

During the last day of trial, Gessia Helfman whispered a secret to her neighboring defendant, Kibalchich. She told him she was sure that she was pregnant by her Narodnaya Volya lover Nikolai Kolodkevitch, the "Purring Cat." Although Helfman also whispered to Kibalcich to keep this information secret, he promptly passed along the news to his court appointed attorney, Vladimir Gerard. Gerard, in turn, informed Helfman's court appointed attorney, who arranged to have a petition for the physical examination of Helfman drawn up and submitted on Monday morning. In response, doctors came to the prison to check her, and confirmed that she appeared to be four months pregnant. The execution of her death sentence was immediately suspended, and soon was deferred until after she could give birth.[547]

Did Perovskaya also have a secret similar to Helfman's? We have no direct evidence on the subject. The question needs to be asked, if only due to the absence of any clear explanation for Sonia's mystery illness, one that required her to buy "medicine," and for her mystery weakness, one that made it "difficult to walk." These symptoms, which can occur during early pregnancy, she exhibited to multiple friends and fellow conspirators in March 1881. For six months, from September of 1880 through February of 1881, Perovskaya enjoyed a live-in relationship with the tall, handsome Andrei Zhelyabov. By the accounts we have, their affair was every bit as impassioned as the relationship between Helfman and the "Purring Cat."

And while the details of Perovskaya's love life with Zhelyabov remain a private matter which she guarded carefully and carried with her into the grave, we know of numerous instances where the sexual relations of couples involved with Narodnaya Volya in the 1879-81 period resulted in pregnancy.[548] Judging from Helfman, it appears women detainees of Narodnaya Volya were not routinely subjected to a medical examination while in custody. Thus, if Sonia decided to die while carrying a secret pregnancy, there was no real impediment to her doing so. It appears she felt a sense of peace and even fulfillment at the thought of dying a public martyr's death alongside her comrades. For this reason, she refused to appeal to the Tsar, or to anyone else, to try to delay her death. Had she revealed herself to be pregnant, very likely she would have died alone.[549]

Rysakov, Mikhailov, and Kibalchich all submitted petitions for clemency of one kind or another that went to the Tsar. Perovskaya and Zhelyabov did not. Rysakov's petition pointed out the help he had given at trial and asked for his execution to be postponed for one year so that he could assist in tracking down more Narodnaya Volya members. Kibalchich said in his petition that he did not protest his execution, but wished to avoid the further reprisals that were likely to follow from his execution and that of the other defendants and therefore urged the Emperor to set the death sentences aside. All of the petitions were denied. The new Tsar wrote on the petition of Kibalchich: "Nothing new here – the fantasy of a sick imagination."[550]

At 8 p.m. on Thursday, April 2, five Orthodox priests entered the House of Detention, one for each of the five remaining condemned. As with earlier assassins and terrorists who had been hanged, starting with Karakozov, the authorities appear to have been concerned with providing them the opportunity to acquiesce, in the end, to sanity. Hence five priests were sent on a mission to urge the "March 1" condemned to prepare for their journey into the abyss by humbly confessing their sins. Rysakov and Mikhailov did so. Kibalchich met and debated with his priest for a good hour, but he did not make any confession, nor did he engage in any part of the ritual of communion. Perovskaya and Zhelyabov declined to see "their" priests. Sonia lay down to go to sleep for the last time at around 11 p.m. [551]

At 6 a.m., the condemned were awakened and given morning tea. They were then escorted one by one into a room in the House of Detention where they were told to change into their execution costumes: state issued clothes consisting of underwear, gray pants, and gray coats, over which was placed a black convict's coat. They wore state issued boots and brimless hats with ear flaps. Perovskaya's clothes were only slightly different from the men's. Instead of gray pants she was issued a black skirt with thin teak-brown stripes sewn on it. Over the skirt she also wore a thin black prison coat. Instead of a hat, her head was wrapped in strips of black cloth that served as a makeshift bonnet. After their hands were pinned to their sides, all of the five prisoners including Perovskaya were draped with special necklaces, large boards to be worn on their chests with black painted lettering that read, "Tsarkiller." [552]

After being dressed and tied in this fashion, the convicts were led out to the prison yard in order to mount chariots that were waiting to take them to the place of execution at Semyonovskaya Square. The journey would cover 18 long blocks, about one mile, along city streets. To better display the prisoners, these large wagons had been fitted with elevated benches for the passengers that were positioned some four meters off the ground. Ivan Frolov, the executioner, had spent the night in the House of Detention so that he could get up in the morning with the condemned. Aided by one of his assistants who was himself a convict, Frolov now supervised and helped the prisoners one by one as they climbed up to their high perches atop the wagons. There each was tied tightly to the vehicle, positioned to ride facing backwards so that the condemned could better see and be seen, with separate straps fastening their arms, legs, and torsos.[553]

On the first wagon were seated Zhelyabov and Rysakov. The positioning of these two next to each other was probably calculated to serve as a reminder of that first terrible day after the assassination, when Zhelyabov had written in a note, "If the new Emperor . . . intends to execute Rysakov, then it would be a grave injustice to spare my life." Rysakov seemed to observers to be very upset. His body was limp and his head hung down. Zhelyabov made a sustained effort to look away from his young protégé, who had talked under interrogation and betrayed his fellow terrorists. Pulled by two horses, the first cart left the gate of the House of Detention at 7:50 a.m.[554]

Right behind the first tumbril followed the second. Riding backwards atop the high bench on this one, Sonia was tied in the middle between Kibalchich and Mikhailov. All three appeared to onlookers to be in good spirits, although Mikhailov was said to be "pale." They lurched each time the springless cart encountered a pothole or an uneven spot on the cobbled street. Several times Mikhailov shouted something at the watchers. Whatever he tried to say was drowned out by the unceasing roll of drums beaten by marching troops who walked alongside the grim cortege. Behind the two wagons carrying the condemned came three more vehicles. In these rode the five priests, who would again attend the prisoners at their execution.[555]

It was a gorgeous spring day, with a bright sun melting patches of ice which still coated the streets of St. Petersburg. All public places in the city had been ordered to remain closed until noon on this Friday. Through streets lined with a solid mass of people, it took the solemn cortege a full hour to travel from the House of Detention to the execution site. Waiting for them there was an enormous crowd that had turned out to see the spectacle of the public execution of the Tsar's assassins.

Thousands of troops and onlookers surrounded the black painted scaffold in Semyonovsky Square. This plaza was then much larger than it is today, being used at that time as a track for winter horse races. The platform, a rectangle ten meters across and eight meters from front to back, had been built about two meters above ground level surrounding a simple gallows structure, two vertical wooden posts planted in the ground with a single wooden crossbar connecting them. To the crossbar were attached six iron rings. Frolov and four convict assistants arrived a half hour before the procession to fit five of these rings with nooses (the last ring to the left, which had been intended for Helfman, was not used). The other end of each noosed rope was to be tied to another ring mounted in the nearest vertical post. Behind the scaffold, in two wagons, were five crudely painted black coffins, each filled with wood shavings. There was also a separate raised dais, about three meters in front of the scaffold, for government dignitaries and foreign diplomats who had been selected to receive front row seats for the ceremony.[556]

At ten minutes to nine, an electric murmur ran through the assembled crowd at Semyonovsky Square as the sound of approaching drums and fifes made themselves heard, faint at first and gradually increasing. Then came into view the sparkle of the sun reflecting off metal tipped spears carried by the Cossack advance guard of the cortege of the condemned. As the wagons slowly rolled their way through the onlookers and approached the scaffold, all eyes strained to catch a glimpse of the face of Perovskaya, this child of nobility who had transformed herself into a hardened leader of terrorists. What they saw impressed them with the lack of any sign of distress. Sonia's cheeks even displayed a faint reddish blush. Her hair, slightly dislodged and tousled from the wind during the ride, tumbled over her forehead. Her arms were pinned alongside her black-clad body; her hands were covered in mittens without fingers. Her eyes glanced about the crowd. Zhelyabov and

Rysakov were dismounted first from their tumbril and led up the steps to the scaffold. Then came the turn of the other three. Perovskaya was helped down from the high bench. She seemed to be the most resolute of the five. Vera Figner would later sum it up: "On the scaffold Perovskaya was firm, with all her steel-hard firmness."[557]

At the back of the platform there were three iron posts that on other occasions served as pillories for the display of convicts who were about to be deported to Siberia. Today, Frolov arrayed the condemned on the back of the platform in the order in which they were to be hanged. Kibalchich was placed on the far right, loosely chained to the railing rather than a post. Mikhailov, Perovskaya, and Zhelyabov, in that order, right to left, were attached to the pillory posts. Rysakov was placed on the far left, also chained to the railing rather than a post. At last the drumming ceased. A hush fell over the crowd and the platform. A military call rang out, "On guard!" From the podium the court secretary, Popov, began reciting the verdicts and death sentences. This took a few minutes. While this was happening, Zhelyabov could be seen leaning in Perovskaya's direction and saying something to her. Sonia, however, stood straight and looked straight ahead.[558]

When Popov finished reading, the dramatic drum rolls resumed. Now the drummers had moved up into a position in front of the dais, between the dais and the scaffold. The priests, dressed in full vestments, strode up onto the platform. Each one carried a large cross, which he held out to his assigned convict to kiss. Kibalchich, Mikhailov and Perovskaya shook their heads and declined. But then Zhelyabov, as a rather surprising gesture, kissed his cross passionately. He did not want the crowd to think the terrorists were opposed to religion. After the priests gave the sign of the cross and left the platform, the prisoners were unchained from their pillories long enough to exchange a final farewell. Zhelyabov, Mikhailov, and Kibalchich each went to Perovskaya and gave her a kiss.

Rysakov also moved toward her, but as he approached Sonia she turned away.[559]

Frolov came to all of the five condemned and led them to their assigned places next to the dangling nooses. He covered Kibalchich first with a grayish death shroud, a sleeveless canvas garment that was pulled over his shoulders, completely covering his head with a hood while leaving a horizontal slit across the throat through which the noose could be inserted. Frolov's assistants quickly shrouded the other four, including Perovskaya. Zhelyabov and Perovskaya, while waiting in their shrouds, shook their heads repeatedly. Rysakov, the last to be hooded, trembled visibly. His knees buckled as the assistants rather forcefully pulled the shroud over his head. Forsaken by the terrorists due to his betrayal, and forsaken by the authorities due to his explosion of the bomb against the beloved Emperor, Rysakov was the most pitiful of the condemned. When his turn came, he would grasp with his feet in a desperate attempt to clutch at the stool, forcing the executioners to yank on his rope while at the same time pushing him from behind to dislodge him.

After all were shrouded, Frolov placed in front of Kibalchich a three-step stool. He then helped him climb to the top, stepped up beside him, and checked to be sure the rope was tight enough and that the noose was sliding freely. Then he got down and, with a flourish, pulled the stool out from underneath. The rope pulled taut. His feet turned just a few small circles in the air before gradually stilling.[560]

With Mikhailov, the executioners had embarrassing difficulties. Under his weight the rope stretched and broke, causing him to fall to the platform. The rope was retied, and the hanging repeated. But the rope broke again. By this time Mikhailov was already only semi-conscious. The executioners had to drag his body up onto the stool while a second noosed rope was rigged to the crossbeam to finish off the hanging.[561] Perovskaya was the third to be hanged, after Mikhailov and before Zhelyabov. It seemed to some of the observers that as soon as she mounted the stool and her noose was in place, she collapsed into it in a welcoming manner.[562]

... Perchance to dream ...

The Lady in Black awakens from her nap and rejoins the party in the salon. Now she tells something of herself. She was born of noble rank, in St. Petersburg. After weighing it well, she made the choice to give up her rank and race for the glory of a cause. Her love was a poor man born for strife, an outlaw. He died a soldier. She must not be sorry. "I was told what to expect."[563]

THE END

Epilogue

Alexander Nikolaevitch Romanov

Alexander III almost immediately declared his intention to erect a church in his father's memory called the Church on the Spilled Blood -- on the very site of the assassination. He also decreed that this new church would be built in "traditional Russian" style - in contradistinction to what he and his circle of close advisors saw as the contaminating Western cultural influence that pervaded the architecture of St. Petersburg. The church's final style drew heavily from St. Basil's Cathedral in Moscow and the Vladimir Cathedral in Kiev. Construction began in 1883. One of the most impressive elements is an extravagant shrine constructed supposedly on the exact spot where Alexander II was fatally wounded, which has maintained a special place within the church's interior. It was completed in July 1907.

After the Revolution, the church was looted and fell into disrepair. It was closed in 1932, and essentially turned into a garbage dump. Rumors circulated that it would actually be torn down. After it sustained damage duiring the siege of

Leningrad during World War II, the church was used as a warehouse for a nearby theater.

Like the Phoenix bird whose multi-colored wings it resembles, the Church on the Spilled Blood rose again from the ashes. In 1970 the church was made a branch of the St. Isaac's Cathedral museum, and 80% of the church's extraordinary restoration was funded by proceeds from St. Isaac's. The project was estimated to cost 3.6 million rubles, but ended up costing 4.6 million rubles, mainly from the extravagant collection of mosaics. Thematically the more than 7,500 square meters of mosaics link Alexander II's murder with the

Church of the Savior of the Spilled Blood, rising from St. Petersburg skyline.
Photo: Dori D. Riggs

crucifixion. The restoration culminated in the dramatic re-opening of the church in August 1997, when thousands of eager visitors swamped the church.[564] The outside of the church is encircled with plaques commemorating the freeing of the serfs and many other reforms that Alexander decreed while he was Emperor.

Alexander Alexandrovitch Romanov

After March of 1881, the fear of new terrorist attacks continued to dampen the spirits of St. Petersburg. For several years, Alexander III virtually refused to come into the city, preferring to remain on his suburban estate at Gatchina. There, he could pursue a relaxed lifestyle centered around hunting and drinking with no real interference from politicians. Pobedonostsev was the key advisor who had Alexander III's ear. He encouraged Alexander III to be constantly security oriented. He lobbied hard against any kind of constitution. "What is a constitution?" he asked rhetorically. "Western Europe gives us an answer to that question. The constitutions that exist are just instruments for more injustice, for more intrigues. One would like to trick us by introducing one of these alien inventions, a constitution, for our unhappiness, for our lost souls. Russia is powerful due to its autocracy, thanks to the mutual confidence and stability that it inspires, thanks to the tight ties that attach the people to their Tsar!" His views carried the day with Alexander III and his cabinet. Leaders open to reform, including Grand Duke Konstantin, Loris-Melikov and D. A. Miliutin gave up on being able to bring about anything approaching a shadow of a constitution or a representative government. Loris-Melikov soon retired from government service and made his way to retirement in the French Riviera.[565]

Alexander III ruled in basically the same conservative fashion for the next 13 years until he died in 1894 at the age of 49. He was succeeded by his oldest son Nikolai, who would turn out to be the last in the line of Russia's Romanov Tsars.

Gessia Helfman

On May 5 (NS), 1881, Helfman was sent to the Trubeskoy Bastion, where she was kept in total solitary confinement. Word that she was malnourished and in poor health came from a rare visitor she was allowed, her attorney Gerke. Large public demonstrations involving more than a thousand people in support of Helfman occurred in France, which had a liberal government at the time, in Paris and Marseille. Victor Hugo wrote an open letter to the Russian government calling for her to be pardoned. In response, on July 14, Alexander III signed a decree commuting her sentence to perpetual servitude.

On August 27 (NS), 1881, Helfman was transferred back to a cell in the House of Detention, where she was under constant surveillance. On October 24 (NS), she gave birth to a baby girl. The girl was afterwards, on February 6 (NS), 1882 taken from her and placed in an orphanage, possibly because by then Helfman was seriously ill with a peritoneal infection. Helfman died one week later, on the night of February 12-13 (NS), 1881. The baby also died one year later, in the orphanage. The baby's father Nikolai Kolodkevitch died in prison August 4 (NS), 1884. [566]

Sergei Nechaev

In the wave of reaction triggered by Alexander II's assassination, the Government put in a new commandant of the Peter and Paul Fortress, General I. S. Ganetsky. Ganetsky cut off Nechaev's liberal treatment. He painted over the window of his cell, discontinued his garden walks, and put him on a diet that resembled bread and water. Still, Nechaev continued to smuggle correspondence out of the Alexei Ravelin until October or November of 1881. But in November and December, the scandal of Nechaev's "staff" was unmasked. Eventually 69 people were arrested for complicity with Nechaev's plot, 44 of them on December 29, 1881.

Nechaev's health worsened dramatically after this

occurred. By a year later, in November of 1882, the prison doctor wrote an alarming note requesting that milk be added to Nechaev's diet, due to his suffering from severe scurvy. Before the end of the month, Nechaev was dead. Upon his death, prison authorities asked the highest government officials what to do with the body. The instructions they received were to incinerate his clothes, to secretly remove his corpse, and to transport it by train, again in the utmost secrecy, for burial someplace where it could never be distinguished if found.[567]

Vera Figner

After the execution of Perovskaya and Zhelyabov, as well as the capture of other Narodnaya Volya Executive Committee members, Vera Figner remained as the unquestioned leader of Narodnaya Volya. But the Executive Committee was now very much weakened and constantly on the run. Figner went first to Odessa, then to Moscow, and then to Kharkov. She was not finally arrested until the summer of 1884, when she was caught through the work of a Narodnaya Volya operative who, after being captured, agreed to help the authorities catch terrorists. Figner was tried and sentenced to death, but shortly afterwards the Emperor commuted her sentence to life in prison. She was sent to Schlüsselburg Prison, 70 kilometers east of St. Petersburg, a facility that had been newly renovated specifically to segregate and house Narodnaya Volya terrorists. There she would remain, along with the other terrorists who did not kill themselves, or die of illness, or get themselves shot as a result of lashing out and attacking prison staff.

By 1902, of the original 40 Narodnaya Volya prisoners, only 13 were left in Schlüsselburg. They formed their own very private and intimate society. On January 13, 1903, Figner's sentence was commuted by the Emperor to 20 years. Thus she was released at the end of September, 1904.[568] She lived on until 1942. Eventually she wrote her memoirs, which are one of our better sources on the personality and activities of Perovskaya and Narodnaya Volya. They are generally well written, filled with meaningful descriptions and vivid images.

Figner's closing thoughts on the events culminating in the assassination of Alexander included the following comments.

> I must here say a few words about the demoralization brought about in society by the methods of the struggle between the government and the revolutionary party. This struggle was accompanied by violence, as is the case with any conflict waged by force rather than ideas. And violence, whether committed against a thought, an action, or a human life, never contributed to the refinement of morals. It arouses ferocity, develops brutal instincts, awakens evil impulses, and prompts acts of disloyalty. Humanity and magnanimity are incompatible with it. And from this point of view, the government and the revolutionary party, when they entered into what may be termed a hand-to-hand battle, vied with one another in corrupting everything and every one around them. On the one hand, the party declared that all methods were fair in the war with its antagonist, that here the end justified the means. At the same time, it created a cult of dynamite and the revolver, and crowned the terrorist with a halo; murder and the scaffold acquired a magnetic charm and attraction for the youth of the land, and the weaker their nervous system, and the more oppressive the life around them, the greater was their exaltation at the thought of revolutionary terror. Since the effects of ideas are hardly perceptible to a revolutionist during the brief span of his lifetime, he desires to see some concrete, palpable manifestation of his own will, his own strength, and at that time only a terroristic act with all its violence could be such a manifestation.[569]

Olga Lyubatovich

After the cataclysmic assassination of March 1, Olga Lyubatovich continued her personal odyssey to try to find the incarcerated "Sparrow" Morozov. Her task was made difficult by the fact that she had no idea what prison he was held in and, in fact, she did not even know under what name he was imprisoned. The aftermath of the assassination of March 1 made it very "hot" for an illegal such as Lyubatovich to live underground anywhere in Russia. It was especially hard for a single unaccompanied woman without a valid internal passport to travel from city to city. Still, Olga persisted in her search for her lover. After a close escape, she make her way to Minsk. There she united herself with Narodnaya Volya sympathizers.

Eventually Lyubatovich learned that Morozov was held in the House of Detention in St. Petersburg. She started a correspondence with him, using a series of intermediaries. This was when she finally learned from Kravchinsky that their daughter left behind in Switzerland had died. Lyubatovich mentioned to a fellow radical that she hoped to come up with a plot to free Morozov. The radical turned out to be a government agent. Morozov was swiftly transferred into the Peter and Paul Fortress.

The government's anti-terrorism campaign was in full swing. The government was easily able to enlist anti-terrorism volunteers, who were hot on the trail of anyone who they detected to be an illegal living in St. Petersburg. The police slowly gained the upper hand on the terrorists and forced them into a defensive battle for survival. Illegals were recognized and then shadowed to find out who else was associating with them. One by one, the illegals were exhausted and isolated and then either succumbed to arrest, or committed suicide.

Lyubatovich, along with Figner and some others in the organization, fled to Moscow where they hoped the government would be less vigilant. However, this was not to be, as the government also had a well-conceived anti-terrorism campaign ongoing in Moscow. The terrorists did not get popular sympathy. Lyubatovich was arrested in the street in Moscow.

During her interrogation, Dobrzhinsky proposed to Lyubatovich that she be released on word of honor if she would agree to negotiate a truce with the Narodnaya Volya terrorists, with the ultimate aim being an amnesty. Lyubatovich perceptively replied that for the terrorists, an amnesty would be perceived as too selfish of an objective. Eventually she suggested that they use a man for the job of negotiating the amnesty. She even met with one of her Narodnaya Volya colleagues, who had been arrested with her. But she was unable to convince him to try. Soon after, Lyubatovich was transferred to the Peter and Paul Fortress, and then she was exiled to Irkutsk. She spent over 20 years there, returning to Russia only after the 1905 Revolution. In 1906, while living in Tiflis, Georgia, she wrote her memoir: "Le proche et le lointain, Souvenirs de la vie des révolutionnaires des années 1878-1881." We know little of her life after that. She died in 1917 in Tiflis at age 64.[570]

Nikolai Morozov

Lyubatovich's lover and the father of her child, Nikolai Morozov, was imprisoned in the Peter and Paul Fortress until 1884. Then, starting in 1884 he was housed for 21 years with the surviving Narodnaya Volya in Schlüsselburg Prison. After his release he married another woman. During his time in Schlüsselburg, Morozov engaged in extensive self-teaching of science and classics. Morozov's chemistry studies while in Schlüsselburg are described by Figner in her Memoirs. Beginning in 1896, these studies also included minerology, geology and paleontology. Morozov ultimately re-invented himself as a psuedo-scientist of considerable international celebrity.

Morozov's seminal and most remembered work, which

remains in print, is titled *Revelation in Thunder and Storms*. It was partially written while he was confined in Schlüsselburg and was first published in 1907. He dedicated the book to his "good friend, Ms. Vera Figner." Revelation is a re-dating of the story of the Bible's New Testament. Morozov placed the events described in the biblical Book of Revelation as happening on September 30 of the year 395, AD, according to the Julian calendar. He supported this conclusion by way of astronomical calculations tied to horoscopes derived from Morozov's re-interpretation of the internal text of Revelations. For example, after pointing out that by some living in some primitive societies the planets were thought to engage in "horse-like" movements, Morozov reasoned,

> While at the present time the author tries to make himself clear to every reader, in the olden days the scientific papers were purposely worded in such a manner that only an initiated person could grasp the true meaning of every paragraph. Thus, if on this basis we could assume that the author of the Apocalypse was really refering to the planets when he wrote "horses," then the "Four Horsemen" of the Apocalypse could be easily deciphered. If this assumption is correct and the author of the Apocalypse merely described a picture including the four planets that he saw in the sky, then it is most likely that there should be a number of other heavenly bodies that he observed, and referred to under some fictitious names that offer only a slight hint for identification of a new star or constellation.

> Could it be a coincidence that in certain places such as southern France, for instance, the constellation of the Big Dipper even until now is called "Chariot of Souls"? Elsewhere, the Big Dipper is known as the "Seven Lanterns." So, if we assume for a minute that the seven burning lamps, mentioned in the fifth verse,

are the seven stars that compose the Big Dipper, then the next assumption suggests itself that the "Throne," in front of which the seven lamps are burning, could not be anything else but the constellation of Cassiopeia.[571]

Based on an elaborate assembly of these kinds of clues, assumptions, hypotheses and deductions, Morozov rejects the accepted chronology of the history of human civilization. Reviewers have observed, "[t]o certain types of minds, Morozov's method appears to be convincing. . . "[572]

Morozov's "method" was adopted by another Russian, Immanuel Velikovsky, who advocated a radically revised "chronology" of ancient times that was featured in his 1950 best seller, *Worlds in Collision.* Morozov's "method" was then explicitly relied upon and expanded (even though the specifics of his logic were modified) by a Russian mathematician named Anatoly T. Fomenko (born 1945). Fomenko became interested in Morozov's theories in 1973 and ultimately published a series of books entitled *History: Fiction or Science?* Fomenko's overall revisionist thesis, called "The New Chronology," has gained a widespread following, although no part of it has found any degree of acceptance in the mainstream scientific community.

Fomenko's contentions are even more fantastic than Morozov's. Whereas Morozov only attempted to re-date events in the "ancient world" prior to the sixth century A.D., Fomenko also, in his chronology, eliminates everything prior to the "Middle Ages." According to Fomenko all events and characters conventionally dated earlier than 11th century are a deliberate falsification, and represent "phantom reflections" of actual Middle Ages events and characters brought about by intentional mis-datings of historical documents. One of the many sensational claims of the New Chronology is that the birth of Christ actually occurred in 1153 AD, and his crucifixion occurred in 1186.[573]

Morozov lived until 1946 when he died at the age of 92. After his release, Morozov disdained any involvement in politics. Following the Bolshevik revolution, Morozov worked for the Institute of Natural Sciences in St. Petersburg. He was admitted to the Russian Academy of Sciences. The asteroid 1210 Morosovia, discovered in 1931, is named in his honor.

Lev Tikhomirov

Morozov's rival as the leading "theoretician" and apologist for Narodnaya Volya's use of terrorism, Lev Tikhomirov, avoided capture. In 1882 he left Russia for Switzerland and joined the emigré community. From there he went to Paris where, with Peter Lavrov, he published "the Narodnaya Volya News." But in 1888 Tikhomirov publicly renounced his revolutionary convictions, writing an editorial entitled, "Why I Stopped Being a Revolutionary." He argued that revolution in Russia was impossible. He urged the opponents of Russian autocracy to change their views and to collaborate with the tsarist regime. He obtained permission to return to Russia. As soon as he reached St. Petersburg he paid homage to the tomb of Alexander II.

Tikhomirov from that point on became an ardent reactionary, continuing to write extensively for Russian publications. Now he became a theoretician for the defense of autocracy. In 1913 he retired from St. Petersburg and moved to a country home about two hours by car north of Moscow. There he wrote a book called *Fundamentals of Religion and Philosophy of History*, in which he argued that all of human history is a constantly evolving development of the idea of religion. He also published recollections of his former pretend fiancée Sofia Perovskaya (1899), of Andrei Zhelyabov (1899), and of Nikolai Kibalchich (1906).[574]

Georgi Plekhanov

After splitting with Narodnaya Volya in the summer of

1879, Georgi Plekhanov moved to Paris. There, in collaboration with Lev Deitch and Vera Zasulitch, he became a fervid Marxist propagandist. He was expelled from France in 1895 and moved to German Switzerland. He collaborated with Vladimir Ilyich Ulyanov, alias Lenin, between 1900 and 1903 in editing a newspaper called Iskra, or Spark. The Group for Liberation of Labor, founded by Plekhanov as an offshoot of Cherny Peredel, was a direct ideological ancestor of Bolshevism. However, he and Zasulitch ultimately rejected Lenin's Bolshevism to become *Men'sheviki*. The key issue in the Bolshevik – Menshevik split was the freedom of the individual to articulate his or her personal views. The Bolsheviks took a totalitarian view which denied that any degree of freedom to dissent should exist. *Bol'sheviki* means "majoritarian" in Russian. *Men'sheviki* means "minoritarian", a name adopted in response to the *Bol'sheviki*.

Plekhanov, as a Menshevik, became an associate of Alexander Kerensky. Plekhanov died of tuberculosis in a suburb of St. Petersburg in 1918.[575]

Vladimir Ilyich Ulyanov, aka Lenin

A 21-year old student from a well-to-do family, named Alexander Ulyanov, was the theoretician for a group called the Terrorists' Faction of the Narodnaya Volya. He and several companions planned to attack Alexander III with bombs on March 1, 1887, the sixth anniversary of his father's assassination. The police, alerted to the plot through an informant, arrested Ulyanov and his co-conspirators as they stood waiting along the route Alexander III planned to travel on the way to a memorial service for his father. At his trial, Ulyanov behaved much like Perovskaya and Zhelyabov. His proclamation in court included the following:

> Terror, this form of struggle devised by the nineteenth century, is the only means of defense to which a spiritually strong minority, convinced of its

righteousness, can resort against the physical power of the majority. . . . I have often thought about the argument that Russian society does not sympathize with terror, in fact is largely hostile to it. But this is a misunderstanding.

Ulyanov and his co-conspirators were hanged on May 8, 1887.[576]

Ulyanov's 17-year old younger brother Vladimir became radicalized as a result of his brother's arrest and execution. Vladimir became obsessed with Chernyskevsky's *What Is to Be Done?* He soon became a devoted follower of the writings and ideas of Georgi Plekhanov. Like his brother, he also became something of a theoretician. However, he disagreed strongly with terrorism as a method of struggle. When a newspaper collaborator proposed to publish a special commemorative tribute on the occasion of the 25th anniversary of the execution of Perovskaya and Zhelyabov, he replied, "They died, so what? Glory and honor to them, but why should we talk about it?"[577]

In 1901 Vladimir Ulyanov, probably to avoid drawing attention to his real identity, began publishing articles under the pen name "N. Lenin." From that point forward he would become known primarily by that name. More than likely "Lenin" was taken from the Lena River in Siberia where Ulyanov and others had been exiled. The next year, "N. Lenin" published his own important essay called "What Is to Be Done?" Lenin eventually split with his mentor Plekhanov, believing that Plekhanov's views were too theoretical and that a more concrete and authoritarian party organization was needed for an effective overthrow of the government.

Although he and his Bolsheviks called on them for support when it was useful to do so, the mature Lenin had no sympathy for the Socialist Revolutionaries, utopian anarchists who were the direct political descendants of Narodnaya Volya. He once wrote: "The majority of anarchists think and write about the future without understanding the present. That is what divides us Communists from them." Lenin admitted that the anarchists were "selfless," but commented that their "empty fanaticism blurred their vision of present and future alike."[578] Ultimately, the Socialist Revolutionaries were banned by the Bolsheviks and their leaders were arrested.

On August 30, 1918 Fanny Kaplan, born Feiga Haimovna Roytblat, a Socialist Revolutionary who had spent 11 years in a Siberian prison, approached Lenin as he was leaving a Moscow factory. She fired three shots, two of which struck him and seriously wounded him. In her confession, Kaplan said she shot Lenin because he was a "traitor to the Revolution." Fanny Kaplan was executed five days later with a bullet to the back of the head. In the next few months of Red Terror, around 800 Socialist Revolutionaries and other opponents of the Bolshevik regime were executed.[579] While Lenin returned to lead the Bolshevik government for five more years, his wounds contributed to his early demise at the age of 54.

Stepan Khalturin

After the Winter Palace explosion of February 1880, the police eventually figured out the real identity of "Stepan Batishkov." They tried to track down Khalturin. His entire family was placed under surveillance. Eventually, having failed to locate him, the authorities believed he had escaped to Romania, and then on to London. His family on the other hand believed that he had finally realized his original objective of going to America.

In reality, Narodnaya Volya had moved him to Moscow, where a family of sympathizers hid him. He was suffering from tuberculosis he had contracted while living in the damp basement of the Winter Palace. It took until the end of the summer of 1880 for him to be able to emerge from the bed where he was being concealed. Eventually he was able to get another job as a woodworker in Moscow. After a lull following the Alexander assassination, Khalturin slowly resumed organizing factory workers of Moscow. In late 1881, still in Moscow, he helped publish a third number of the "Worker's Gazette" which Zhelyabov and Perovskaya had initiated in St. Petersburg in the winter of 1880-81.

At around that same time, the Executive Committee of Narodnaya Volya headed by Vera Figner sent Khalturin to Odessa. The latest target of NV's wrath was the chief prosecutor of Odessa and an implacable enemy of terrorists, Major General Vasily Stepanovich Strelnikov. Figner, having "sentenced" Strelnikov to death, personally conducted a surveillance of his routine in Odessa. Khalturin and Nikolai Zhelvakov volunteered to take charge of the assassination. Zhelvakov was a rather typical profile terrorist, a product of the upper middle class and former student who had met Zhelyabov and Perovskaya in St. Petersburg.

On March 18, 1882, at around 4 p.m., Strelnikov finished an early dinner and went for a walk in the main part of town. He decided to sit on a bench and look out at a view of the Black Sea. While he was sitting there, at around 5 p.m., Zhelvakov ran up to him from behind and fired a revolver from close range into the back of his neck and head. Strelnikov died within minutes. Zhelvakov ran down a steep hill and jumped into a waiting carriage being driven by Khalturin. The two tried to escape but the populace, being alerted to the terrorist murder by the cries of Strelnikov's adjutant, rapidly surrounded the vehicle and kept it from moving. Khalturin tried shouting to the crowd that he was a socialist and that he was fighting for all of them. Nobody tried to help him and, in fact, the crowd held him down tightly until he could be handed over to police.

At the police station Khalturin was identified as a 31-year old resident of Tiflis named Konstantin Stepanov, and Zhelvakov was identified as a noble, 21-year old Nikolai Kosogorsky. Alexander III, from Gatchina, ordered that the terrorists should be summarily executed. At 5 a.m. on March 22, 1882, Khalturin, still identified as "Stepanov," was hanged along with "Kosogorsky." He was so weak with tuberculosis that he had to be helped to stand on the stool.

Bust of Stepan Khalturin, destroyed in 2010

After the Bolshevik Revolution, Soviet propaganda portrayed Khalturin as a model workers' hero. The city of Orlov was renamed "Khalturin" in 1923. But with the fall of the Soviet regime, the newly liberated public consciousness recognized the undesirable aspect of the hero worship of a murderous terrorist. The town of Khalturin was restored to its original name. The bust of Khalturin that had been prominently displayed there was smashed to bits.

Sofia Perovskaya

Perovskaya's legacy has undergone a parallel transformation. Under Soviet Russia, she was recognized as being a heroine bordering on sainthood. Among other enconmiums, she was the featured subject of a 1962 biography by Elena Segal, written for inclusion as part of the standard reading for Russian teenaged children. Alexandra Nazarova played the role of Sonia in a full length motion picture directed by Lev Arnshtam in 1967. Most who lived in Russia between 1967 and 1991 have seen the film. In every major Soviet city a street was named after Perovskaya. Over 400 monuments to her were erected. In St. Petersburg, a main street across the canal from the site of the assassination – the route traveled by the carriage carrying the mortally wounded Alexander to the Winter Palace – was renamed after Perovskaya.

After the fall of the Soviet regime in 1991, the public perception of Perovskaya changed dramatically. Now she was recognized as having been a terrorist, a person many no longer felt it appropriate to elevate into a national icon. Numerous streets that had been named after her were returned to their pre-revolutionary names.[580]   Today, the St. Petersburg street is called Konyushennaya Place [Конюшенная Площадь].

Endnotes & Bibliography

ENDNOTES TO INTRODUCTION

[1] Defining "terrorism" has presented a challenge for students of the phenomenon. The term has grown to have an overwhelmingly negative connotation, which lends itself to political overtones. In the classical formulation of the issue, "One man's terrorist is another's freedom fighter." For interesting discussions of the definitional problems surrounding the concept of terrorism, see E. Ahmad, *Terrorism: Theirs and Ours* (1998), republished in Geopolitics Review, Vol. n2, Issue 3 (Oct. 2001); G. Martin, *Understanding Terrorism, Challenges, Perspectives and Issues* (Sage Publications, Thousand Oaks, California, 2nd Edition 2006), pp. 33-74; L. Z. Freedman, *Terrorism, Problems of the Polistaraxic*, in *Perspectives on Terrorism*, L. Z. Freedman and Y. Alexander, eds., (Scholarly Resources, Inc., Wilmington, DE 1983), pp. 3-11. An ultimate truth may lie in Justice Potter Stewart observation relative to trying to define obscenity. We are "faced with the task of trying to

define what is undefinable." *Jacobellis v. Ohio*, 378 U.S. 184, 197 (1964) (Stewart, J., concurring). While much legitimate debate exists about who are the "real" terrorists, there is at least a general consensus that terrorism consists of sudden acts of violence against unarmed people and property, where the violence has political content (distinguishing "terrorism" from other sudden violent phenomena such as "mall shootings," which it resembles to some degree). The protagonists discussed in this book more or less obviated the definitional issue when they themselves explicitly characterized their tactic as "political killing."

[2] Letter to Benjamin Thomson, quoted in A. Roberts, *Napoleon, a Life*, p. 330 (Penguin Books, New York, NY, 2015).

[3] See generally W. Laqueur, in his June 2001 Introduction to the "Transaction Edition" of A History of Terrorism (Transaction Publishers, New Brunswick (U.S.) and London (U.K.), 2007).

[4] Laqueur, "Introduction to the Transaction Edition," at p. ix.

[5] Laqueur, p. 6.

ENDNOTES TO CHAPTER 1: THE POWER OF A LITERARY WORK

[6] Michael Andrew Drozd, *Chernyshevskii's What Is to Be Done, a Reevaluation*, Northwestern University Press, 2001, pp, 5-8.

[7] *What Is to Be Done?*, by Nikolai Chernyshevsky, with introduction by Kathryn Fever, translated in 1886 by N. Dole & S. S. Skidelsky, Ardis Publishers, Ann Arbor, Mich., 1986 ("Ardis Edition"), pp. 1-4.

[8] *What Is to Be Done?*, Ardis Edition, pp. 4-8.

[9] *What Is to Be Done?*, Ardis Edition, pp. 8-10.

[10] *What Is to Be Done?*, Ardis Edition, p. 11.

[11] *What Is to Be Done?*, Ardis Edition, pp. 11-15, 56.

[12] *What Is to Be Done?*, Ardis Edition, pp. 15-16.

[13] *What Is to Be Done?*, Ardis Edition, pp. 22-27.

[14] *What Is to Be Done?*, Ardis Edition, pp. 27-30.

[15] *What Is to Be Done?*, Ardis Edition, pp. 30-47.

[16] *What Is to Be Done?*, Ardis Edition, pp. 47-53.

[17] *What Is to Be Done?*, Ardis Edition, pp. 53-54.

[18] *What Is to Be Done?*, Ardis Edition, pp. 55-65.

[19] *What Is to Be Done?*, Ardis Edition, pp. 65-72.

[20] *What Is to Be Done?*, Ardis Edition, pp. 72-75.

[21] *What Is to Be Done?*, Ardis Edition, pp. 75-94.

[22] *What Is to Be Done?*, Ardis Edition, pp. 95-102.

[23] *What Is to Be Done?*, Ardis Edition, pp. 103-04.

[24] *What Is to Be Done?*, Ardis Edition, pp. 105-08.

[25] *What Is to Be Done?*, Ardis Edition, pp. 108-21.

[26] *What Is to Be Done?*, Ardis Edition, pp. 121-22.

[27] *What Is to Be Done?*, Ardis Edition, pp. 121-25.

[28] *What Is to Be Done?*, Ardis Edition, pp. 59, 125-36.

[29] *What Is to Be Done?*, Ardis Edition, p. 136.

[30] *What Is to Be Done?*, Ardis Edition, pp. 136-41.

[31] *What Is to Be Done?*, Ardis Edition, pp. 141-45.

[32] *What Is to Be Done?*, Ardis Edition, pp. 145-50.

[33] *What Is to Be Done?*, Ardis Edition, pp. 150-53.

[34] *What Is to Be Done?*, Ardis Edition, pp. 153-55.

[35] *What Is to Be Done?*, Ardis Edition, pp. 155-57.

[36] *What Is to Be Done?*, Ardis Edition, pp. 157-63.

[37] *What Is to Be Done?*, Ardis Edition, pp. 163-72.

[38] *What Is to Be Done?*, Ardis Edition, pp. 172-78.

[39] *What Is to Be Done?*, Ardis Edition, pp. 178-81.

[40] *What Is to Be Done?*, Ardis Edition, pp. 181-85.

[41] *What Is to Be Done?*, Ardis Edition, p. 185.

[42] *What Is to Be Done?*, Ardis Edition, pp. 185-88.

[43] *What Is to Be Done?*, Ardis Edition, pp. 189-91.
[44] *What Is to Be Done?*, Ardis Edition, pp. 191-94.
[45] *What Is to Be Done?*, Ardis Edition, p. 195.
[46] *What Is to Be Done?*, Ardis Edition, pp. 195-202.
[47] *What Is to Be Done?*, Ardis Edition, pp. 202-08.
[48] *What Is to Be Done?*, Ardis Edition, pp. 208-17.
[49] *What Is to Be Done?*, Ardis Edition, pp. 217-19.
[50] *What Is to Be Done?*, Ardis Edition, pp. 219-24.
[51] *What Is to Be Done?*, Ardis Edition, pp. 224-29.
[52] *What Is to Be Done?*, Ardis Edition, pp. 230-36.
[53] *What Is to Be Done?*, Ardis Edition, pp. 236-41.
[54] *What Is to Be Done?*, Ardis Edition, pp. 241-46.
[55] *What Is to Be Done?*, Ardis Edition, pp. 246-53.
[56] *What Is to Be Done?*, Ardis Edition, pp. 253-58.
[57] *What Is to Be Done?*, Ardis Edition, pp. 258-61.
[58] *What Is to Be Done?*, Ardis Edition, pp. 261-64.
[59] *What Is to Be Done?*, Ardis Edition, pp. 264-68.
[60] *What Is to Be Done?*, Ardis Edition, p. 269.
[61] *What Is to Be Done?*, Ardis Edition, pp. 270-72.
[62] *What Is to Be Done?*, Ardis Edition, pp. 272-82.
[63] *What Is to Be Done?*, Ardis Edition, pp. 282-85.
[64] *What Is to Be Done?*, Ardis Edition, pp. 285-89.
[65] *What Is to Be Done?*, Ardis Edition, pp. 289-92.
[66] *What Is to Be Done?*, Ardis Edition, pp. 292-309.
[67] *What Is to Be Done?*, Ardis Edition, pp. 309-12.
[68] *What Is to Be Done?*, Ardis Edition, pp. 312-16.
[69] *What Is to Be Done?*, Ardis Edition, pp. 316-28.
[70] *What Is to Be Done?*, Ardis Edition, p. 329.
[71] *What Is to Be Done?*, Ardis Edition, p. 329.
[72] *What Is to Be Done?*, Ardis Edition, pp. 329-35.
[73] *What Is to Be Done?*, Ardis Edition, pp. 335-36.
[74] *What Is to Be Done?*, Ardis Edition, pp. 336-37.
[75] *What Is to Be Done?*, Ardis Edition, p. 337.

[76] *What Is to Be Done?*, Ardis Edition, pp. 337-53.

[77] *What Is to Be Done?*, Ardis Edition, pp. 353-56.

[78] *What Is to Be Done?*, Ardis Edition, pp. 356-60.

[79] *What Is to Be Done?*, Ardis Edition, pp. 360-63.

[80] *What Is to Be Done?*, Ardis Edition, pp. 363-75.

[81] *What Is to Be Done?*, Ardis Edition, pp. 374-87.

[82] *What Is to Be Done?*, Ardis Edition, pp. 387-88.

[83] *What Is to Be Done?*, Ardis Edition, pp. 389-97.

[84] *What Is to Be Done?*, Ardis Edition, pp. 397-400.

[85] *What Is to Be Done?*, Ardis Edition, pp. 400-15.

[86] *What Is to Be Done?*, Ardis Edition, pp. 416-19.

[87] *What Is to Be Done?*, Ardis Edition, pp. 422-23.

[88] *What Is to Be Done?*, Ardis Edition, pp. 423-24.

[89] *What Is to Be Done?*, Ardis Edition, pp. 424-28.

[90] *What Is to Be Done?*, Ardis Edition, pp. 428-30.

[91] *What Is to Be Done?*, Ardis Edition, pp. 430-36.

[92] *What Is to Be Done?*, Ardis Edition, p. 437.

[93] *What Is to Be Done?*, Ardis Edition, pp. 437-44.

[94] *What Is to Be Done?*, Ardis Edition, p. 445.

[95] *What Is to Be Done?*, Ardis Edition, pp. 445-48.

[96] Drozd, p. 175.

[97] *What Is to Be Done?*, Ardis Edition, pp. 448-49.

[98] *What Is to Be Done?*, Ardis Edition, pp. 449-50.

[99] *What Is to Be Done?*, Ardis Edition, pp. 450-54.

[100] *What Is to Be Done?*, Ardis Edition, pp. 454-55.

[101] *What Is to Be Done?*, Ardis Edition, pp. 455-60.

[102] Chernyshevsky himself termed the Conclusion and Epilogue of *What Is to Be Done?* his most "treasured . . . artistic ruse." Ardis Edition, preface, p. xxxviii (quoting Chernyshevsky note).

[103] *What Is to Be Done?*, Ardis Edition, pp. 461-62.

[104] Drozd, pp. 11-12, 16.

[105] Drozd, p. 12.

[106] Drozd, pp 11-13; A. Siljak, *Angel of Vengeance* (St. Martin's Press 2008). p. 71. The term "nihilist" was in fact used in France as early as the 18th century, and had been used in Russia at least since 1829 to refer to a person who "knows nothing and understands nothing." M. Grawitz, *Bakhounine Biographie* (Calmann-Lèvy, 2000.) Interestingly, John Wilkes Booth was an active adherent of the populist "Know Nothing" party, which enjoyed brief success in the United States during the mid-1850's. Asia Booth Clarke, *The Unlocked Book, a Memoir of John Wilkes Booth*, (G.P. Putnam & Sons, New York, 1938), p. 105. The party's somewhat xenophobic beliefs were sometimes referred to as "Kni-ism."

[107] *Artemisia cina*, commonly known as santonica, Levant wormseed, and wormseed, is an herbaceous perennial of the daisy family. Its dried flowerheads are the source of the vermifugic drug santonin since ancient times. Its common names arise from its known ability to expel worms. The powder is grayish-green in colour with an aromatic odour and a bitter taste.

[108] For additional discussions on the pervasive importance of Chernyshevsky's *What Is to Be Done?* within the framework of the "Generation of the Sixties," see, e.g., N. Kolchevska, introduction to S. Kovalevskaya, *Nihilist Girl*, pp. x, xiii, xvi (Modern Language Assn of America, 2001); C. Porter, *Fathers and Daughters, Russian Women in Revolution* (Virago, 1975), pp. 77-80, 97, 120, 136, 158, 177; Siljak, pp. 71-73, 84-85.

[109] A. B. Ulam, *In the Name of the People* (Viking Press, 1977), pp. 53-55; Siljak, p. 72.

[110] Siljak, pp. 71-72.

[111] Drozd, p. 10; Siljak, p. 85.

ENDNOTES TO CHAPTER 2: THE NEW TSAR LIBERATOR

[112] H. Troyat, *Alexandre II, Le Tsar Liberateur* (Flammarion, 1990), pp. 18-19.

[113] A. Tarsaidze, *Katia, Wife Before God* (MacMillan, 1970), p. 39.

[114] Troyat, pp. 23-24.

[115] Troyat, p. 60.

[116] Troyat, p. 58.

[117] Ulam, p. 40.

[118] Troyat, p. 36.

[119] Samuel D. Kassow, *The University Statutes of 1863,* reprinted in *Russia's Great Reforms* (anthology), (B. Eklof, J. Bushnell & L. Zakharova editors), Indiana Univ. Press 1994, p. 261 fn. 15.

[120] P. Pomper, *Sergei Nechaev* (Rutgers Univ. Press 1979), p. 47.

[121] Troyat, pp. 63-67.

[122] Troyat, p. 68.

[123] On Alexander II's initiative to free the serfs, described here, see generally, C. De Grunwald, *Le Tsar Alexandre II et Son Temps* (Editions Berger-Levrault, 1963), 61-70.

[124] Troyat, pp. 68-69.

[125] Troyat, pp. 70-75.

[126] Troyat, pp. 75-76.

[127] Troyat, p. 77.

[128] Troyat, pp. 61-62.

[129] De Grunwald, pp. 103-05.

[130] Troyat, p. 84.

[131] De Grunwald, pp. 104-07.

[132] Troyat, pp. 91-92.

[133] E. Radzinsky, *Alexandre II, La Russie Entre L'Espoir e Le*

Terreur, (A. Coldefy-Foucard tr., le cherche midi 2009), p. 173.

[134] Ulam, pp. 86-87.

[135] Troyat, pp. 92-93.

[136] Ulam, pp. 46-47; Troyat, p. 113.

[137] Ulam, p. 50.

[138] Siljak, pp. 57-58.

[139] Drozd, introduction p. xiii.

[140] Porter, p. 53.

[141] Ulam, pp. 102-05.

[142] Ulam, p. 112.

[143] De Grunwald, p. 163; Troyat, pp. 116-17.

[144] Unless otherwise stated, dates of events mentioned in this work are given in terms of the Julian calendar that was used in Russia until 1918 (sometimes called "Old Style," or "OS"). During the period covered here, the Russian dates were 12 days behind the Gregorian calendar based days used in the rest of the western world. Thus, May 28, 1862 was June 9, 1862 elsewhere. Dates prior to January 1, 1900 that are given here according to the Gregorian calendar are labeled "NS" for "New Style".

[145] Ulam, pp. 111-12.

[146] Troyat, pp. 102-03.

ENDNOTES TO CHAPTER 3: THE PROPHET OF ANARCHISM, MIKHAIL BAKHUNIN

[147] M. Grawitz, *Bakounine, Biographie* (Calmann-Levy, 2000) pp. 10-15.

[148] Grawitz, pp. 30-37.

[149] Grawitz, pp. 24-27.

[150] Grawitz, pp. 82-84.

[151] Grawitz, pp. 92-96.

[152] Grawitz, pp. 114-18.
[153] Grawitz, pp. 120-26.
[154] Grawitz, p. 131.
[155] Grawitz, p. 132.
[156] Grawitz, p. 136.
[157] Grawitz, pp. 137-39.
[158] Grawitz, pp. 143-44.
[159] Grawitz, pp. 168-69.
[160] Grawitz, pp. 171-75.
[161] Grawitz, p. 186.
[162] Grawitz, p. 210.
[163] Grawitz, pp. 192-97.
[164] Grawitz, p. 210.
[165] Grawitz, p. 214.
[166] Grawitz, pp. 215-22.
[167] Grawitz, pp. 224-31.
[168] Grawitz, pp. 231-33.
[169] Grawitz, p. 236.
[170] Grawitz, p. 242.
[171] Grawitz, pp. 247-50.
[172] Grawitz, pp. 262-67.

ENDNOTES TO CHAPTER 4: BIRTH OF A PRINCESS

[173] N. A. Troitsky, *Sofia Lvovna Perovskaya, A Life, Personality, Fate* (Saratov State University, 2014), p. 38. Prior biographers, including Troitsky and Perovskaya's other Russian biographers, missed the fifth child. The author uncovered the existence of Varvara, the oldest girl and named after her mother, who was born October 4, 1846, from a review of the Formulary List of Service of Lev Nikolaevitch Perovsky (hereafter, "List of Service") at the Central State Historical

Archive in St. Petersburg. This List of Service is in essence a *curriculum vitae* prepared on behalf of Lev Nikolaevitch Perovsky for his application for a position in the Russian customs office on Oct. 12, 1850. Varvara apparently died in early childhood and she is not mentioned further in accounts of Sofia Perovskaya's family.

[174] Troitsky, p. 38.

[175] The background information in this chapter on the Razumovsky family is taken primarily from K. Valishevsky, *The Razumovsky Family* (St. Petersburg, 1880).

[176] See https://ru.wikipedia.org/wiki/Разумовский,_Кирилл_Григорьевич (Wikipedia page).

[177] Another of Kirill's sons was Andrei Razumovsky, who became the Russian ambassador to the Congress of Vienna in 1815. Andrei Razumovsky, in addition to being a prominent diplomat, was an accomplished musician who commissioned three string quartets now bearing his name by Ludwig von Beethoven.

[178] V. Leontosovich, *The History of Liberalism in Russia* (Univ. of Pittsburgh Press, 2012), pp. 85, 135.

[179] W. Moss, *Russia in the Age of Alexander II, Tolstoy and Dostoevsky*, pp. 44-45 (Anthem Press, London 2002). Moss comments that although the Perovskys were influenced by post-Napoleonic war reformist hopes, they did not go so far as to join the Decembrists. Vasily Perovsky stood by Nicholas and personally took part in putting down the Decembrists.

[180] Troitsky, p. 32.

[181] List of Service, pp. 2-3.

[182] List of Service, pp. 1-3; Troitsky, p. 34; see also V. Perovsky, *Vospominia o Sestre* (Moscow 1927), p. 6.

[183] Perovsky, p. 4; see also Troitsky, p. 40.

[184] Quoted in T. Cymrina, *Sofia Perovskaya, a Political Portrait* (Tagenrog 2006), p. 37.

[185] Troitsky, pp. 35-36.
[186] Cymrina, p. 36.
[187] Troitsky, p. 35.
[188] Troitsky, p. 34.
[189] List of Service, pp. 2-6.

ENDNOTES TO CHAPTER 5: HE CALLED HER GLOOMY GIRL

[190] Troitsky, p. 41.
[191] Troitsky, pp. 43-44 (citing Perovsky memoirs).
[192] Perovsky, pp. 14-15.
[193] Troitsky, pp. 45-47 (citing Perovsky)
[194] Perovsky, pp. 14-15, 22-23; see also Troitsky, p. 50.
[195] Perovsky, pp. 22-23; see also Troitsky, p. 50.
[196] Troitsky, p. 53.
[197] Perovsky, pp. 4-7; see also Porter, pp. 179-80.
[198] Troitsky, pp. 40 (quoting Perovsky), 48; see also List of Service, p. 2.
[199] Perovsky, p. 25.
[200] Perovsky, p. 23; see Radzinsky, p. 156.
[201] Troitsky, p. 51.
[202] Perovsky, p. 29.
[203] Perovsky, pp. 15-16.
[204] Perovsky, p. 28; Troitsky, p. 54 (quoting Perovsky).
[205] Troitsky, p. 57; see Radzinsky, pp. 424-25.
[206] Troitsky, p. 54.
[207] Perovsky, p. 31; Troitsky, p. 57.

ENDNOTES TO CHAPTER 6: A SHOT THAT CHANGED RUSSIA FOREVER

[208] Ulam, pp. 2-3; Troyat, p. 119; C. Verhoeven, *The Odd Man*

Karakozov (Cornell Univ. Press 2009), p. 72.

[209] Verhoeven, pp. 136-38; Ulam, p. 159.

[210] Verhoeven, pp. 19, 43.

[211] Verhoeven, p. 146; Ulam, p. 60.

[212] Verhoeven, pp. 20-22.

[213] Verhoeven, pp. 22, 130-32. To the conspiracy minded, this evidence could well point in the direction of a plot by neo-Decembrist liberals to kill Alexander II and, after seizing power, to install Constantine (referred to as "K" in the letter found in Karakozov's possession) on the throne.

[214] Verhoeven, pp. 130, 143. Ulam, pp. 162-63 & fn. 29, questions whether the pamphlet was written by Karakozov, and suggests it was in fact written by Khudiakov, who also was responsible for getting it printed. Regardless, it represents Karakozov's ideation and state of mind.

[215] Ulam, p. 166.

[216] Verhoeven, pp. 16, 17;

[217] Troyat, pp. 122-23.

[218] Porter, pp. 179-80. Some historians have assumed that Perovsky's demotion was due to lax security that allowed Karakozov access for the assassination attempt. But this is not credible. Alexander frequently took walks by himself without any special security detail. Tarsaidze, p. 91.

[219] S. Kravchinsky, *Underground Russia* (Scribner & Sons 1883), p. 118; Cymrina, p. 39.

[220] Perovsky, pp. 37-38.

[221] Cymrina, p. 39.

ENDNOTES TO CHAPTER 7: A SELECT HARVEST OF REBELLIOUS SEEDLINGS

[222] Kravchinsky, p. 107.

[223] V. Zasulitch memoir, reprinted in C. Fauré, *Quatre Femmes*

Terroristes Contre le Tsar (François Masparo, Paris 1978), pp. 32-36.

[224] Zasulitch, in *Quatre Femmes, op. cit.*, pp. 36-38.

[225] Zasulitch, in *Quatre Femmes, op. cit.*, p. 37.

[226] Zasulitch, in *Quatre Femmes, op. cit.*, p. 42.

[227] Zasulitch, in *Quatre Femmes, op. cit.*, pp. 41-44.

[228] Grawitz, p. 339.

[229] Pomper, pp. 25-28, 45.

[230] Pomper, pp. 125, 141.

[231] Zasulitch, in *Quatre Femmes, op. cit.*, pp. 46-49; Pomper, pp. 62-64.

[232] Pomper, pp. 66, 69.

[233] Grawitz, pp. 340, 347.

ENDNOTES TO CHAPTER 8: TERRORISM GETS A CATECHISM

[234] Grawitz, pp. 264, 278-79.

[235] Grawitz, pp. 282-83.

[236] Grawitz, pp. 307-08.

[237] Grawitz, pp. 321-24.

[238] Pomper, pp. 90-91.

[239] Grawitz, p. 347.

[240] Pomper, pp. 96-97.

[241] Pomper, p. 102. February 19, 1870 was the ninth anniversary of the decree emancipating the serfs and, under the decree, it was scheduled to mark the final phase of the prescribed land settlement. Nechaev and others theorized, altogether erroneously, that because the duplicitous nature of the decree would become apparent on that date, peasant revolt was certain to occur.

[242] M. Prawdin, *The Unmentionable Nechaev* (Roy Publishers, New York, 1961), p. 37.

[243] Pomper, pp. 103-05.

[244] Pomper, p. 112.

[245] Pomper, pp. 113-15; R. Seth, *The Russian Terrorists* (Barrie & Rockliff, London, 1966), p. 35.

[246] Pomper, pp. 109, 117-19.

[247] Pomper, pp. 140-41.

[248] Pomper, p. 143.

[249] Pomper, pp. 143-44.

[250] Grawitz, pp. 338, 349-50.

[251] Pomper, pp. 151-52.

[252] Grawitz, pp. 351-67; Pomper, pp. 147-62.

[253] Pomper, pp. 181-82.

[254] Pomper, pp. 183-214; Prawdin, pp. 97-107.

ENDNOTES TO CHAPTER 9: GOING TO THE PEOPLE

[255] V. Figner, *Memoirs of a Revolutionist* (Moscow, 1925), pp. 17-18.

[256] Porter, pp. 64, 67.

[257] Porter, p. 90.

[258] A. Lindenmeyr, *The Rise of Voluntary Associations During the Great Reforms*, reprinted in *Russia's Great Reforms*, op. cit., p. 264; Porter, p. 92.

[259] M. Maxwell, *Narodniki Women* (Pergamon Press 1990), p. 61 & fn. 17.

[260] Cymrina, p. 41.

[261] E. Kovalskaya, in *Quatre Femmes*, p. 271.

[262] Kravchinsky, in *Underground Russia*, p. 115.

[263] Writings of Tikhomirov, as quoted in Ulam, p. 301, indicate that the feelings of Perovskaya's one time fictitious husband, Lev Tikhomirov, for her were more than platonic, and were unrequited to his dismay. Goldenberg, from his time spent

with her in Moscow, also was reported to have a big crush on Perovskaya. Trifonov, pp. 262, 321; see also Footman, pp. 160, 163.

[264] An unflattering police report at the end of the decade described the typical nihilist woman in the following fashion: "She has cropped hair, wears blue glasses, is slovenly in her dress, [and] rejects the use of comb and soap." Moss, p. 78.

[265] Porter, p. 182; Maxwell, p. 62; Perovsky, p. 41.

[266] Elizabeth Kovalskaya, in *Quatre Femmes*, pp. 272-73.

[267] Perovsky, p. 44.

[268] Figner, *Memoirs*, p. 109.

[269] Perovsky, pp. 44-50; Porter, p. 184.

[270] Perovsky, p. 51; see also Ulam, pp. 201-05; Figner, *Memoirs*, p. 108; L. Kern, *Die Zaren Morderin* (Osburg Verlag Hamburg 2013), p. 115.

[271] Kovalskaya, in *Quatre Femmes*, p. 274.

[272] Porter, pp. 186-87; Cymrina, p. 44.

[273] Kravchinsky, pp. 119-20.

[274] Porter, p. 187, 238; Kravchinsky, pp. 120-21.

[275] Kropotkin is quoted in De Grunwald, p. 308.

[276] D. Footman, *Red Prelude: The Life of Russian Terrorist Zhelyabov ("Red Prelude")*, p. 42 Yale Univ. Press 1945); A. Kornilov, *Modern Russian History*, Vol. II, (Alfred A. Knopf 1917), pp. 212-13.

[277] Ulam, pp. 209, 221; Troyat, pp. 181-82; A. Svobodin, in the Introduction to Y. Trifonov, *The Impatient Ones* (Progress Publishers 1978), p. 14; Kern, p. 49.

[278] This village is not to be confused with the larger Stavropol that is situated in the Crimea. Perovskaya herself added a note at the end not to confuse the two in the letters we quote here. The Stavropol in the province of Samara was founded in 1780 and existed under that name until 1924. But now it is renamed Tolyatti [Тольятти]. It is a small city (11,000 sq. kilometers),

with current population by nationality being Russian 150,907, Mardva, 26,145, Chuvash, 8,779, Tatars, 32,354, total, 280,185. https://ru.m.wikipedia.org/wiki/Ставропольский_уезд_(Самарская_губерния).

[279] "Unpublished Letters of S. L. Perovskaya," with introductory historical notes and comments by R. M. Kantor, published in: *Krasnyi arkhiv (Red Archive)*, vol 3. (1923), pp. 243-250 (hereafter, "Perovskaya Unpublished Letters").

[280] Perovskaya Unpublished Letters, p. 245. The quoted memoir states that the people in Stavropol described Perovskaya's cheeks as "two pots on the face," a quaint Russian expression meaning rosy healthy looking cheeks.

[281] Footman, *Red Prelude*, pp. 42-43; see generally Ulam, pp. 219-33; Troyat, p. 183.

[282] Perovskaya Unpublished Letters, pp. 246-47. Translation by the author, with assistance from V. Kourova.

[283] The identity of "Mikhail Fedovich" is unknown. Probably he was another Chaikovsky adherent who had "gone to the people."

[284] Perovskaya Unpublished Letters, p. 248. Translation by the author with assistance from V. Kourova.

[285] Nikolai Vasilyevich Vereshchagin (1839 - 1907) was an agronomist and cheesemaker. In the spirit of the Generation of the Sixties, he organized a series of communal, artisanal cheese-making enterprises, of which the largest was in the region of Corcescom, Tver province. This is where Obodovskaya was then working as a teacher.

[286] Perovskaya Unpublished Letters, p. 249. Translation by the author with assistance from V. Kourova.

[287] A Discourse delivered at the Royal Institution, on Friday, the 19th of March, 1858 (reprinted from "Fraser's Magazine," for April, 1858). This text is from *The Miscellaneous and Posthumous Works of Henry Thomas Buckle* (1872).

[288] Edited by Terry Heller, Coe College. Downloaded at http://www. public.coe.edu/~theller/soj/u-rel/buckle.html (Dec. 26, 2016).

[289] Porter, p. 193.

[290] Porter, pp. 188, 194.

[291] Perovsky, pp. 58-59; Porter, p. 194; Cymrina, p. 54.

[292] Perovsky, p. 64.

[293] Kern, p. 64.

[294] Porter, pp. 194-95; Perovsky, p. 63.

[295] Cymrina, pp. 60-61; Perovsky, pp. 78-79.

[296] Perovsky, pp. 78-84.

[297] Footman, *Red Prelude*, p. 41; Troyat, p. 182; Kornilov, p. 219.

[298] Troyat, p. 183; Kornilov, p. 220 (citing statistics in a report by Count Pahlen). Many of the others were dealt with by "administrative" decisions such as de facto confinement to a particular city or province.

[299] Porter, p. 205.

ENDNOTES TO CHAPTER 10: THE TSAR'S SECOND FAMILY

[300] Tarsaidze, pp. 15, 100.

[301] Tarsaidze, pp. 106-09, 134, 148.

[302] Troyat, pp. 144-47.

[303] Troyat, p. 151.

[304] Moss, pp. 147, 157.

[305] Porter, pp. 177-78; Kravchinsky, pp. 116-22.

[306] Figner, *Memoirs,* p. 53; Troyat, pp. 184-86.

[307] Radzinsky, p. 335.

[308] Ulam, p. 263; D. Footman, *The Alexander Conspiracy, a Life of A. I. Zhelyabov* (*"Alexander Conspiracy"*), p. 83 (Barrie & Rockliff, London, 1944).

[309] Kravchinsky, p. 38.

[310] Ulam, p. 280.

[311] Footman, *Alexander Conspiracy,* pp. 90-91; Porter, pp. 207-08. On Masha Kolenkaya's beauty, see Porter, p. 202. The quote is from Figner, *Memoirs*, p. 56.

[312] See Kovalskaya, in *Quatre Femmes,* p. 275.

[313] Y. Trifonov, *The Impatient Ones* (Progress Publishers 1978), p. 71.

[314] Kovalskaya, in *Quatre Femmes*, pp. 275-76.

ENDNOTES TO CHAPTER 11: DISORGANIZING

[315] Maxwell, p. 25.

[316] Zasulitch, in *Quatre Femmes,* pp. 94-98.

[317] Footman, *Alexander Conspiracy*, p. 92; Svobodin, in *The Impatient Ones*, p. 16.

[318] Maxwell, pp. 3-18; Porter, p. 217; Seth, p. 55; Footman, *Alexander Conspiracy*, pp. 92-93. It is interesting that after spending several years abroad, Zasulitch eventually turned out to be a staunch opponent of terrorism. She would ally herself closely with the "moderate" faction of *Zemlya i Volya* that opposed the terrorist path of Zhelyabov, Mikhailov and, later, Perovskaya.

[319] Kravchinsky, pp. 158-65; Footman, *Alexander Conspiracy*, pp. 99-104.

[320] A. Kornilov, *Modern Russian History*, Vol. II, (Alfred A. Knopf 1917), p. 218.

[321] Footman, *Alexander Conspiracy*, pp. 104-05; Cymrina, p. 73; Porter, p. 251.

[322] Radzinsky, p. 347; Trifonov, p. 104. Additional color on Kovalsky may be found in Trifonov, pp. 75-84.

[323] Ulam, pp. 275-76; Footman, *Alexander Conspiracy*, pp. 107-09; Cymrina, pp. 74-76; Porter, pp. 223-24, 290; Kern, p.

111.   On the impact of Mezentsov's assassination on the policies of the Tsar and his immediate circle of ministers, see P. A. Zaionchkovsky, *The Russian Autocracy in Crisis, 1878-1882* (Academic International Press, Gulf Breeze, Florida, 1979), pp. 45-47.

[324] Perovsky, p. 86.

[325] Perovsky, pp. 86-88; Lyubatovich in *Quatre Femmes*, p. 149; Kovalskaya in *Quatre Femmes*, p. 277; Cymrina, pp. 74-75; Kravchinsky, p. 124; Porter, p. 222; Footman, *Alexander Conspiracy*, pp. 105-06; http://it. wikipedia.org/wiki/ Sof'ja_L'vovna_Perovskaja, accessed July 8, 2015 (hereafter, "Italia Wikipedia Perovskaya"). There are some inconsistent details between Perovsky, Kovalskaya and Lyubatovich, each of whom gives an account of Sofia's subsequent description of the escape.

[326] Lyubatovich, in *Quatre Femmes*, pp. 149-51.

[327] Footman, *Alexander Conspiracy*, p. 106.

[328] Footman, *Red Prelude*, p. 91.

ENDNOTES TO CHAPTER 12: TERRORISTS SPLIT OFF

[329] Figner, *Memoirs*, p. 48.

[330] Radzinsky, p. 354.

[331] Figner, *Memoirs,* passim. Her account of Solovyev's visit to her in Saratov is found at pp. 62-65.

[332] Lyubatovich in *Quatre Femmes*, p. 146.

[333] Footman, *Alexander Conspiracy,* pp. 122-23; Radzinsky, pp. 357-58.

[334] Radzinsky, pp. 359-60.

[335] Troyat, pp. 189-91.

[336] Zaionchkovsky, pp. 50-53.

[337] Zaionchkovsky, p. 56.

[338] Footman, *Alexander Conspiracy*, p. 130. On the time of

Osinski's arrest, see Cymrina, p. 78.

[339] Radzinsky, pp. 364-65; Trifonov, p. 153.

[340] Radzinsky, p. 365.

[341] Figner, *Memoirs*, p. 69; Cymrina, p. 81.

[342] Figner, *Memoirs*, pp. 56, 67 (Voronezh as location of populist commune), 69; Footman, *Alexander Conspiracy*, p. 126.

[343] Porter, pp. 230-31; Footman, *Alexander Conspiracy*, pp. 126-27.

[344] Footman, *Alexander Conspiracy*, pp. 3-4.

[345] Footman, *Alexander Conspiracy*, p. 13; Trifonov, pp. 90-91.

[346] Trifonov, pp. 50-53; Footman, *Alexander Conspiracy*, pp. 14-15.

[347] Indications are, to the contrary, that Zhelyabov as an adult got on decently with Lorentsov. Trifonov, p. 90.

[348] Footman, *Alexander Conspiracy*, p. 28.

[349] Footman, *Alexander Conspiracy*, pp. 41-45.

[350] Footman, *Alexander Conspiracy*, p. 47; Trifonov, p. 26.

[351] Trifonov, p. 111 (quoting Pimen Semenyuta).

[352] Trifonov, pp. 32, 60.

[353] Footman, *Alexander Conspiracy*, pp. 64-67.

[354] Footman, *Alexander Conspiracy*, 68-70; Trifonov, pp. 29-32, 36-41, 75-76.

[355] Footman, *Alexander Conspiracy*, pp. 89-91; Trifonov, pp. 41-42.

[356] Footman, *Alexander Conspiracy*, pp. 91-92; Trifonov, pp. 69-72.

[357] Trifonov, p. 113.

[358] Footman, *Alexander Conspiracy*, p. 127; Trifonov, pp. 109-10.

[359] Footman, *Red Prelude*, p. 72,

[360] Trifonov, pp. 113-16 (summarizing first person account by

Semenyuta).

[361] Trifonov, pp. 110-18 (account of Semenyuta); Footman, *Alexander Conpsiracy*, p. 127.

[362] Trifonov, pp. 152-53.

ENDNOTES TO CHAPTER 13: THE FORMATION OF NARODNAYA VOLYA

[363] Ulam, p. 323.

[364] Trifanov, pp. 55, 156.

[365] Lyubatovich, in *Quatre Femmes*, p. 145; see also *id.* at 211 ("Boris").

[366] Radzinsky, p. 382.

[367] Trifonov, p. 156; Lyubatovich in *Quatre Femmes*, p. 191; see also Porter, p. 236.

[368] Footman, *Alexander Conspiracy*, pp. 134-36; Trifonov, pp. 164-80.

[369] Porter, p. 234.

[370] Kravchinsky, *Underground Russia*, p. 126.

[371] On the fundamental acceptance of anarchy as the underlying political philosophy by the Chaikovsky Circle and other populists who emerged out of the Generation of the Sixties, see generally the discussion in G. Gamblin, *Russian Populism and Its Relation With Anarchism 1870-81* (doctoral thesis, University of Birmingham, 1999), pp. 88-127 (accessed at http://etheses.bham.ac.uk/1401/1/PhD1999Gamblin.pdf, Aug. 11, 2015.

[372] Footman, *Alexander Conspiracy*, p. 141, citing Deitch; Italia Wikipedia Perovskaya, citing Deitch Memoirs, pp. 407-08.

[373] Cymrina, p. 83; Footman, *Alexander Conspiracy,* pp. 137-42; Porter, pp. 233-37; Figner, *Memoirs,* p. 110.

[374] Kravchinsky, in *Underground Russia,* p. 116.

[375] Footman, *Alexander Conspiracy*, p. 142, citing Kovalskaya.

[376] Porter, pp. 237-39; Figner, *Memoirs*, pp. 73-74.

[377] Dynamite had been invented in 1867 in Sweden by Alfred Nobel. Radzinsky, p. 382.

[378] Seth, pp. 65-66; Footman, *Alexander Conspiracy,* pp. 148-50; Porter, p. 247.

[379] Footman, *Alexander Conspiracy*, pp. 151-57.

[380] Kravchinsky, p. 140.

[381] Kravchinsky, p. 147.

[382] Porter, p. 251; Footman, *Alexander Conspiracy,* pp. 261-62.

[383] Quoted in Cymrina, p. 86.

[384] Radzinsky, p. 399.

[385] Radzinsky, p. 394.

[386] Footman, *Alexander Conspiracy*, pp. 158-64; Seth, pp. 68-71; Radzinsky, pp. 395-96.

ENDNOTES TO CHAPTER 14: ATTACK IS MADE ON A TRAIN OF MARMALADE

[387] Footman, *Alexander Conspiracy*, pp. 165-67; Radzinsky, p. 396.

[388] Trifonov, pp. 235-36, 244; Radzinsky, p. 402.

[389] Radzinsky, pp. 398-402.

[390] Lyubatovitch in *Quatre Femmes*, p. 191.

[391] Footman, *Alexander Conspiracy*, pp. 201-11; Radzinsky, pp. 402-03.

[392] Ulam, pp. 310-11, 316; Footman, *Alexander Conspiracy*, pp 108-09, 120-21, 122, 333.

[393] Ulam, pp. 292, 305.

[394] Trifonov, p. 160.

[395] Ulam, p. 361.

[396] Quoted in Ulam, pp. 290-91.

[397] Ulam, p. 292.

[398] Footman, *Alexander Conspiracy*, pp. 87-90 (citing Kletochnikov's own writings); Radzinsky, pp. 477-79 (citing account of Anna Korba); Trifonov, pp. 119-49.

[399] Italia Wikipedia article, *Stepan Nikolaevič Chalturin*, accessed at url, https://it.wikipedia.org/wiki/Stepan _Nikolaevi%C4%8D_Chalturin, July 8, 2015 ("Italia Wikipedia Khalturin"), citing Ju. Z. Polevoj, *Stepan Chalturin. Nel 100° anniversario dell'Unione settentrionale.de.*

[400] Italia Wikipedia Khalturin, citing Georgi V. Plekhanov, *L'operaio russo nel movimento rivoluzionario*, in «Works», vol. III, Moscow, 1923, p. 195.

ENDNOTES TO CHAPTER 15: DYNAMITE IN THE WINTER PALACE

[401] Italia Wikipedia Khalturin, citing *Stepan Khalturin: The Family, Childhood and Adolescence. Interesting Details* (in Russian), url http://tornado-84.live journal.com/80575.html.

[402] Italia Wikipedia Khalturin, citing Polevoj.

[403] Italia Wikipedia Khalturin, citing Plekhanov and Polevoj.

[404] Italia Wikipedia Khalturin, citing Plekhanov.

[405] Italia Wikipedia Khalturin, citing Ju. A. Pelevin, *The Attempt of Khalturin and Narodnaya Volya on the Winter Palace*, ttp://www.nivestnik.ru/2011_1/13_pelevin_10.shtml.

[406] Footman, *The Alexander Conspiracy*, p. 176; Italia Wikipedia Khalturin, citing *History of the Governate of Vjatka*; Trifonov, pp. 273-74.

[407] Trifonov, pp. 235-36; Footman, *Alexander Conspiracy*, p. 167.

[408] Italia Wikipedia Khalturin, citing Tikhomirov; Footman, *Alexander Conspiracy*, pp. 179-80.

[409] Ulam, p. 340; Footman, *Alexander Conspiracy*, p. 176; Troyat, p. 197; Lyubatovich in *Quatre Femmes*, p. 212.
[410] Footman, *Alexander Conspiracy*, pp. 180-81; Figner, *Memoirs*, pp. 85-86.
[411] Radzinsky, pp. 412-15.
[412] Italia Wikipedia Khalturin, citing V. Burvev, *The Trial of the Sixteen Terrorists*, and Pelevin; Footman, Alexander Conspiracy, pp. 181-82.
[413] Italia Wikipedia Khalturin, citing *Literature of the Narodnaya Volya Party*, published Paris, 1906.

ENDNOTES TO CHAPTER 16: A DICTATOR TAKES THE HELM

[414] Radzinsky, pp. 430-31.
[415] Radzinsky, pp. 425-28.
[416] Radzinsky, pp. 431-33; Troyat, pp. 203-05.
[417] Radzinsky, p. 434; Troyat, p. 205.
[418] Radzinsky, p. 440.
[419] Footman, pp. 183-84.
[420] Zaionchkovsky, pp. 164-69.
[421] Radzinsky, pp. 442-47.
[422] Zaionchkovsky, pp. 141-42; Radzinsky, p. 458.
[423] Trifonov, pp. 259-62; Footman, *Alexander Conspiracy*, pp. 184-85; Ulam, p. 344.
[424] Trifonov, pp. 326-30.
[425] Radzinsky, pp. 449-57.
[426] Radzinsky, pp. 457-61; Troyat, pp. 215-16.
[427] Radzinsky, p. 462; Troyat, pp. 215-16.
[428] Footman, *Alexander Conspiracy*, pp. 209, 210; Trifonov, p. 330.
[429] Sympathetic writers have argued that Narodnaya Volya slowed the pace of its attacks on Alexander after Loris-

Melikov's appointment. E.g., Footman, *Alexander Conspiracy*, p. 207-08. They point to a document signed by others on the Narodnaya Volya Executive Committee to the effect that a constitutional government that included the Tsar would be respected. They have, however, adduced no evidence that Perovskaya ever personally approved of a decision to relent in the campaign to kill Alexander. They admit she was away from St. Petersburg, working on a plot to assassinate Alexander in Odessa, when the document stating Narodnaya Volya would support a constitution was produced. She was personally responsible for heading off any thought of moderation within the Executive Committee. Footman, *Alexander Conspiracy*, p. 221. In the end, as further discussed below, Perovskaya personally pulled off the assassination of Alexander on the eve of his granting of local representation on two new advisory commissions.

[430] Figner, *Memoirs*, pp. 88-89.

ENDNOTES TO CHAPTER 17: THE NARODNAYA VOLYA LOVE AFFAIRS

[431] Radzinsky, pp. 345-46; *Mothers and Daughters: Women of the Intelligentsia in Nineteenth Century Russia*, by Barbara Alpern Engel (Northwestern University Press 1983), p. 178.

[432] Lyubatovich, in *Quatre Femmes*, pp. 157, 173, 179.

[433] Footman, *Alexander Conspiracy*, pp. 130-32; Trifonov, pp. 153-54.

[434] Lyubatovich, in *Quatre Femmes*, pp. 143-46, 215-17, 218; Trifonov, p. 239.

[435] Italia Wikipedia article, *Aleksandr Aleksandrovič Kvjatkovskij*, accessed at https://it.wikipedia.org/wiki/ Aleksandr_Aleksandrovi%C4%8D_Kvjatkovskij, retrieved July 28, 2015, citing Chronos, *Biographical Notes on Ivanova;*

Trifonov, pp. 290-91; Lyubatovich, in *Quatre Femmes*, p. 184. Kviatkovsky was already married to Ekaterina Konstantinovna Tonjaeva, who had chosen to remain in Tomsk rather than return to the St. Petersburg underground with Kviatkovsky. His son by this marriage, also named Alexander Kviatkovsky, also turned out to be a radical and eventually was shot after the Bolshevik revolution.

[436] Porter, pp. 247-48.

[437] Porter, p. 252; Kravchinsky, p. 210 (confirming "husband and wife" relationship between Kolodkevitch and Helfman); Trifonov, p. 304 (calling Kolodkevitch "the Purring Cat"); Footman, *Alexander Conspiracy*, p. 315.

[438] Anna Korba went to great lengths to stress Zhelyabov's physical attributes. Unlike other radicals, she described Zhelyabov primarily on a level of physical, rather than spiritual, idolization. "He was enormously beautiful and handsome," she wrote. "His teeth were white. Beautiful hair. Beautiful beard. White, high forehead. Cheeks – rosy. Eyebrows were beautiful. He had a straight nose that was an ideal form. When he was talking and smiling, you could see his bright, fresh teeth. He had a great posture – held his head up high. He had an energetic, powerful appearance." She also emphasized his size and his "broad shoulders." A.P. Pribilyova-Korba, *Narodnaya Volya, Memoirs, 1870 – 1880's* (Mospolygraph, Government publisher, Moscow, 1926), p. 82.

[439] Porter, p. 257 says this happened in the "summer" of 1880. Footman, in *Alexander Conspiracy* at p. 204 gives the date when Epstein moved out and Zhelyabov moved in as September 1880. Trifonov, p. 367, gives the date when Zhelyabov moved in as Sonia's "brother" as October 1880. The author chooses to put credence in the words of Perovskaya herself, who told the authorities after her arrest that Zhelyabov had moved in with her in "September" of 1880. Footman,

Alexander Conspiracy, p. 286.

[440] L. B. Croft, *Nikolai Ivanovich Kibalchich: Terrorist Rocket Pioneer* (Tempe, Arizona, 2006) p. 77.

[441] Yuri Trifonov, in his 1978 historical novel called *The Impatient Ones*, gave this account of the development of the relationship between Boris and Sonia. Boris showed interest in Sonia as early as Lipetsk, asking Tikhomirov if the two of them were still engaged, to which Tikhomirov immediately responded that they were not. (Trifonov, pp. 177-78.) In the aftermath of Voronezh, even though Boris and Sonia had clashed, they each admired the other's revolutionary ardor. They continued to engage in heated discussions about tactics, but in the course of doing so, became interested in each other's company. (Trifonov, pp. 189-92.) After Sonia returned to St. Petersburg from her first assassination attempt in Odessa in late November, 1879, the two definitely fell for each other. They had sex for the first time on the night of the Narodnaya Volya New Year's celebration, the early morning of Jan. 1, 1880. (Trifonov, pp. 276-82.) From that point forward, they were desperately in love. Trifonov does not cite any sources for his narrative on these points.

[442] Perovsky, p. 93 (translation by author); see also as translated in Porter, p. 258.

[443] Cymrina, p. 111, citing Kravchinsky; Kern, p. 184, citing Praskovya Ivanovskaya.

[444] Figner, *Memoirs*, p. 112.

[445] Quoted in Ulam, pp. 300-01.

[446] L.A. Tikhomirov, *Sofia Lvovna Perovskaya*, Carouge (Geneva), 1906, p. 27; see also Porter, p. 258; Footman, *Alexander Conspiracy*, p. 204.

[447] Trifonov, pp. 361-65; Footman, *Alexander Conspiracy*, pp. 189-90; Figner, *Memoirs*, p. 90. As for the haste to head off a "tsar-liberator" initiative, see the insightful analysis by Ulam,

p. 344.

[448] Footman, *Alexander Conspiracy*, pp. 212-15.

[449] Footman, *Alexander Conspiracy*, pp. 217-19.

[450] Seth, pp. 79-80; Radzinsky, pp. 394-95; Footman, *Alexander Conspiracy*, pp. 172, 186; Ulam, pp. 344-45; Trifonov, pp. 347-50.

[451] Trifonov, p. 374.

[452] Trifonov, pp. 374-75, 378.

[453] Trifonov, p. 375.

[454] An eyewitness account of the executions of Kviatkovski and Presnyakov which appeared in the daily newspaper *Nation* ("Nation Account") may be found on line at http://historydoc.edu.ru/catalog.asp?cat_ob_no=16500&ob_no=16566.

[455] See Trifonov, p. 334.

[456] Radzinsky, pp. 479-80 (quoting General Bogdanovich); see also Nation Account, *op. cit.*

ENDNOTES TO CHAPTER 18: "OUR GIRLS ARE FIERCER THAN OUR MEN"

[457] Quoted in Footman, *Alexander Conspiracy*, p. 221.

[458] Ibid.

[459] Porter, p. 262, quoting Kibalchich.

[460] Porter, pp. 243-44.

[461] Porter, p. 264.

[462] Porter, p. 261; Footman, *Alexander Conspiracy*, pp. 226-27.

[463] Footman, *Alexander Conspiracy*, p. 222; Trifonov, pp. 384-86.

[464] Lyubatovich, in *Quatre Femmes*, pp. 215-18.

[465] Footman, *Alexander Conspiracy*, p. 187.

[466] Footman, *Alexander Conspiracy*, p. 230; Trifonov, p. 406.

[467] Kravchinsky, p. 94.

[468] Kravchinsky, pp. 92-99; Figner, p. 74; Trifonov, pp.178-79; Italia Wikipedia article with citations, found 12-5-15 at https://it.wikipedia.org/wiki/Dmitrij_Andreevi%C4%8D_Lizogub; Ulam, pp. 319-22.

[469] Footman, *Alexander Conspiracy*, p. 231.

[470] Figner, *Memoirs*, pp. 96-98; Footman, *Alexander Conspiracy*, pp. 230-31; Trifonov, pp. 399-401.

[471] Trifonov, pp. 406-07.

[472] Figner, *Memoirs*, p. 98.

[473] Trifonov, p. 408; Footman, *Alexander Conspiracy*, p. 240; Croft, p. 85.

[474] Kern, p. 67, translated these Narodnaya Volya "program guidelines" as:

Every Committee member undertakes:

1. to give all mental and spiritual powers to the revolutionary cause, forsaking all family ties, abandoning sympathy, love and friendship;

2. if necessary, to give his life, and without regard to others;

3. to possess nothing that is not part of the organization;

4. to renounce his personal will and to subordinate it to the majority vote of the organization;

5. to keep all matters, plans, intentions and membership of the organization strictly secret;

6. in all respects of a public and private character, and in all official acts and declarations to never describe oneself as a member, but always only be described as representative of the Executive

Committee; and

7. in the case of withdrawal from the society maintain inviolable silence to preserve above all the activity of the company concerned.

[475] Pomper, pp. 196-201.

[476] Pomper, p. 200; Footman, *Alexander Conspiracy*, pp. 232-34.

[477] Pomper, pp. 201-04: Footman, *Alexander Conspiracy*, pp. 232-33. Trifonov, pp. 428-33, gives a more extended version in which Zhelyabov actually went to the wall of the Ravelin itself one night and spoke with Nechaev, with the assistance of his "staff." There is no independent historical support for this aspect of Trifonov's narrative.

[478] An "envoy" whom Zhelyabov, at this time, sent to Switzerland to deliver a letter to a former revolutionary associate, Mikhail Dragomanov, told Dragomanov that Zhelyabov explicitly fancied himself in the role of a "Parnell," a reference to Charles Stewart Parnell, the Irish Fenian nationalist who, like Zhelyabov, was a stirring speaker. Trifonov, p. 356; Footman, *Alexander Conspiracy*, p. 211. Parnell served as a representative of the Irish separatist movement in the British Parliament.

[479] Zaionchkovsky, pp. 181-82.

[480] Zaionchkovsky, pp. 178-85.

[481] Ulam, pp. 337-38, 349; Footman, *Alexander Conspiracy*, pp. 152-57, 234; Trifonov, p. 375, 378, 381-82. For another's recognition of the insight that class guilt played a role in the discontent of the typical product of the landed nobility who took part in the Generation of the Sixties, see Kern, p. 49.

[482] Footman, *Alexander Conspiracy*, p. 235; Croft, p. 84; Troitsky, p. 285.

ENDNOTES TO CHAPTER 19: DEATH OF A TSAR

[483] Figner, *Memoirs*, p. 97.

[484] Footman, *Alexander Conspiracy*, pp. 243, 245; Croft, pp. 85, 103.

[485] Footman, *Alexander Conspiracy*, pp. 244-45, 326, 328; Trifonov, p. 393.

[486] Footman, *Alexander Conspiracy*, pp. 252-53; Trifonov, p. 439.

[487] Footman, *Alexander Conspiracy*, pp. 246, 340.

[488] Footman, *Alexander Conspiracy*, pp. 247-48.

[489] V. Laferté, *Alexandre II, Détails Inédits Sur La Vie e La Mort* (1882), pp. 6-26; Troitsky, p. 288.

[490] Figner, *Memoirs*, p. 99; Footman, *Alexander Conspiracy*, pp. 253-54; Croft, p. 85; Troitsky, p. 284; Mravinsky, for his incompetence, was later stripped of his military position and exiled to the far north.

[491] See, e.g., A. Kornilova-Moroz, *Sofia Lvovna Perovskaya* (Uzdatelstvo Politkatorzhan, Moscow, 1930), pp. 19-20.

[492] See P. Yablonskii, A. Vizel, V. Galkin & M. Shulgina, *Tuberculosis in Russia, Its History and Status Today*, American Journal of Respiratory and Critical Care Medicine, Vol. 191, No. 4 (2015), pp. 372-76. Furthermore, it is quite possible that Sonia's father Lev Nikolaevitch Perovsky also suffered from tuberculosis. This would explain his repeated and otherwise unexplained bouts of "illness," for which he went on an extended visit to a German sanitarium in 1869, as we have seen. The sanitarium was a nineteenth century method of choice for treating tuberculosis, particularly among the upper classes. See http://exhibits.hsl.virginia.edu/alav/tuberculosis/, "Early Research and Treatment of Tuberculosis in the 19th Century."

[493] Trifonov, pp. 394, 403, 433, 436; Kravchinsky, pp. 211-13

(reporting eyewitness account of Rina Epstein); Figner, Memoirs, p. 109; Footman, *Alexander Conspiracy*, p. 209, 273-74 (reporting eyewitness account of Arkady Tyrkov) N. Asheshov, *Sofia Perovskaya, Materials for Biography* (Government Publisher, St. Petersburg, 1920), p. 110.

494 Croft, p. 86.

495 Figner, *Memoirs,* pp. 100-01.

496 Figner, *Memoirs*, p. 101; Footman, *Alexander Conspiracy*, p. 255.

497 Maxwell, p. 70; Figner, *Memoirs*, p. 101; Footman, *Alexander Conspiracy*, pp. 255-56.

498 Quoted in Footman, *Alexander Conspiracy*, p. 256.

499 Footman, *Alexander Conspiracy*, p. 257.

500 Lafertè, pp. 23-24; Radzinsky, pp. 505-06.

501 Lafertè, pp. 25-26.

502 Troitsky, p. 314, quoting confession of Perovskaya from her interrogation of March 11, 1881.

503 Radzinsky, pp. 508-09; Lafertè, p. 28; Footman, *Alexander Conspiracy*, p. 259.

504 Radzinsky, p. 509 (citing Tyrkov); Troitsky, p. 293 (citing Tyrkov).

505 Footman, *Alexander Conspiracy*, p. 100; Radzinsky, p. 510; Lafertè, p. 30; Croft, pp. 91-92. Footman, probably relying on a figure casually thrown in by Lafertè, states that Rysakov was "100 yards" down the embankment when he threw his bomb. This does not exactly fit with other reports that the bombers were "evenly spaced." The entire length of the quay between Inzhenernaya Street and the Moika River, where the cortege was to turn left, was measured by the author at approximately 264 yards.

506 Croft, pp. 91-95; Footman, *Alexander Conspiracy*, pp. 259-63; Radzinsky, pp. 511-14; Lafertè, pp. 34-37. Footman, pp. 263-65, pointed out that it is impossible to reconcile the

eyewitness accounts of the assassination, because they have impossible contradictions in the sequence of events. We lack tangible photographic evidence such as the Zapruder film. What is stated here is considered to be the most plausible amalgamation.

[507] Footman, *Alexander Conspiracy*, pp. 262-63.

ENDNOTES TO CHAPTER 20: "SONIA HAS LOST HER HEAD"

[508] Troitsky, pp. 292-93 (quoting Tyrkov); Footman, *Alexander Conspiracy*, p. 265 (quoting Tyrkov).

[509] Footman, *Alexander Conspiracy*, p. 266.

[510] Quoted in Footman, *Alexander Conspiracy*, p. 268.

[511] Porter, p. 271.

[512] Footman, *Alexander Conspiracy*, pp. 270-71; Troitsky, p. 305.

[513] Troitsky, pp. 294-98; Footman, *Alexander Conspiracy*, pp. 272-73; Porter, p. 271.

[514] Quoted in, Footman, *Alexander Conspiracy*, p. 274.

[515] Kravchinsky, pp. 214-18 (recounting letters from Epstein); Troitsky, pp. 322-23.

[516] Kravchinsky, pp. 219-20 (recounting letters from Epstein).

[517] Figner, *Memoirs*, pp. 112-13; Kornilova-Moroz, p. 37.

[518] Troitsky, pp. 299-301; Cymrina, pp. 106-07. The full text of the "Letter of the Executive Committee of the Will of the People to Tsar Alexander III" is published in English translation as an appendix to Figner's *Memoirs of a Revolutionist* (pp. 311-16).

[519] Figner, *Memoirs*, p. 131.

[520] Troitsky, p. 311; Footman, *Alexander Conspiracy*, p. 277.

[521] Troitsky, pp. 312-13.

[522] Cymrina, p. 113; Footman, *Alexander Conspiracy*, p. 286.

The characterization of the attitude of Perovskaya and other *Narodnaya Volya* "martyrs" as one of the spirit of "sacrifice for humanity" is taken from the writings of a Narodnaya Volya member, Lyubatovich, in *Quatre Femmes Terroristes Contre Le Tsar*, p. 129.

[523] Perovsky, pp. 102-03.

[524] Perovsky, p. 106, gives a third hand account of the meetings which is somewhat different in that it implies a more extensive outpouring of emotion by Sonia occurred during her visits with Varvara Stepanovna. The author chooses to credit the report by prison matrons who were actually present that in reality very little was said during these meetings, with a "sick" Sonia merely resting the whole time on her mother's lap. Figner, *Memoirs*, p. 109. Much of what Vasily ascribes to Sonia from the meetings essentially summarizes what she said to her mother in her March 22 letter.

[525] English translation of letter is from Kravchinsky, pp. 131-33, with several corrections by the author's research assistant Maria Hoffman from her review of the handwritten image of the letter in V. Perovsky, following p. 103.

[526] Croft, p. 103; Footman, *Alexander Conspiracy*, p. 286.

[527] See, e.g., https://en.wikipedia.org/wiki/ United_States_v._ Khalid_Sheikh _Mohammed (detailing the various faltering steps that occurred over a period of a decade in connection with the trial of the "9-11" terrorists, as well as the terrorists' own attitude welcoming a "prolonged" martyrdom).

[528] See, e.g., *People v. Allen* (Cal. Ct. of Appeal, 2ndApp.Dist. 2009) 2009 Cal.App.Unpub. LEXIS 9592 (depublished opinion) (example of upholding hate crime enhancement of punishment for racist terrorists whose professed aim was to overthrow U.S. Government); *United States v. Gregory* (D. Utah 2007) 2007 U.S. Dist. LEXIS 62413 (upholding upward departure from federal sentencing guideines for defendant

whose avowed purpose in robbing banks was to obtain the funds needed to operate a terrorist organization whose aim was to overthrow the U.S. Government). On the reaction of even so-called "progressive" organizations such as the American Civil Liberties Union favoring the enhanced punishment of terrorism as a "hate crime," see generally, R. Riggs, *Punishing the Politically Incorrect Offender Through "Bias Motive" Enhancements: Compelling Necessity or First Amendment Folly?*, 21 Ohio N.U.L. Law Review (1995).

[529] Letter of Leo Tolstoy to Alexander III, marked "draft," dated March 8, 1881, found on line at http://tolstoylit.ru/tolstoy/pisma/18801886/letter33.htm. Translation is by the author.

[530] Troitsky, p. 329.

[531] Croft, p. 111; Troitsky, pp. 323-25; Footman, *Alexander Conspiracy*, p. 287.

[532] Quoted in Footman, *Alexander Conspiracy*, pp. 289-90; Troitsky, pp. 323-24.

[533] Footman, *Alexander Conspiracy*, p. 290; Troitsky, pp. 327-28.

[534] Footman, *Alexander Conspiracy*, p. 291.

[535] Footman, *Alexander Conspiracy*, pp. 294, 309; Troisky, p. 340; on Perovskaya's admissions at trial, see Kornilova-Moroz, p. 42.

[536] Perovsky, p. 12; Porter, p. 274; Troitsky, pp. 43, 325.

[537] Porter, p. 275, translating report from Asheshov, p. 127.

[538] Footman, *Alexander Conspiracy*, pp. 296-99; Troitsky, pp. 329-31; Croft, pp. 113-14; Porter, p. 275.

[539] Footman, *Alexander Conspiracy*, p. 296.

[540] Footman, *Alexander Conspiracy*, p. 310.

[541] Croft, p. 114.

[542] Footman, *Alexander Conspiracy*, p. 311; Croft, p. 114.

[543] Footman, *Alexander Conspiracy*, p. 301.

[544] *Le Figaro*, April 9, 1881 p.2 (Paris, France)
[545] Footman, *Alexander Conspiracy*, p. 311; Troitsky, p. 338.

ENDNOTES TO CHAPTER 21: RESOLUTE TO THE END

[546] Приговор по делу 1 марта 1881 года и казнь осужденных ["The verdict in the case on March 1, 1881 and the execution of the convicts"], p. 20 (Nizhny Novgorod, 1906) [retrieved from National Library of Russia as Card Catalog Item No. 34.48.7.1164] (this 32 page document, hereafter, "Verdict and Execution," is referred to by Troitsky, p. 359, and by E. Segal, *Sofia Perovskaya*, p. 386 (Moscow 1962) as "the official report of the execution;" it is referred to by Footman as "*Protsess 1 Marta*" (Trial of March 1)); Footman, *Alexander Conspiracy*, pp. 311-12; Kern, p. 230. An account published in the *Times of London* on Monday, April 11 (NS), 1881 gives slightly different versions of the bizarre hours of the proceedings, stating that the judges were sent out to consider the sentence at 2 a.m., and returned the death sentences at 7 a.m.

[547] Croft, p. 116. Croft notes, fn. 175, that the attribution of the "whispered news" to Kibalchich as the source of the discovery that Helfman was pregnant is found only in one source, a 1995 biography of Kibalchich by Ivachenko & Kravets. Italia Wikipedia, https://it.wikipedia.org/wiki/Gesja_Meerovna _Gel%27fman, also accepts this version. Whether or not Kibalchich indeed disclosed the secret of Helfman's pregnancy without her consent, the indisputable fact is that Helfman concealed her pregnancy for a period of 26 days that she spent in custody following her arrest on March 3, 1881. Thus, it would appear she was not given a thorough physical examination.

[548] That we know of, Russian women "revolutionaries" living underground, besides Helfman (and Kolodkevitch), to whom children were born out of wedlock during this period include: Fanny Litchkous (and Serge Kravchinsky); Olga Lyubotovitch (and Nikolai Morozov); Sofia Ivanova (and Alexander Kviatkovsky), and Anna Yakimova (and Grigory Isaev) (see Porter, pp. 277-78). It is also of interest that Lyubatovich, who spent time with Helfman in early 1881, described her as being "not in good health," presumably because she was carrying an early stage pregnancy under highly stressful circumstances with her sex partner having been arrested. Lyubatovich, in *Quatre Femmes*, pp. 220-21. Olga's comment on Helfman's poor "health" is reminiscent of what various persons said about Perovskaya in early March 1881.

[549] The subject probably can still be investigated forensically if Perovskaya's body could be located. Historians to date have been unable to say exactly where her remains are located, reporting only that the five who were hanged on April 3, 1881 were placed in unmarked graves somewhere within the Preobrazhensky cemetery in St. Petersburg. Footman, *Alexander Conspiracy*, p. 322; Kern, p. 328; Troitsky, p. 363.

[550] Footman, *Alexander Conspiracy*, pp. 314-17; Croft, pp. 121-22.

[551] Verdict and Execution, p. 25; Croft, p. 123; Footman, *Alexander Conspiracy*, p. 317.

[552] Verdict and Execution, pp. 24, 25; Troitsky, p. 350.

[553] Verdict and Execution, pp. 24-26.

[554] Verdict and Execution, p. 23.

[555] Verdict and Execution, pp. 24-25, 26.

[556] Figner, p. 107 (Figner did not attend the execution, but she commented on the lovely weather); *Execution des Assassins du Czar*, an eyewitness account by a "correspondent" dated April 15 (NS), 1881 published in *Le Figaro*, April 16, 1881 p. 1

(Paris, France) ("Le Figaro account"); Verdict and Execution, p. 26; Footman, *Alexander Conspiracy*, p. 320.

[557] Le Figaro account, p. 1; Verdict and Execution, pp. 29-30; account in the *Times of London*, published Monday, April 16 (NS), 1881.

[558] Le Figaro account, p. 1; Verdict and Execution, p. 30; Kern, p. 236 (quoting eyewitness acount of Andrej Brejtfus); Footman, *Alexander Conspiracy*, p. 320.

[559] Footman, *Alexander Conspiracy*, p. 320; Kern, p. 236 (quoting Brejtfus); Le Figaro account, p. 1; Verdict and Execution, p. 30.

[560] Verdict and Execution, p. 31; Le Figaro Account, p. 1; Kern, p. 236; Asheshov, p. 140.

[561] Interestingly, multiple eyewitness accounts, specifically, the *Le Figaro* correspondent, the St. Petersburg "official record," and 14-year old Andrej Brejtfus, fail to make any mention of this dramatic incident. The *Times of London*, in its editions of Saturday, April 16 (NS), 1881, and Monday, April 18 (NS), 1881, included the description about Mikhailov's hanging that is relied on here. Perovskaya's prior biographers are divided in terms of whether or not they include the account that "Mikhailov fell twice while hanging" prior to Perovskaya's death. Her earliest real biographer, N. Asheshov, writing in 1920, did not mention such an incident (see pp. 139-40). Neither did Elena Segal, writing in 1962 (see pp. 385-89). Segal's actively pro-Soviet viewpoint almost certainly would have resulted in her emphasizing any such event. Two more recent Russian biographers, Tatiana Cymrina (p. 115, citing a 1913 account by L. A. Planson), and Nikolai Troitsky (pp. 360-61, also citing Planson) do include the "Mikhailov fell twice" version. However, Liliana Kern, in her 2013 German language biography of Perovskaya, relies on the Brejtfus eyewitness account and does not mention that "Mikhailov fell twice" (see

pp. 236). There is a small possibility that the account that "Mikhailov fell twice" could be a semi-hagiographic retelling based on the story of the execution of five Decembrists on July 13, 1826. On that occasion, three of the martyrs' ropes broke, requiring re-hanging.

[562] Le Figaro account, p. 1; Verdict and Execution, p. 31; Troitsky, p. 362; Kern, pp. 236-37; Footman, *Alexander Conspiracy*, p. 322.

[563] *What Is to Be Done?,* Ardis Edition, p. 459.

ENDNOTES TO EPILOGUE

[564]   http://www.saint-petersburg.com/cathedrals/church-resurrection-jesus-christ/ .

[565] Troyat, pp. 241-42.

[566] Lyubatovich, in *Quatre Femmes*, pp. 222-23; see also, https://it.wikipedia.org/wiki/ Gesja_Meerovna_Gel%27fman.

[567] Pomper, pp. 201-14.

[568] Figner, *Memoirs*, pp. 277-93.

[569] Figner, *Memoirs*, p. 120.

[570] Lyubatovich, in *Quatre Femmes*, pp. 223-48; see also Fauré, in *Quatre Femmes*, p. 126.

[571] Kissell, Michael S., *The Revelation in Thunder and Storm,* in *Popular Astronomy*, v. 48 (Dec. 1940), pp. 538-41.

[572] N. T. Bobrovnikoff, *Pseudo-Science and Revelation*, in *Popular Astronomy*, Vol 49 (May 1941), p. 252.

[573] A. Fomenko, *History, Fiction or Science? Chronology 1*, (Mithec 2007), retrieved at https://archive.org/details/bub_gb_YcjFAV4WZ9MC.

[574]   https://it.wikipedia.org/wiki/Lev_Aleksandrovi%C4%8D_Tichomirov; Footman, *Alexander Conspiracy*, pp. 344, 347.

[575]   Ulam, p. 325; https://it.wikipedia.org/wiki/Georgij_Valentinovi%C4%8D_Plechanov.

[576] Ulam, pp. 392-93.

[577] Ulam, pp. 392-94.

[578] P. Avrich, *Anarchist Portraits* (Princeton University Press, 1988) (in his chapter on Makhno), p. 112 (quoting Lenin). Portions of the text are based on https://en.wikipedia.org/wiki/Vladimir_Lenin and https://it.wikipedia.org/wiki/Lenin.

[579] See https://en.wikipedia.org/wiki/Fanny_Kaplan.

[580] Kern, p. 239.

BIBLIOGRAPHY

Part I – Primary Sources

Account of the executions of Alexander Kviatkovski and Andrei Presnyakov which appeared in the newspaper *Nation*, found on line at http://historydoc.edu.ru/catalog.asp?cat_ob_no= 16500&ob_no=16566. In Russian. Russian language translations in this work are by the author and his credited research assistants unless otherwise indicated.

Account of the execution of the March 1 Regicides, titled *Execution des Assassins du Czar*, an eyewitness account by a "correspondent" dated April 15, 1881 (NS) published in *Le Figaro,* April 16, 1881, p.1 (Paris, France). In French. French language translations in this work are by the author unless otherwise indicated.

Accounts of the execution of the March 1 Regicides, published in the *Times of London*, in its editions of April 16, 1881 (NS), and April 18, 1881 (NS).

Account of the trial of the March 1 Regicides, published in *Le Figaro*, April 9, 1881 (NS), p.2 [in French] (Paris, France).

Account of the trial of the March 1 Regicides, published in the *Times of London*, April 11, 1881 (NS) (London, England).

Account of the trial of the March 1 Regicides, and their execution, published as Приговор по делу 1 марта 1881 года и казнь осужденных ["The verdict in the case on March 1, 1881 and the execution of the convicts"] (Nizhny Novgorod, 1906) [retrieved from National Library of Russia as Card Catalog Item No. 34.48.7.1164]. In Russian. Translations given here are by the author.

Formulary List of Service of Lev Nikolaevitch Perovsky [in Russian], located at the Central State Historical Archive, St. Petersburg, Russia, reviewed March 15, 2016.

Letter from Sofia Perovskaya to her mother Varvara Stepanovna Veselovskaya, reproduced in Kravchinsky, *Underground Russia* (*op. cit.*), pp. 131-33, with several corrections by author's research assistant Maria Hoffman from review of the handwritten Russian language image of the letter published in V. Perovsky, *op. cit.*, following p. 103.

Memoirs of Osip V. Aptekman, published as *Organization Zemlya i Volya 70's* [in Russian] (2nd edition, Kolos, Petrograd, 1924).

Memoirs of Vera Figner, published in V. Figner, *Memoirs of a Revolutionist* (Moscow, 1925); reprinted in English as an "authorized translation from the Russian," Greenwood Press, New York, 1968.

Memoirs of Elisabeth Kovalskaya, reprinted in Christine Fauré, *Quatre Femmes Terroristes Contre le Tsar* [in French] (François Masparo, Paris 1978).

Memoirs and accounts of Serge Kravchinsky, published in S. Kravchinsky, *Underground Russia: Revolutionary Profiles and Sketches from Life* (Scribner's Sons, New York 1883). The 1883 edition reviewed for this work was "translated from the Italian" by an uncredited translator.

Memoirs of Alexandra Kornilova-Moroz, published as A. Kornilova-Moroz, *Sofia Lvovna Perovskaya* [in Russian] (Uzdatelstvo Politkatorzhan, Moscow, 1930).

Memoirs of Olga Lyubatovich, reprinted in Christine Fauré, *Quatre Femmes Terroristes Contre le Tsar* [in French] (François Masparo, Paris 1978).

Memoirs of Anna Pribilyova-Korba, published as A. P. Pribilyova-Korba, *Narodnaya Volya, Memoirs, 1870 – 1880's* [in Russian] (Mospolygraph, Government publisher, Moscow, 1926); also additional memoirs published as A. P. Pribilyova-Korba, *Alexander Dmitrievitch Mihailov, a Member of Narodnaya Volya* [in Russian] (Government publisher, Leningrad, 1925 [Moscow]).

Memoirs of Vasily Perovsky, published as *Memoirs About Sister (Sofia Perovskaya)* [in Russian], by V. L. Perovsky (Government Publisher, Moscow & Leningrad (St. Petersburg), 1927).

Memoirs of Lev A. Tikhomirov, published as Tikhomirov, Lev

A, *Sofia Perovskaya* [in Russian] (Carouge: M. Elpidine, 1899).

Memoirs of Vera Zasulitch, reprinted in Christine Fauré, *Quatre Femmes Terroristes Contre le Tsar* [in French] (François Masparo, Paris 1978).

Memoirs by Unattributed Woman Author Who Knew Perovskaya, published as *Sofia Perovskaya* [in Russian] (Izdanie Gugo Steinitz, Berlin, 1903).

"Unpublished Letters of S. L. Perovskaya," with introductory historical notes and comments by R. M. Kantor, published in: *Krasnyi arkhiv (Red Archive)*, vol 3. (1923), pp. 243-250. These letters were seized and confiscated from the property of the two friends of Perovskaya to whom she had sent them, both of whom were arrested on charges of subversive activity and later tried with her in the "Trial of the 193." The letters were kept in the files of these defendants, and were discovered there after the Revolution of 1917.

What Is to Be Done, an inspirational novel by Nikolai Chernyshevsky, with introduction by Kathryn Fever, translated into English in 1886 by N. Dole & S. S. Skidelsky (Ardis Publishers, Ann Arbor, Mich., 1986).

Part 2 – Secondary Sources

Asheshov, Nikolai. *Sofia Perovskaya, Materials for Biography* [in Russian] (Government Publisher, St. Petersburg, 1920)

Bobrovnikoff, N.T. *Pseudo-Science and Revelation*, in *Popular Astronomy*, Vol 49 (May 1941), p. 252.

Clarke, Asia Booth. *The Unlocked Book, a Memoir of John Wilkes Booth*, (G.P. Putnam & Sons, New York, 1938).

Croft, Lee B. Nikolai Ivanovich Kibalchich: Terrorist Rocket Pioneer (Tempe, Arizona, 2006).

Cymrina, Tatiana. *Sofia Perovskaya, a Political Portrait* [in Russian] (Tagenrog 2006)

Drozd, Michael Andrew. *Chernyshevskii's What Is to Be Done, a Reevaluation* (Northwestern University Press, 2001).

Footman, David. Red Prelude: The Life of Russian Terrorist Zhelyabov. (Yale Univ. Press 1945).

Footman, David. *The Alexander Conspiracy, a Life of A. I. Zhelyabov* (Barrie & Rockliff, London, 1944).

Gamblin, Graham J. *Russian Populism and Its Relation With Anarchism 1870-81* (doctoral thesis, University of Birmingham, 1999), pp. 88-127 (accessed at http://etheses.bham.ac.uk/1401/1/PhD1999Gamblin.pdf, Aug. 11, 2015).

Grawitz, Madeline. *Bakhounine Biographie* [in French] (Calmann-Lèvy, 2000).

Kassow, Samuel D. *The University Statutes of 1863,* reprinted in *Russia's Great Reforms* (anthology, B. Eklof, J. Bushnell & L. Zakharova editors) (Indiana Univ. Press 1994).

Kern, Liliana. *Die Zaren Morderin* (Osburg Verlag Hamburg 2013). In German; translations given here are by the author.

Kissell, Michael S. The Revelation in Thunder and Storm, in Popular Astronomy, v. 48 (Dec. 1940).

Kolchevska, Natasha. Introduction to S. Kovalevskaya, *Nihilist Girl* (a historical novel) (Modern Language Assn of America, 2001).

Kornilov, Alexander. *Modern Russian History*, Vol. II,

(Alfred A. Knopf, 1917).

Laferté, Victor. Alexandre II, Détails Inédits Sur La Vie e La Mort [in French] (1882)

Leontosovich, Victor. *The History of Liberalism in Russia* (Univ. of Pittsburgh Press, 2012).

Lindenmeyr, Adele. *The Rise of Voluntary Associations During the Great Reforms*, reprinted in *Russia's Great Reforms* (anthology, B. Eklof, J. Bushnell & L. Zakharova editors) (Indiana Univ. Press 1994).

Maxwell, Margaret. Narodniki Women: Russian Women Who Sacrificed Themselves for the Dream of Freedom (Pergamon Press, New York 1990).

Moss, Walter. Russia in the Age of Alexander II, Tolstoy and Dostoevsky (Anthem Press, London 2002).

Pomper, Philip. *Sergei Nechaev* (Rutgers Univ. Press 1979).

Porter, Cathy. Fathers and Daughters, Russian Women in Revolution (Virago, 1975).

Prawdin, Michael. *The Unmentionable Nechaev* (Roy Publishers, New York, 1961).

Radzinsky, Edvard. *Alexandre II, La Russie Entre L'Espoir e Le Terreur,* [in French] (A. Coldefy-Foucard translation from the Russian, le cherche midi 2009).

Segal, Elena. *Sofia Perovskaya* [in Russian] (Moscow 1962). Segal's work is a hybrid of a historical novel and a researched biography.

Seth, Roland. The Russian Terrorists: The Story of the Narodniki (Barrie & Rockliff, London, 1966).

Siljak, Ana. *Angel of Vengeance* (St. Martin's Press 2008).

Svobodin, A. Introduction, titled "*A Feeling of Time,*" to Y. Trifonov, *The Impatient Ones* (Progress Publishers 1978).

Tarsaidze, Alexandre. *Katia, Wife Before God* (MacMillan , 1970).

Trifonov, Yuri. *The Impatient Ones* (Progress Publishers 1978). Trifonov's work is a hybrid of a historical novel and a researched biography. The edition reviewed for this work was translated from the Russian by Robert Daglish.

Troitsky, Nikolai A. *Sofia Lvovna Perovskaya, A Life, Personality, Fate* [in Russian] (Saratov State University, 2014).

Troyat, Henri. *Alexandre II, Le Tsar Liberateur* [in French] (Flammarion, 1990)

Verhoeven, Claudia. *The Odd Man Karakozov* (Cornell Univ. Press 2009)

Ulam, Adam B. *In the Name of the People* (Viking Press, 1977)

Zaionchkovsky, P. A. *The Russian Autocracy in Crisis, 1878-1882* (Academic International Press, Gulf Breeze, Florida, 1979).

Part 3 – General Reference

Avrich, Paul. *Anarchist Portraits* (Princeton University Press, 1988).

Avrich, Paul, ed. *The Anarchists in the Russian Revolution* (anthology and collected materials) (Thames & Hudson, Ltd., London, 1973).

Box, Steven. *Deviance, Reality and Society* (Holt, Rinehart & Winston, Ltd., East Sussex (UK), 1971.)

Chernevskaya-Bochanovsaya, G.F., *Maria Nikolaevna Olovennikova* [in Russian] (Moscow 1930).

Court decisions:

People v. Allen (Cal. Ct. of Appeal, 2nd App.Dist. 2009) 2009 Cal.App.Unpub. LEXIS 9592 ("depublished" opinion).

United States v. Gregory (D. Utah 2007) 2007 U.S. Dist. LEXIS 62413.

Davies, Norman. *God's Playground: A History of Poland* (Vol. II) (Clarendon Press, Oxford, 1981).

De Grunwald, Constatin. *Le Tsar Alexandre II et Son Temps* [in French] (Editions Berger-Levrault, 1963)

Easley, Roxanne. The Emancipation of the Serfs in Russia: Peace arbitrators and the development of civil society (Routledge, London & New York, 2009).

Eysenck, H. J., *Crime and Personality* (London 1970).

Fomenko, Anatoly. *History, Fiction or Science? Chronology 1*, (Mithec 2007), retrieved at https://archive.org/details /bub_gb_YcjFAV4WZ9MC.

Freedman, Lawrence Zelic and Alexander, Yonah, editors. *Perspectives on Terrorism* (anthology) (Scholarly Resources, Wilmington (US) 1983).

Gaucher, Roland. *Les Terroristes* [in French] (Editions Albin Michel, Paris, 1965).

Hudson, Rex A., Majeska, Marilyn, Savada, Andrea M., and Metz, Helen C., *The Sociology and Psychology of Terrorism: Who Becomes a Terrorist, and Why?* (Library of Congress,

Washington, 1999).

Kohn, Hans. *The Mind of Modern Russia* (Rutgers Univ. Press, New Brunswick, 1955). Includes a collection of English-translated letters from Russian writers of the 19th century.

Kovalevskaya, Sofia. *Nihilist Girl* (historical novel, translated into English by Natasha Kolchevska with Mary Zirin) (Modern Language Assn of America 2001).

Laqueur, Walter. *A History of Terrorism* (Transaction Publishers, New Brunswick (U.S.) and London (U.K.), 2007).

Martin, Gus. *Understanding Terrorism: Challenges, Perspectives and Issues* (Sage Publications, Thousand Oaks (U.S.), 2nd Edition 2006).

Massari, Roberto. *Il Terrorismo: Storia Concetti Metodi* (Rome 1979). In Italian. All Italian language translations are by the author.

Marshall, Peter. *Demanding the Impossible: A History of Anarchism* (PM Press, Oakland, 1992).

Parry, Albert. *Terrorism from Robespierre to Arafat* (Vanguard Press 1976).

Payne, Robert. *The Terrorists: The Story of the Forerunners of Stalin* (Funk & Wagnalls, New York, 1957).

Rapaport, David C. and Alexander, Yonah. *The Morality of Terrorism: Religious and Secular Justifications* (Columbia University Press, New York, 1989.)

Rhodes, Richard. *Why They Kill: The Discoveries of a Maverick Criminologist* (Alfred A. Knopf, New York, 1999).

Riggs, Robert. *Punishing the Politically Incorrect Offender*

Through "Bias Motive" Enhancements: Compelling Necessity or First Amendment Folly?, 21 Ohio N.U.L. Law Review (1995).

Sand, Georges. *Histoire de Ma Vie* [in French] (Editions Gallimard 2004).

Valishevsky, K. *The Razumovsky Family* [in Russian] (St. Petersburg, 1880).

Villemin, Jean-Antoine & Koch, Robert. *"Early Research and Treatment of Tuberculosis in the 19th Century,"* accessed at http://exhibits.hsl.virginia.edu/alav/tuberculosis/.

Wikipedia pages:

https://ru.wikipedia.org/wiki/Разумовский,_Кирилл_Григор ьевич [in Russian] (accessed Sept. 17, 2016).

http://it. wikipedia.org/wiki/Sof'ja_L'vovna_Perovskaja (accessed July 8, 2015). In Italian; all Italian sources mentioned here were translated by the author.

https://it.wikipedia.org/wiki/Stepan_Nikolaevi%C4%8D_Cha lturin [in Italian] (accessed July 8, 2015).

https://it.wikipedia.org/wiki/Aleksandr_Aleksandrovi%C4%8 D_Kvjatkovskij [in Italian] (accessed July 28, 2015).

https://it.wikipedia.org/wiki/Dmitrij_ Andreevi%C4%8D_ Lizogub [in Italian] (accessed Sept. 17, 2016).

https://en.wikipedia.org/wiki/United_States_v._Khalid_Sheik h_Mohammed (accessed June 15, 2016).

https://it.wikipedia.org/wiki/Gesja_Meerovna _Gel%27fman [in Italian] (accessed July 2, 2016).

https://it.wikipedia.org/wiki/Lev_Aleksandrovi%C4%8D_Tic homirov [in Italian] (accessed July 2, 2016).

https://it.wikipedia.org/wiki/Georgij_Valentinovi%C4%8D_P lechanov [in Italian] (accessed July 2, 2016).

https://en.wikipedia.org/wiki/Fanny_Kaplan (accessed July 2, 2016).

Woodcock, George. *Anarchism, A History of Libertarian Ideas and Movements* (Meridian Press, Cleveland and New York, 1962).

Yablonskii, P., Vizel, A., Galkin V. & Shulgina, M. *Tuberculosis in Russia, Its History and Status Today*, published in American Journal of Respiratory and Critical Care Medicine, Vol. 191, No. 4 (2015), pp. 372-76.

Zabel, Richard B. & Benjamin, James J. *In Pursuit of Justice: Prosecuting Terrorism Cases in the Federal Courts* (a white paper) (Human Rights First, Washington & New York, 2008)

Zilboorg, Gregory. *The Psychology of the Criminal Act and Punishment* (Harcourt, Brace and Company, New York, 1954).

Index

CPSIA information can be obtained
at www.ICGtesting.com
Printed in the USA
BVHW01*2106080218
507675BV00001B/1/P